THE EMPEROR'S NEMESIS

LIU HEPING

Translated by
Wen Huang

SINOIST

ACA Publishing Ltd
University House
11-13 Lower Grosvenor Place,
London SW1W 0EX, UK
Tel: +44 20 3289 3885
E-mail: info@alaincharlesasia.com
www.alaincharlesasia.com
www.sinoistbooks.com

Beijing Office
Tel: +86(0)10 8472 1250

Author: Liu Heping
Translator: Wen Huang

Published by Sinoist Books (an imprint of ACA Publishing Ltd) in arrangement with Guangdong Flower City Publishing House Co., Ltd.

Original Chinese Text © 大明王朝 1566 *(Da Ming Wang Chao 1566)* 2016, Guangdong Flower City Publishing House Co., Ltd, Guangdong, China

English Translation text © 2021 ACA Publishing Ltd, London, UK

ALL RIGHTS RESERVED. NO PART OF THIS PUBLICATION MAY BE REPRODUCED IN MATERIAL FORM, BY ANY MEANS, WHETHER GRAPHIC, ELECTRONIC, MECHANICAL OR OTHER, INCLUDING PHOTOCOPYING OR INFORMATION STORAGE, IN WHOLE OR IN PART, AND MAY NOT BE USED TO PREPARE OTHER PUBLICATIONS WITHOUT WRITTEN PERMISSION FROM THE PUBLISHER.

This novel is entirely a work of fiction. The names, characters and incidents portrayed in it are the work of the author's imagination. Any resemblance to actual persons, living or dead, events or localities is entirely coincidental.

Paperback ISBN: 978-1-910760-66-6
eBook ISBN: 978-1-910760-65-9

A catalogue record for *The 1566 Series (Book Four): The Emperor's Nemesis* is available from the National Bibliographic Service of the British Library.

THE EMPEROR'S NEMESIS

Book Four of the 1 5 6 6 series

LIU HEPING

Translated by
WEN HUANG

Sinoist Books

CHIEF CHARACTERS

The Imperial Family

- **Emperor Jiajing:** 12th emperor of the Ming dynasty
- **Prince of Yu:** son of Emperor Jiajing
- **Princess Li:** consort of the Prince of Yu

The Imperial Court

- **Lu Fang:** chief of the interior ministry, Emperor Jiajing's most senior eunuch
- **Yan Song:** grand secretary of the Privy Council
- **Yan Shifan:** son of Yan Song
- **Xu Jie:** deputy grand secretary of the Privy Council and head of the Imperial Treasury
- **Tan Lun:** the Prince of Yu's chief of staff
- **Zhang Juzheng:** head of the Ministry of Defence
- **Gao Gong:** deputy minister of the Imperial Treasury
- **Mao Qing:** deputy minister of justice
- **Feng Bao:** commander of the Imperial Secret Police
- **Luo Wenlong:** director of the Imperial Post Office and Yan Song's confidant

The Zhejiang Provincial Government

- **Hu Zongxian:** governor of Zhejiang Province
- **Zheng Bichang:** imperial inspector of Zhejiang Province
- **Zhao Zhenji:** governor and imperial inspector of Nanjing; successor to Zheng Bichang as imperial inspector of Zhejiang Province
- **Ho Maocai:** head of the Zhejiang Provincial Justice Department
- **Gao Hanwen:** mayor of Hangzhou City
- **Wang Yongji:** magistrate of Jiande County
- **Hai Rui:** magistrate of Chun'an County
- **Tian Youlu:** deputy magistrate of Chun'an County

Other Characters

- **Yang Jinshui:** head of the South China Textile Bureau and the Zhejiang Provincial Maritime Affairs Department
- **Shen Yishi:** silk mill owner and Zhejiang's wealthiest businessman
- **Chee Dazhu:** leader of rebel farmers in Chun'an County
- **General Qi Jiguang:** regional military commissioner responsible for fighting Japanese pirates in southeast China
- **Dr Li Shizhen:** legendary doctor, considered to be the founder of Chinese medicine
- **Inoue Jusaburo:** Japanese pirate commander
- **Inoue Toushirou:** Japanese pirate
- **Warden Wang:** warden of Chun'an County prison
- **Officer Xu:** squad leader of troops in Chun'an County
- **Officer Jiang:** police officer in Hangzhou City

I

In 1562, the forty-first year under the reign of Emperor Jiajing, Yan Song and his son, who had dominated the Imperial Government for twenty years, fell from power. Feeling indebted to his unswerving loyalty, Emperor Jiajing removed Yan Song from office without sending him to prison. In fact, historians say that the formerly powerful grand secretary was allowed to retire with a handsome pension of five thousand kilograms of rice a year.

While other core members of the Yan Clan, such as Yan Shifan, Luo Wenlong and Yan Maoqing were either imprisoned or exiled, the majority remained in power. As a consequence, corruption continued unabated. In the forty-fourth year of Emperor Jiajing's reign, natural disasters struck many provinces. Since the state's coffers were nearly empty, the Imperial Government had no choice but to impose heavy taxes, which roused widespread discontent. The Privy Council, led by Grand Secretary Xu, pressured the commissioner of Audit and Inspection to file another lengthy report with Emperor Jiajing relating to rampant corruption within the Imperial Government. To appease public anger, Emperor Jiajing ordered the execution of Yan Shifan and the imprisonment of more corrupt officials. Even so, Emperor Jiajing was widely denounced as a fatuous ruler.

In July that year, Hai Rui was transferred to Beijing as an auditor at the Ministry of Treasury.

The large plaque bearing the words 'Home of Six Necessities', which had been inscribed by Yan Song, still hung high on the lintel over the pickle store's three-winged black wooden door. Under the hot summer sun, Yan Song's gold-embossed calligraphy glittered. Even though the store was located on a busy shopping street in Beijing, it looked deserted. Shoppers who happened to walk past always lifted their heads and glanced at the plaque before hastening away. Few people would dare enter the store. The Imperial Palace issued a secret decree, forbidding the store owner from taking down the plaque because Emperor Jiajing wanted to hear what the world was saying about Yan Song, or more specifically about himself.

On this morning, a hooded horse-drawn carriage carrying Hai Rui and his family arrived in Beijing. It was one of the hottest months the city had experienced. The heat inside the small, crammed carriage cabin had become unbearable. Hai Rui, who was wearing a conical bamboo hat and a long grey linen gown, sat on the cowling next to the coachman, who was brandishing a whip. Hai Rui's beard had turned grey but he was brimming with vigour, and his eyes remained sharp. As the carriage drove past the pickle store, he caught sight of Yan Song's plaque.

"Stop," he told the coachman.

The coachman pulled the reins on the horse. The carriage drew up outside a teahouse across the street from Home of Six Necessities.

Hai Rui jumped off the carriage and fixed his gaze at the store.

"Have we arrived at our destination?" asked Amu from inside the curtained cabin.

"Not yet, Amu," replied Hai Rui, putting his head close to the cabin. "I'm thinking of buying some pickled vegetables here. When we get home, we can eat them with our porridge."

"That's a good idea."

"Please go inside and buy a pot of cold tea for my family," said Hai Rui, handing two copper coins to the coachman.

"Master, where are you going?" asked the puzzled coachman as he took the money.

"I'm going into that pickle store," Hai Rui answered.

The coachman watched nervously as Hai Rui crossed the street. Several passers-by peered at Hai Rui warily.

Inside the teahouse, in front of which Hai Rui's carriage was parked, several men sitting around a table near the door stared intently at Hai Rui. Even though they were wearing casual gowns, the owner could easily tell from their cold and tense demeanours that they were spies from the Imperial Palace. The one in the middle was a eunuch working for the Criminal Investigative Division. Sitting either side of the eunuch were two imperial secret agents.

Before entering the teahouse, Hai Rui's coachman noticed the three suspicious-looking characters. Intimidated by their presence, he abruptly turned around and went back to the carriage. With Hai Rui's two copper coins in his hand, he stood by his vehicle motionless, as if his feet had been nailed to the ground.

Pausing in front of Home of Six Necessities, Hai Rui raised his head to squint at the plaque. Just then, a pedestrian almost bumped into him. He glanced at Hai Rui furtively before scurrying away. Hai Rui's gaze shifted from the plaque above the door to the inside of the shop. Taking off his conical hat and holding it behind his back, he strolled through the door.

Curiously, the owner and store assistants seemed to be idling about. None of them bothered to greet Hai Rui or invited him to come in and buy their pickled vegetables. Nor did anyone chase him away. All they did was to stare at him blankly.

Inside the teahouse across the street, the eunuch and the two imperial agents rose from their table. They stepped out and swaggered towards Home of Six Necessities.

Seeing that the palace spies had left, the coachman quickly inserted his whip into a holder on the cowling. Placing the two copper coins next to the whip holder, the coachman abandoned his carriage and crept away. A few steps down the street, he started to run as fast as his legs could carry him.

The conspicuous presence of the imperial secret agents on the street sent pedestrians scurrying away. Shoppers coming from the east turned around and headed back east, while those arriving from the west turned around and went west. A few bold and curious onlookers hung around and watched the secret agents from a distance. What was about to unfold inside the pickle shop would no doubt enliven their after-dinner conversations.

Hai Rui walked up to the counter. His gaze swept across the earthen jars on rows of sturdy wooden shelves. Several shop assistants were lounging on a long bench. No one stood up to serve him.

Zhao, the owner, happened to come in from the back door. "What can I do for you?" he asked coldly.

"I want to buy some pickled vegetables for an old person and a patient. What kinds do you recommend?"

"They're all equally good," Zhao answered indifferently.

From a side glance, Hai Rui noticed that all the shop assistants who had been sitting around were now looking at the door behind him. Then, they rose from their chairs and bowed slightly in that direction. Hai Rui became keenly aware that some important figures were about to enter.

The palace spies were standing at the door. The eunuch gave a knowing wink to the two imperial agents before he strutted through the doorway. The agents remained outside. The eunuch picked a square table against a wall on the left and sat down quietly. A shop assistant darted out from behind the counter and approached the eunuch with a porcelain teapot and a cup. Filling the cup with tea, he placed the pot on the table, bowed and returned to his bench behind the counter.

Hai Rui pretended not to have seen the mysterious visitor. Taking out ten copper coins from his pocket, he placed them on the counter. "Please get me ten copper coins' worth of pickled vegetables."

Zhao removed a cover from a bamboo basket that held a stack of dried lotus leaves. He pulled out one leaf and placed it at the bottom of a white porcelain bowl. Lifting the lids off two earthen jars, he used a sifting spoon to scoop out two different kinds of pickled vegetables into the bowl.

"I heard that the pickled vegetables at your store are more

expensive than meat," Hai Rui stated. "You're giving me a lot. I didn't realise that ten copper coins could buy so much."

"Didn't you just tell me that you're buying them for a patient?" the owner replied. "That's why I'm giving you a bit more than I would to other customers."

Hai Rui did not argue. He watched with fascination as Zhao pulled out a large lotus leaf from the bamboo basket and spread it out on the counter. Then, he took the pickled vegetables and the smaller lotus leaf out of the bowl and placed them on top of the large lotus leaf. After Zhao wrapped them up, he retrieved three thin strips of palm leaves from under the counter and tied a perfect six-loop bow. "Here you are," Zhao said. "Take care."

Hai Rui picked up the packet and turned around. Instead of leaving, he strolled over to the square table and sat down opposite the eunuch. Pointing at the teapot on the table, he said to the shop assistant behind the counter: "Could you bring me a cup as well? I've been on a long trip and I'm dying for some tea."

The shop assistant didn't dare answer and turned to Zhao for instructions. But Zhao quickly looked to the eunuch who pretended that he didn't see Hai Rui. When the eunuch realised that the pickle store owner was fixing his eyes on him, waiting for a signal, he nodded grudgingly.

Zhao uttered a silent sigh. Picking up a cup, he pushed open the counter door and walked over to the table. "Sir, please have your drink, take your stuff and continue on your way," Zhao said with a hint of impatience in his tone as he filled Hai Rui's cup with tea.

"May I bother you with a question," Hai Rui asked before Zhao stepped away.

Zhao paused and looked at Hai Rui.

"I heard that your store used to called Home of Six Hearts. Why did you change it to Home of Six Necessities?"

Fear flashed across Zhao's face. The eunuch who was sitting across the table tilted his head and glared at Hai Rui.

The two imperial agents outside also heard Hai Rui's question. They peered at him vigilantly.

The shop assistants either cast their eyes downwards or deliberately looked away.

Hai Rui could sense the tension in the room, but he persisted. Zhao gave no response. Instead, he turned around and went back to the counter. Soon he returned with the ten copper coins that Hai Rui had left on the countertop. "Sir, please take your money," he said as he tossed the coins on the table and went to grab the packet from Hai Rui. "I'm not selling you these pickled vegetables today. Please leave."

"What kind of rule is this?" Hai Rui asked, pushing Zhao's hands away. "I paid my money and you delivered the goods. Why are you cancelling the sale?"

The two of them had reached an impasse. "If you are here to buy my pickled vegetables, you should get your stuff and leave," said Zhao. "You and I don't even know each other. Why are you giving me trouble?"

"This is my first time in Beijing. I'm merely curious about some local traditions and customs. I'm not giving you trouble, am I?"

Zhao became desperate. "Sir, we're just a few streets away from the Son of Heaven. As an out-of-towner, it's better you don't make trouble here."

"You are wrong!" said Hai Rui, standing up. "I never instigate trouble. I'm only calling your attention to some obvious facts. For example, your store offers some of the best pickled vegetables, but nobody dares come in and buy them. So I feel obligated to offer you some suggestions."

"Who says nobody dares come in to buy my pickled vegetables?" Zhao countered nervously as he glanced at the eunuch. "Sir, please leave us alone. Don't hang around and disrupt my business."

Hai Rui decided to reveal his true intention: "Maybe I'm just being too nosy, but while I was working in the south, I heard that your store used to be called Home of Six Hearts and that business was brisk. But since you changed its name, people are afraid to come in. That being the case, why did you change the word 'hearts' to 'necessities'?"

Who would dare answer such a sensitive question? Zhao and his assistants were dumbfounded. All they did was glance at the dour-looking eunuch. The two imperial agents were ready to pounce on Hai Rui.

Unconcerned by the owner's fearful reaction, Hai Rui continued: "I heard a few more rumours about the name change on my way to Beijing. The problem is that when you add a throw to the middle of the character for 'hearts', 心, and change it to 必 or 'necessities', it's almost like you're stabbing a knife though the 'heart' character. No wonder your business has gone downhill. Don't you agree?"

The eunuch sprang to his feet. The two imperial agents burst in and stopped in front of Hai Rui.

Hai Rui's remarks terrified Zhao and his assistants.

"Go… go ahead with your comments," urged the slightly alarmed eunuch.

Hai Rui ignored the eunuch and the towering presence of the imperial agents. Adjusting his chair, he straightened his back and said to the eunuch: "Actually, changing the characters is not necessarily a bad thing. But when you failed to convey its significance to the public, you allowed rumours to flourish and overtake the truth. All you need to do is add a couple of footnotes to expound the new character. Once you clarify the situation to the public, you can dispel any rumours and your business will naturally recover. Bring me a piece of paper and a calligraphy brush, and I'll do it for you."

With the palace spies standing nearby, Zhao was too scared to respond.

"Bring some paper and a calligraphy brush for him," the eunuch encouraged Zhao. "Let him write down his ideas."

Paper and ink brushes were readily available in the store because Zhao needed them for bookkeeping. He beckoned to one of his assistants behind the counter: "Get him a calligraphy brush and some paper."

The assistant grabbed the stationery from the countertop and waddled over to the table.

"Go ahead and write," the eunuch said to Hai Rui.

Dipping the brush in an ink bowl, Hai Rui explained to Zhao: "Based on what I have heard, the pickled vegetables here are unique because you're very particular about six things. First, your raw vegetables are grown in places with favourable weather and soil conditions. Second, the vegetables are always in season. Third, you have a good mix of squash and vegetables. Fourth, you use a unique sweet sauce. Fifth, you store them in particular containers, and lastly the vegetables are pickled in a special type of spring water. Are these points accurate?"

Despite his fear, Zhao was pleasantly surprised that a stranger who had never visited his store would summarise the strengths of his products so succinctly. He looked touched and sought permission from the imperial agents to speak to Hai Rui.

"You may answer him," the eunuch said to Zhao.

"Yes," uttered Zhao. The word was meant both as an answer to the eunuch's order and to Hai Rui's observations.

"Since you agree with my comments, I'm going to write them down for you," said Hai Rui.

Now that the calligraphy brush was charged with ink, Hai Rui lifted it from the bowl and started writing. Zhao and the imperial agents couldn't help peeking at the characters that were appearing on the paper. Their eyes immediately lit up. While none of the three spies had sat for the imperial examinations, they were literate. During their careers, they had interrogated countless imperial officials and imperial scholars who had been charged with crimes, and pored over their confessions. Seldom had they seen such beautiful calligraphy. Surprised, the eunuch gave his two colleagues a knowing glance. They surmised that this stranger was no ordinary person. He looked like someone who might have powerful political connections.

When he finished, Hai Rui put down the calligraphy brush and showed his writing to Zhao. At the same time, he gave the three imperial spies a sideway glance.

"This is how I interpret the name 'Home of Six Necessities'. What do you all think?"

"Could you read it aloud to us?" the eunuch asked. His tone turned reverential.

"'Six necessities' mean that the location of production must be authentic, the season must be in harmony, the squash and vegetables must be fresh, the sweet sauce must be mellow, the containers must be clean and the water must be pristine."

Zhao nodded.

"These attributes should be publicised as the true reasons for your name change," said Hai Rui. "I hope you can inscribe what I have written on another plaque and hang it up. I guarantee your business will pick up in no time."

Before Zhao could respond, Hai Rui picked up his conical hat and the packet of pickled vegetables, and headed for the door.

The eunuch signalled for the imperial agents to intercept Hai Rui.

"Sir, you haven't left your name and address," said an imperial agent who caught up with Hai Rui and tapped him on the shoulder. "The owner can contact you if they decide to inscribe your writings on a plaque."

"He can come and look for me at the Ministry of Treasury."

"You're with the Ministry of Treasury?" the eunuch asked. "What do you do there?"

"My name is Hai Rui and I'm going to be an auditor at the ministry," he said, pushing the imperial agent's hand off his shoulder.

"Don't leave yet," the eunuch called out. "If you are an auditor at the Ministry of Treasury as you claim to be, let's go there now to verify your identity."

"Of course." Hai Rui paused and turned around. "In fact, I'm about to go there now and register my arrival. If it's not too much trouble, I'd like you to guide me and my coachman there. I don't know the city at all. Please allow me to take care of my family first. They're inside the carriage over there. We can go together."

The two imperial agents were at a loss about what to do.

"Let's follow him," said the eunuch.

Together, the four of them walked out of the store.

Inside the shop, Zhao had finally recovered his wits and bent over to examine Hai Rui's writings. The ink on the paper was still wet. The shop assistants rose from their chairs and stood behind Zhao on tiptoes, hoping to get a glimpse at the calligraphy.

All of a sudden, the eunuch barged back in. "Grab me another piece of paper," he ordered.

An assistant rushed over with a sheet of blank paper.

The eunuch put the paper gently on top of Hai Rui's writings.

Then, he rolled up all the papers and walked out with them without any explanation.

Zhao plopped down on a bench, looking dejected.

"Are you all right?" asked an assistant who darted out from behind the counter.

"It looks like we might be in trouble again," Zhao said. "Pack up your stuff. Go find a job elsewhere. I'll probably have to close the store."

As Hai Rui approached his horse-drawn carriage outside the teahouse, he saw the long whip on the cowling but the coachman was nowhere to be seen.

Looking around, he caught a glimpse of several curious onlookers on both sides of the street. They were staring at him from a distance.

"My coachman has abandoned me," Hai Rui said to the imperial agents who walked behind him. "How do I get to Qianliang Alley? Do you mind guiding me there?"

The two imperial agents did not respond. They were waiting for the eunuch to come back.

"What kept you so long?" Amu asked from inside the carriage. "Has the coachman abandoned us?"

"Amu, I was delayed at the store because I bought some extra kinds of pickled vegetables. The coachman had to leave and take care of an emergency. Don't worry, I met a couple of folks at the store. They'll take us to our residence."

"All right," Amu said without further questioning.

The eunuch came over with a roll of papers in his hands. "You two can take him to his residence first and then to the Ministry of Treasury."

"What about you?"

"I need to run back to the palace and present this to Chen Gonggong because I see his writing as a veiled attack on His Majesty," he said before waving vigorously to someone who was waiting with a horse in the distance. "Come over here," the eunuch shouted in his high-pitched voice.

The man with the horse trotted over. The eunuch took the reins from him, jumped onto the horse and squeezed his legs. The horse galloped in the direction of Qianmenwai Street.

Since Hai Rui had no idea how to drive a carriage, he simply grabbed the reins and said to the imperial agents. "Please go first. I'll follow you."

The imperial agents were a bit mystified that Hai Rui, a newly appointed official at the Ministry of Treasury, would be bold enough upon his arrival in Beijing to speak disrespectfully of Emperor Jiajing. While they had been ordered to watch him, they sensed that this new hire must know some powerful figures inside the palace. Otherwise, he wouldn't have acted with such brash confidence. The two agents softened their tone and said politely: "All right, let's go then."

Hai Rui led the horse-drawn carriage and the two imperial agents flanked him. Thus, an odd scene occurred. One of Beijing's most bustling streets rapidly emptied of pedestrians. As the carriage and agents trudged along a deserted street, they were watched from afar, with the bystanders presuming that Hai Rui was a captured criminal.

The Ming government enforced stringent traffic rules within the inner city of Beijing. On main thoroughfares, non-ministerial officials were not allowed to ride large sedan chairs with four or more carriers. Except for senior military officers or city police patrolling the streets, no one was authorised to ride a horse. Horse riders who entered the inner city had to get off and walk. Therefore, each time a rider was spotted galloping on the street, residents would know that he was either a messenger from the Ministry of Defence, a senior-ranking eunuch or a palace official who was taking care of important business.

At this point, Hai Rui heard the urgent sound of hoofbeats behind him. Pedestrians quickly retreated to the side. A few patrons at a teahouse poked their heads out from behind the door. They saw three horses dashing towards them, and the men on horseback were wearing civilian clothes.

"That's Master Thirteen," one customer at the teashop shouted. "He must be here to arrest a big criminal."

"Which one is Master Thirteen?" the man sitting next to him asked.

"The person on the first horse," the customer said, pointing his finger outside. "His Majesty has just anointed him as one of the Thirteen Warriors at the Imperial Investigative Agency. I wonder if he's rushing over to arrest that chap leading the carriage."

Several customers thronged to the door and watched. The three horses caught up with Hai Rui's carriage and gradually slowed down.

The two imperial agents who were escorting Hai Rui urged him to stop the carriage. Then they turned around to salute the person on the horse: "Master Thirteen!"

"Is this the new official at the Ministry of Treasury who just bought pickled vegetables at Home of Six Necessities?"

"Yes," one imperial agent replied. "How did you find out so fast?"

Master Thirteen sized up the familiar figure under the large conical hat before dismounting his horse. "This is my saviour!" he shouted, dropping to his knees in the middle of the street. Master Thirteen's sudden act took the imperial agents by surprise. Based on palace etiquette, imperial agents only knelt to the emperor or genuflected to their superiors at the Interior Ministry and the Imperial Investigative Agency. For other senior-ranking officials, a palm-over-fist salute would suffice. Kneeling to a low-ranking auditor at the Ministry of Treasury was unheard of. However, when they heard Master Thirteen addressing Hai Rui as his saviour, they figured that he was kneeling for a personal reason and didn't follow his example. They simply stood to the side, with their heads down.

Hai Rui soon recognised that Master Thirteen was actually Chee Dazhu. For a fleeting moment, he became emotional. "Please rise," Hai Rui said, trying to compose himself. "This is not the place for such courtesy."

Chee Dazhu stood up and asked excitedly: "Where is Amu? What about Mrs Hai and your little girl? Are they all inside the carriage?"

"Who is that?" Hai Rui's mother enquired from inside the carriage. "Why are we stopping again?"

Chee Dazhu dashed over to the carriage.

"Amu, this is your other son, Chee Dazhu. I'm here to welcome you to Beijing."

Hai Rui's mother lifted the carriage curtain. She now had a head of grey hair.

Chee Dazhu was about to kowtow to Amu when Hai Rui stopped him. "Didn't I say this is not the place for such rituals?" he said.

Hai Rui held the curtain for Amu while she reached out her right hand. "Dazhu, is that you?" she cried out.

Chee Dazhu stepped forward and held Amu's arm with his large hands. "Amu, it is I," he said. "Last month, when I heard that my saviour and you were coming to Beijing, my wife and I rented a courtyard house for you. We have scrubbed the floor very clean. Initially, we thought you might have travelled by boat. So we waited for you at the pier near Dongbianmen Gate. We didn't realise that you would come here in a carriage."

"Thank you for thinking of us," Mrs Hai said. "How is your wife?"

"She's waiting for you at home. As soon as she heard about your arrival several days ago, she's been so excited that she couldn't get to sleep!"

"Mother," said Hai Rui, interrupting the conversation, "Dazhu is now an official at the Imperial Investigative Agency. He's working for His Majesty. So we mustn't delay him. Let him go now. We can catch up later."

From Hai Rui's tone and expression, Amu sensed that something had gone wrong. "I understand," she said, pulling the curtain down. "I will see you another time."

"Let's forget what I have done for you in the past," Hai Rui said to Chee Dazhu. "Since you're now employed by the Imperial Investigative Agency, it's important you don't come looking for me. Even if you do, I won't see you."

Confounded by Hai Rui's change of tone, Chee Dazhu stammered: "But you're my saviour... how could I..."

"I'm nobody's saviour," Hai Rui said with a grim look on his face. "Please leave."

Grabbing the reins of the horse, Hai Rui moved on. "Let's go," he said to the two imperial agents, who were supposed to escort him to his new residence and then to the Ministry of Treasury.

The imperial agents found themselves in a dilemma. They were supposed to follow Hai Rui. At the same time, they were also afraid of offending their Master Thirteen.

Prior to his arrival, Chee Dazhu had heard that two imperial agents were monitoring a new appointee at the Ministry of Treasury. He had guessed it was Hai Rui, but he had no idea what had just happened. "Do you know what the fuss is about?" he asked his two colleagues.

The two imperial agents appeared awkward. "Master Thirteen, this person made some blasphemous remarks about His Majesty at the pickle store," one agent whispered to Chee Dazhu. "He also wrote them down on a piece of paper. Liu Gonggong from the Criminal Investigative Division has instructed us to escort him home first before delivering him to the Ministry of Treasury for investigation."

"What did he write?" Chee Dazhu asked, looking alarmed. "Where is Liu Gonggong?"

"Well, His Majesty changed the store name from Home of Six Hearts to Home of Six Necessities. Your friend there reinterpreted His Majesty's words and issued a new statement, claiming that his words would enable the store to 'set the record straight and dispel rumours'. Liu Gonggong took his writing and went to see Chen Gonggong at the Interior Ministry's duty room."

Chee Dazhu stamped his feet. "When did Liu Gonggong leave?" he asked. "Was he on a horse?"

"It's too late," one agent replied. "He left on his horse. There's no way you can catch up with him."

Chee Dazhu thought about it for a moment. "Why don't you go with Mr Hai?" he suggested. "Help him out and make sure he gets to his new place safely. There's no need to take him to the Ministry of Treasury today."

"Understood," the two imperial agents said. They turned around and went to chase Hai Rui's carriage.

"Let's go back to the Imperial Investigative Agency," Chee

Dazhu said to his two colleagues. He mounted his horse and galloped west, towards Qianmen Gate.

His two peers also got on their horses and followed him.

Many pedestrians who had been watching from a distance swarmed out onto the street. It was as if nothing had happened. Normal life resumed.

明

For masters of martial arts, the extreme heat of summer and the freezing cold of winter are optimal for endurance training. Zhu Qi, who happened to be on duty at the Imperial Investigative Agency, took advantage of the hot weather and an uneventful shift by practising his 'horse stance' in the yard. Under the scorching sun, he was standing on one foot, with a thick bamboo pole on one of his shoulders. Two gigantic stone locks were strung onto each side of the pole. His pectoral and bicep muscles resembled pieces of cast iron.

Chee Dazhu rushed in, sweating profusely. Instead of interrupting Zhu Qi's practice, he stood there and waited quietly.

Zhu Qi propped up the bamboo pole with both palms and shifted it to a different shoulder without moving his leg. "What's happening?" he said calmly.

"Master, I've run into a problem," Chee Dazhu reported anxiously.

Zhu Qi gave him a side glance with the pole on his shoulder. "Did anyone die?" he asked.

"No, not exactly."

"So if nobody's died, what's the rush?" Zhu Qi said as he shifted his weight onto a different leg.

"This incident happened at Home of Six Necessities. Someone issued a statement, trying to reinterpret the character 'necessities'. You know the store's original name was Home of Six Hearts."

Zhu Qi was stunned. Standing on both feet now, he propped up the bamboo pole and threw it onto the ground. "Was it a verbal statement or a written one?" he asked Chee Dazhu.

"Unfortunately, it was written down. Someone at the Criminal

Investigative Division has delivered the piece of paper to Chen Gonggong. Master, the person who issued that statement is my saviour."

"Who is that?"

"Mr Hai Rui."

"Him? I thought he was in Jiangxi Province."

"After Yan Shifan was executed, the Privy Council transferred a group of regional officials to Beijing. Mr Hai will be joining the Ministry of Treasury as an auditor."

Zhu Qi realised this was a serious matter. "Do you know what he wrote?"

"I was told that he issued a new interpretation for the store name, Home of Six Necessities."

Zhu Qi stood pensively.

"Master, could you talk with Chen Gonggong and see if we can sweep this incident under the carpet?" Chee Dazhu begged.

"You idiot. Who would dare cover up something that directly concerns the Son of Heaven? Besides, Chen Gonggong is probably waiting for something like this to happen."

"If His Majesty learns about this, my saviour will probably be thrown into jail."

"Don't ever call him your saviour again," Zhu Qi warned with a stern voice. "If you work here, there is only one saviour, and that's His Majesty."

Chee Dazhu lowered his head.

"Do you know why he went there and made those remarks?" Zhu Qi asked in a softened tone.

"I wasn't there. Two of our colleagues said Mr Hai intended his statement to set the record straight and dispel any rumours."

Zhu Qi continued to stand, staring into the distance.

Chee Dazhu became impatient. Beads of sweat streamed down his face.

"I think I understand the situation now. Hai Rui was appointed by the Prince of Yu. This has nothing to do with you. I do want you to report this matter to Grand Secretary Xu immediately. From now on, I won't allow you to see Hai Rui again. Bring me my clothes."

Chee Dazhu ran over to a bench under the eaves and picked up Zhu Qi's undershirt and official gown.

"Let's go," Zhu Qi said as he put on his clothes.

"Where are you going?" Chee Dazhu asked as he helped Zhu Qi tie his belt.

"Where else can I go? Didn't you tell me that someone has reported the matter to Chen Hong? If that's the case, I have to notify Lu Gonggong right away."

四

Emperor Hongwu was born to a family of impoverished peasants. After founding the Ming dynasty in 1368, he set very meagre salary levels for Imperial Government officials. Those who passed the imperial examinations and entered officialdom often lived in poverty if they refused to take bribes. Regional officials tended to fare better because local governments covered many of their living expenses such as their horses or horse-drawn carriages. In the capital city of Beijing, junior officials below grade four received an annual salary of no more than several dozen taels of silver. When the state coffers ran low, the Imperial Government paid officials in salt, pepper or fabrics. Since Beijing was an expensive city and officials had to purchase their own sedans, it was difficult for an imperial official to raise a family on his government salary.

Hai Rui had taught in a school for several years in Nanping, Fujian Province, before the Prince of Yu appointed him as a magistrate in Chun'an County, Zhejiang Province. Subsequently, he was transferred to Xingguo County in Jiangxi Province. As an imperial official, he lived a frugal life. In the aftermath of the political upheaval of 1562, he was offered a job in Beijing as an auditor at the Ministry of Treasury. By then, he was nearly impecunious. Since the Imperial Government only offered a limited amount of money to cover his relocation cost, he could not afford to travel by boat. He and his family ended up taking a carriage. Every thirty or forty kilometres, the carriage would drop him off at a government guesthouse, where, as a grade-six imperial official, he could enjoy free food and accommodation. Then he would change to a different carriage that would take him north.

Before departing Xingguo, Hai Rui wrote a letter to Wang Yongji, who had been transferred to Beijing the previous year and worked as an inspector at the Audit and Inspection Commission. In the letter, he asked Wang to find him a small courtyard house, specifically stating that the monthly rent could not exceed five strings of copper coins, equivalent to about five taels of silver. It was an impossible task. The minimum rent for a crude courtyard house in the northeast of the city was about eight strings of copper coins. Those houses were normally far away from the Imperial Government office complexes. In the end, Wang came up with an idea. He decided to sign two leases with the landlord. The first lease between Wang and the landlord would show the actual amount of eight strings of copper coins, and Wang promised to subsidise three strings. The amount of rent listed in a separate lease between Hai Rui and the landlord would show only five strings.

Even for eight strings of copper coins, Wang was only able to find a small, dilapidated courtyard house with an empty yard and unfurnished rooms. Wang hired a crew of masons and carpenters, who fixed the broken doors and windows, and repaired the leaky roof and the peeling walls. On the morning of Hai Rui's arrival, the workers were completing the repair work.

"The tenants will be here soon," Wang told two carpenters who were installing the last window frame. "Do it quickly!"

After the carpenters finished nailing the last window frame, Wang went to check the masons who were mending the walls inside a room on the east side.

"Are you finished?" he asked anxiously. "Pack up your equipment. You can go now. The tenants will be here any minute."

When the crew gathered in the courtyard, Wang beckoned to his aide who was standing at the door to wait for Hai Rui. "Come back here and pay the workers their remaining wages," he said.

The aide pulled out five strings of copper coins from his sleeve pocket and handed them to the head of the group.

"Thank you for the money," said the crew leader who then bowed before leaving.

"The cleaners are waiting outside," Wang said to the aide. "Ask them to move the furniture and cookware into the rooms. One more thing, wash and scrub the floor in the east room. That's Mrs Hai's room."

"Yes sir." Soon, a group of cleaners stepped into the courtyard, carrying several baskets containing pots, pans and bowls. Wang directed them to a small kitchen attached to the east room. Two were instructed to move a table and four chairs into the guest room in the middle. Another walked over to a well in the far right corner of the courtyard, and used a bucket to draw water so he could scrub the floor of Mrs Hai's room.

"Hurry up and use two buckets," he told the cleaners, instructing them to fetch water from the well.

The landlord, a middle-aged man in a long gown, went up to Wang. "Your Highness, thanks for your generosity," he said with an ingratiating smile. "This ancestral home of mine gets a free makeover."

Wang handed the landlord a copy of the lease. "When Mr Hai arrives, show this copy to him and then ask him to sign it for you," he said.

"Your Highness, didn't you sign the lease with me yesterday?"

"The lease I signed yesterday is for you and me. Don't tell Mr Hai about it. You need to sign this lease with Mr Hai today."

The landlord skimmed through the document and his expression changed to one of incredulity. "Your Highness, didn't you agree to pay eight strings of copper coins a month? Why have you changed the amount to five strings here?"

"This colleague of mine is an extremely honest and upright official, and he doesn't have a lot of money. So he can't afford eight strings of copper coins a month. The most he can pay is five strings."

"But you agreed to pay eight strings," the landlord complained in a raised voice. "I'm not going to rent him this house, even if you put a gun to my head."

"Let me finish. You'll still get eight strings. He'll pay you five strings and I'll pay you the remaining three."

"Wait, let me think about it…" said the landlord, who widened his eyes while trying to understand Wang's plan. "Are you saying that I'll still be receiving eight strings of copper coins as we agreed yesterday. Mr Hai will pay me five strings and you'll give me three without his knowledge?"

"I'm glad you've finally figured it out, but promise me that you won't tell Mr Hai about it. Also, let him know that the furniture in the house is all yours. Someday, when his family moves out, you can have all the furniture."

"Understood," the landlord replied with a beaming smile. "I will do accordingly."

"Sir, a carriage is coming this way," the aide shouted from outside the courtyard. "It must be Mr Hai's."

Wang strode out of the courtyard door and saw a carriage rumbling towards him. A man wearing a long linen gown and a conical hat came into view. Wang ran up to greet Hai Rui.

Seeing that Wang Yongji was coming towards him, Hai Rui took off his hat and quickened his steps.

The two friends paused a few feet away from each other, smiling. Wang stared at Hai Rui, shaking his head.

"I know what you're going to say," Hai Rui teased.

"What?"

"You're going to tell me that I should dress nicely because I'm now an official in Beijing, not a rustic county magistrate. Am I right? Last time we met, you promised to gift me two sets of silk gowns."

"You've guessed right, but since you don't want the silk gowns, I won't buy them. But first, let's get Amu and your wife off the carriage."

By then, Amu had lifted the carriage curtain. Wang waved at her and dashed over. He held her arm as she slowly disembarked. As he was helping her to the courtyard door, he caught a glimpse of Hai Rui's wife who was sitting quietly inside the carriage. Her face was as white as a sheet.

"We have a patient in the carriage," Wang said to his aide. "Bring a chair over."

"That's not proper," Amu said before turning to Hai Rui. "You should carry your wife inside. Don't worry about me."

"Yes, Amu," said Hai Rui, who gave Wang a helpless glance.

"There's no need," said someone behind them. Wang and Hai Rui turned around and saw that the two imperial agents had already disengaged the horse from the carriage. They lifted the carriage inside which Mrs Hai was sitting, and carried it all the way into the courtyard.

Everyone watched them in awe.

The two imperial agents paused in the middle of the courtyard, looking calm and effortless as if they were holding an empty wooden box. "Where do you want us to put it?" the agent in front asked.

"Would you please place it outside the west room?" Hai Rui said. The agents complied. Putting the carriage down gently by the west room, they dusted off their hands and stepped outside.

Wang noticed that the two imperial agents were standing either side of the courtyard door. He led Amu to the east room and sat her down on a chair near the window. Then, he pulled Hai Rui aside and asked in a near whisper: "Who are they?"

"Can't you tell? They're imperial secret agents," Hai Rui replied with a look of indifference.

"You've just arrived in Beijing! What have you done to provoke them into following you all the way home?"

"As I mentioned in my letter to you, I'm going to get in trouble with them sooner or later," Hai Rui said in a playful tone. "So I decided that the sooner, the better."

The presence of the imperial agents made the landlord nervous. When he overheard the conversation between Wang Yongji and Hai Rui, he was nonplussed.

Hai Rui strolled around, taking a real liking to the small courtyard house that Wang had secured for him. There were three south-facing rooms. He and his wife occupied the west room, and Amu slept in the east room. The guest room in the middle had two additional side doors, one leading to the couple's bedroom and the other to Amu's room. At night, when Hai Rui needed to take care of his mother, he could keep Amu's door open and lie on a folding bamboo recliner in the guest room.

The most precious thing in the courtyard was a luxuriant locust tree, which provided welcome shade. A small table with a few chairs would allow them to eat outside or simply enjoy the cool air. To the east of the courtyard was a three-metre-deep well that supplied clear drinking water, a rare luxury in a city that frequently suffered drought. For Hai's mother, who washed and scrubbed the floor every day, the well was a convenient addition.

By now, it was already noon. Wang's aide went out and bought food from a nearby restaurant. After Hai's family finished their lunch in the guest room, the aide collected the chopsticks and bowls, and carried them to the kitchen to wash. Hai Rui set up a bed in the east room for Amu to rest. As he and Wang stepped out of the drawing room, they bumped into the landlord, who waved at them with a feigned smile.

"Who is this gentleman?" Hai Rui asked Wang.

"Ah, I was so busy that I forgot to introduce you two. This is your landlord. Now that both of you are here, why don't you sign your lease?"

Hai Rui and Wang Yongji sauntered over to the small table under the shade and sat down on the bamboo chairs. The landlord followed them, but refused to take his seat.

"Please sit down," said Wang. "You need to sign the lease as well."

The landlord appeared a bit reluctant. Sneaking a glance at the courtyard door, he said in a low voice: "The two strangers are still here. They are waiting in the alley."

Hai Rui and Wang looked at each other without responding.

The landlord thought that Hai Rui and Wang did not comprehend what he was telling them. Gesticulating wildly, he whispered: "Those two are imperial secret agents, I mean, they are in the alley, monitoring everything…"

"Don't let them scare you," said Wang. "They're not watching you. Sign the lease please."

The landlord peered at the courtyard door and suddenly fell to his knees. "Your Highness, I know you two are kind people, but I don't think I… As you know, this house was built by my great-great-grandfather. My family has lived here for generations. We make an honest living and we have no intention of getting into trouble with the law. Please have mercy and keep my family safe."

Even though the landlord spoke in a roundabout way, Hai Rui and Wang quickly grasped what he was insinuating. Wang's face fell. "What do you mean?" Wang asked. "Are you saying that we're posing a risk to your family?"

"Your Highness, you serve His Majesty at the Audit and Inspection Commission. How could you not understand my plight? Please leave and find another house for your friend. I'm willing to reimburse all of the money you spent on repairs and renovation."

Wang lost his patience. "Nonsense! How dare you order a tenant to move out after he has just moved in!"

The landlord simply knelt there and refused to sign the lease.

The landlord's plea put Hai Rui in an awkward situation. "We have not signed the contract yet," he said to Wang. "If he's unwilling to rent the house to me, I have no choice but to leave. But I have an elderly person and a patient. They have just gone to rest. There's no way I can move out today."

Wang felt that he had to reveal the truth to Hai Rui: "Don't worry, we're not going to move. I signed a one-year lease with him yesterday. You can stay as long as you like."

Before Hai Rui had time to respond, Wang turned to the landlord. "You don't have to sign the fake lease. Get out of here right away!"

The landlord was close to tears. "Mr Wang and Mr Hai, both of you work for the Imperial Government, and His Majesty pays you good salaries. As the saying goes, a scholar official dies from remonstrance, and a warrior dies on the battlefield. You're both brave and fearless because of your loyalty to His Majesty. But I'm a mere commoner. I can't afford to court trouble."

As the landlord went on with his plea, the mild-mannered Wang Yongji lost his temper. "What you are asking is unacceptable," he scolded. "Are you leaving or not? If you don't, I'm going to get up and summon the two imperial secret agents. I'll have them talk with you."

"Please don't," the landlord implored, springing to his feet. "I'll go now…"

As he was leaving, a cicada in the locust tree produced a

piercing buzz, startling the landlord. He crept out, looking utterly wretched.

Wang sat down quietly, with his head down.

Hai Rui did not speak. By now, he had figured out the story about the fake lease, and understood the meticulous arrangements that Wang had made for him. More important, he saw how courageous it was for Wang to stand by him at a time when he could be taken away by the imperial agents at any second.

The cicada's shrill chirping accentuated the silence in the courtyard.

Wang's aide walked over with a pot of tea and two cups.

"Please wait for me outside," Wang said to the aide. "And close the door behind you."

"Well, we always say that national affairs are difficult to manage," said Wang. "So are family affairs."

Hai Rui picked up his cup and raised it to Wang. They both took a sip and put their cups down on the table.

"You're a true friend who never hesitates in sharing his wealth, but I have nothing to give back. You know I'll never be able to repay the money you've spent on me. You don't even get a proper 'thank you' from me. Regardless, I accept and deeply appreciate your generosity and kindness. I didn't mean to provoke anyone and cause trouble when I got here, but our country is seriously ill. If every official treats the health of our nation with liquorice root, a sweet but useless herbal remedy, the Great Ming Empire will die. When a nation is suffering, no family is spared. Now that the Imperial Palace has brought both of us to Beijing, we'll get through these tough times together."

"You always put me to shame," Wang said. "It's been almost a year since I started with the Audit and Inspection Commission. During this period, I've handled a few cases and submitted several censure reports. I guess you can regard my work as offering useless liquorice roots. I admire the fact that you were able to prescribe a dose of bitter medicine upon your arrival and target the true cause of our country's disease. The Imperial Palace is like a pond of stagnant water. If you're brave enough to throw a stone into the water and stir it up, that's not a bad thing."

"Oh come on, I'm not that powerful," said Hai Rui, waving his hand. "I just want to tell the truth. If something is black, I want to tell people it's black. If it's white, I'll say it's white. Nowadays, people are afraid of speaking honestly about what is white and what is black, let alone reforming the Imperial Government. While I was in Xingguo County, I tried to do some meaningful things for ordinary people. But every move I made was met with resistance. In the end, I hardly accomplished anything. When the Imperial Palace is corrupt and dysfunctional, the whole country loses its moral compass."

"I have no problems with your passion for state affairs, but you can't ignore your family. Allow me to be frank. During the three years you were in Xingguo, you failed your family. Your little girl drowned in a river. If you had been home at the time of the accident, she would have been rescued. Your wife wouldn't have suffered a miscarriage and become so ill like this. Like Mencius once said: 'There are three ways to be unfilial, and the worst is to not produce an offspring.'"

"I deserve the blame," Hai Rui said, his deep voice conveying remorse.

"Now that you're in Beijing, I'm sure things will improve," said Wang, who was an optimist by nature. "I almost forgot to share some good news with you. Can you guess what it is?"

"Has Doctor Li Shizhen arrived in Beijing?"

"He's been here for a month now," Wang bragged like a true insider. "The Prince of Yu has been ill for some time. He ostentatiously invited Dr Li to Beijing to offer him treatment. But the Crown Prince's true intent is to send Dr Li to Yuxi Palace and treat His Majesty. Let's hope that Grand Secretary Xu and Lu Gonggong can persuade His Majesty to grant Dr Li an audience. Even though Dr Li is opposed to the practice of alchemy, he truly cares about His Majesty and he is a patriot at heart. As a filial son, the Prince of Yu has gone out of his way to bring Dr Li to Beijing to save His Majesty's health. I assume His Majesty will appreciate his son's painstaking efforts."

"There are very few people who truly understand Dr Li. He wanders the land, but his mind always dwells at the court of Ming," said Hai Rui, who was becoming emotional. "Remember what I told you when we were all in Zhejiang? I have lived over half of my life. You and Dr Li are my only true friends."

"I don't deserve that honour," Wang said. "I assume that your remarks at Home of Six Necessities will cause a stir in the next few days. Once the dust settles, I'll invite Dr Li to come and visit your family. He can use the occasion to examine your wife and prescribe some medicine for her."

Hai Rui's face turned sombre at the mention of his wife. "Yongji, let me say something from the heart. If you hadn't been in Beijing, I wouldn't have dared say and write those words at Home of Six Necessities. There's a possibility they might arrest me and send me to the Imperial Prison either today or tomorrow. If that happens, I'm entrusting my family to your care. I'm serious."

Hai Rui's words saddened Wang. "First, if anything happens, I promise to take care of your family. Second, I don't think we'll ever reach that point. Since I've been here for a year now, I probably have a better grasp of palace politics and know more about His Majesty's personality than you do. Even though your writing was directed at His Majesty, he knows you were motivated by a sense of loyalty and dedication towards the Great Ming Empire. His Majesty is a wise ruler, and I'm sure he'll understand your good intentions. As I said just now, if you prescribe the right medicine, His Majesty won't turn against you."

Hai Rui's wife, who was resting in the west room, started a coughing fit. Soon, the coughing aggravated and she was gasping for breath. Hai Rui rose from his chair and rushed into the room.

While Wang was standing by Hai Rui's bedroom door, waiting for his friend, he saw Amu come out of the guest room. He stepped over and greeted her.

"Mr Wang, I'm afraid we have to bother you again," Amu pleaded. "Could you send for a doctor?"

"Don't worry, I've already made arrangements," Wang reassured her as she walked towards the west room.

明

Emperor Jiajing was also afflicted with an illness.

Large chunks of ice were sitting inside two containers next to the altar, reducing the temperature in the meditation room to a comfortable level. At this moment, Lu Fang was soaking a snow-white cotton velvet face towel in a basin of ice water. He wrung it slightly and folded the towel into a strip. Holding the wet towel in his left hand and a dry one in his right hand, he tiptoed towards Emperor Jiajing. He wiped the sweat from Emperor Jiajing's face with the dry towel, before placing the cold, wet towel on the emperor's forehead.

In May 1562, Yan Song retired to his native village in Jiangxi Province. Upon taking over the Privy Council, Grand Secretary Xu Jie dug out the previously censored reports submitted by officials in the two capital cities and thirteen provinces, and reviewed all the reports that Yan Song had discarded or hidden. Only then did he realise that the political and fiscal situation in the country was much worse than he had imagined. Little by little, Grand Secretary Xu, Gao Gong and Zhang Juzheng leaked their findings to Emperor Jiajing. Daily accounts of the country's dire financial and political problems debilitated the emperor. As his health worsened, he began to take more and more of his 'elixirs of immortality', which contained poisonous substances such as mercury and arsenic.

Meanwhile, the Privy Council was facing tremendous challenges in salvaging the fiscal crisis. All they could do was to 'rob the Wang's to pay the Li's'. In the beginning of the year, multiple disasters struck, threatening to rock the very foundation of the Great Ming Empire. Since the military experienced severe funding shortages, the troops stationed along the northern borders failed to fend off a series of erratic raids from the Tartars. A few tribes east of the Liao River had also started provoking the imperial troops. In the south, government forces under Governor Hu had conquered the pirates along the coastal regions in China's southeast. However, different groups of pirates popped up in Guangdong and Fujian Provinces, plundering and destroying many local villages there. In Beijing and many large provinces, discontent was brewing among imperial officials, who had not been paid for months. In the north-western province of Sha'anxi, about a hundred and fifty people working for one of the imperial lords besieged the imperial inspector's yamen after their demands for unpaid wages went unanswered. The protesters beat up the head of the Provincial Civil Affairs Department and set his house on fire. Elsewhere, when the Imperial Government imposed higher taxes to replenish the state coffers, corrupt officials exploited the situation to line their own pockets. As a consequence, residents living in Wanping and Daxing Counties near Beijing fled in droves to escape the heavy tax burdens. In some places, entire villages became abandoned.

The dire situation prompted Grand Secretary Xu to submit another censure report against Yan Shifan, Luo Wenlong and several senior-ranking officials. Upon reading the report, Emperor Jiajing ordered the execution of Yan Shifan and the imprisonment of a large number of corrupt officials. Authorities raided their homes and confiscated their assets.

In June, the beleaguered emperor became so weak that he found it hard to conceal his illness. The summer heat made him sweat profusely. Nevertheless, he listened to the advice of his trusted Taoist priests and refused to open the windows for fresh air. In a deliberate effort to defy the seasons, he wore a thick cotton gown. Even though he refused to give up his usual meditation routine, he could sit in the lotus position for no longer than half an hour before laying down to rest. His gown was always soaked with sweat.

In the midst of chaos, Grand Secretary Xu felt overwhelmed. Despite his hectic schedule, he always made a point of visiting the emperor after he had finished handling major issues of the day in the Privy Council's duty room. When sitting next to Emperor Jiajing, he tried all means to get the emperor to approve or acquiesce to proposals by cabinet members such as Gao Gong and Zhang Juzhen to remedy the current problems facing the nation.

Instead of sitting on his prayer mat as usual, Emperor Jiajing was today lying on a bamboo recliner. With a large stack of papers on his knees, Grand Secretary Xu was sitting by the recliner on Yan Song's old embroidered pouf. The emperor's eyes, with dark circles underneath them, were half closed. His forehead beaded with sweat.

Grand Secretary Xu's mission today was multifold. Over the past month, Treasury officials had made an inventory of the assets confiscated from members of the Yan Clan. They had planned to redistribute the money and support different initiatives. Grand Secretary Xu had intended to come in and brief Emperor Jiajing on the plan in the afternoon. However, after Chee Dazhu tipped him off about the incident at Home of Six Necessities, he changed his mind and showed up at Yuxi Palace before noon. Obviously, Hai Rui had stirred up a hornets' nest. With the help of Lu Fang, Grand Secretary Xu hoped to mend the situation and spare the Prince of Yu a stinging rebuke.

The cold, wet towel that Lu Fang had placed on Emperor Jiajing's forehead helped ease his fever. Even though he still furrowed his eyebrows, he felt well enough to speak. When he talked, he lost his usual calculated calmness. "Feel free to spill all the bad news you have. I enjoy listening to it," he said, sounding irritated. "It's just a war in the east and a flood in the west. The sky won't fall."

Grand Secretary Xu and Lu Fang exchanged knowing glances.

"Your Majesty, I agree," Grand Secretary Xu replied. By then, he had long acquired the skills of maintaining a perpetual pleasant face to cope with the emperor's unpredictable mood swings. Rising from the pouf, he bowed before discussing the asset inventory in his stiff Mandarin with a thick Wu dialect: "Your Majesty, we have catalogued the assets of nearly a thousand corrupt officials, including those of Yan Shifan, Luo Wenlong and Yan Maoqing. In total, we were able to collect three hundred and seventy thousands taels of gold, six million, four hundred thousand taels of silver, and various antiques and jewellery items that are worth nearly three million taels of silver."

"Please go on," said Emperor Jiajing, who had by now opened his eyes.

"Your Majesty, the Privy Council has convened several meetings with senior ministerial officials. We have decided to allocate three million, six hundred thousand taels of silver to the Ministry of Defence. This includes one million, six hundred thousand to purchase military supplies for the troops of Generals Yu Dayou and

Qi Jiguang, who are now battling the pirates in Guangdong and Fujian Provinces, and an additional two million for our troops guarding the northern border."

Emperor Jiajing thought about the plan for a moment before giving his assent. Then he closed his eyes.

Grand Secretary Xu handed the two spending requests to Lu Fang, who brought them over to Emperor Jiajing's desk and started reviewing each item.

"At the moment, several provincial governments owe salaries to their officials," Grand Secretary Xu continued. "In the provinces of Shanxi, Sha'anxi, Henan, Yunnan and Guizhou, the governments have been in arrears for over a year. The Ministry of Personnel has requested two million, seven hundred thousand for these provinces as salary payments."

Emperor Jiajing remained silent. Lu Fang sat at the emperor's desk and did not come over to collect the Ministry of Personnel's requests from Grand Secretary Xu.

"I assume that other provinces are also experiencing similar difficulties," Emperor Jiajing said after a long pause. "Give me the full list. We can divide up the remaining amount and give it all away!"

"Your Majesty, the situation in the other provinces is slightly better. I've had meetings with the governors of these provinces. We will figure out ways to help them address these problems at a later date."

The emperor's face softened. "All right then. You have the final say. Distribute the money to the provinces you just listed so they can pay their employees."

"I wouldn't dare make a decision without your approval, but I will do so accordingly," replied Grand Secretary Xu as he drew out the spending item from his pile and handed it to Lu Fang who took the request grudgingly.

"Get me another cold towel," Emperor Jiajing instructed Lu Fang.

Putting his calligraphy brush on the desk, Lu Fang scurried over to the gold basin on a wash stand and fetched another wet towel for the emperor. As Lu Fang was changing the towel, Emperor Jiajing closed his eyes again. "We have given money to the military and the governments," the emperor mumbled. "Do we have anything left for my subjects?"

"The benevolence and righteousness of a wise ruler," said Grand Secretary Xu. "Your Majesty, Jiangxi Province was struck by a series of natural disasters earlier in the year. During the rainy season in March, four prefectures and counties were flooded. In the summer, seven more prefectures suffered severe drought. The governor of Jiangxi has requested that we provide tax relief for people in these disaster areas and allocate some money so his government can purchase grain from neighbouring provinces to prevent a possible famine..."

"Please finish your report," Emperor Jiajing urged when Grand Secretary Xu paused.

"Since the second half of last year, some local governments have started to increase taxes. For example, in Wanping and Daxing Counties in Shuntian Prefecture, the taxes last year increased threefold. As a consequence, people have fled in droves. Nine in ten houses are now abandoned. It is hard to believe these things are happening right outside Your Majesty's home territory!"

Emperor Jiajing sighed. Grand Secretary Xu became emotional. Pulling out a silk handkerchief from his sleeve pocket, he wiped his tears. "The Ministry of Treasury has requested two million taels of silver for the local governments to reimburse taxpayers," he stated. "Out of this total, about six hundred thousand will be set aside for people in Wanping and Daxing Counties. We hope that the money will bring vagrants back to their villages so they can resume farming."

"That's enough!" said Emperor Jiajing as he removed the wet towel from his forehead. "Have you put the magistrates of Wanping and Daxing under arrest?"

"Your Majesty, they have been dismissed from their positions. As far as I know, they're under investigation."

"Raid their homes first. Distribute the money to local residents and reimburse their overpaid taxes."

"Yes, Your Majesty, but the amount of money we have confiscated from the two magistrates is only a drop in the bucket. It'll help, but not much. The two million taels of silver we have budgeted is not enough to cover all of the refunds. The important thing is to reassure the public that Your Majesty cares about them."

Lu Fang did not accept the Ministry of Treasury's tax relief proposal when Grand Secretary Xu handed it to him. Looking a bit bewildered, the chief eunuch stared at Emperor Jiajing.

"If I'm willing, why are you hesitating?" Emperor Jiajing said to Lu Fang sarcastically. "Let's distribute everything we have. I don't mind living inside this ramshackle palace. If the worst comes to the worst, all my palace staff can put on rags and go out begging for food on the street."

Lu Fang felt obligated to speak up on behalf of the emperor. "Grand Secretary Xu, we're in the middle of repairing His Majesty's Longevity Palace and Palace of Eternal Longevity. The projects are only half completed. Besides, we have to feed the one hundred thousand palace employees. Are they covered in your plan?"

Grand Secretary Xu stood up. "No matter how tough things get, we cannot let His Majesty and his staff suffer. The royal court will receive the remaining two million taels of silver. Part of it will be used to repair and renovate the two palaces. You can use the rest to cover various palace expenses."

Emperor Jiajing closed his eyes again. Grand Secretary Xu and Lu Fang waited anxiously. Silence fell in the meditation room.

Knowing that the Privy Council had tried their best to balance the competing needs of different groups with the confiscated money, Emperor Jiajing still had a tough time accepting the harsh reality. "There's a popular saying among commoners: one gives away one's wealth in exchange for peace and good health," he said. "Now that we have distributed every penny we have confiscated, do you think the Heavenly God will agree to restore my health? Lu Fang, sign off on all the budget requests."

Grand Secretary Xu knelt down next to Emperor Jiajing. Lu Fang also dropped to his knees but he did not sign the final spending request.

"The Heavenly God has granted longevity to my benevolent ruler, but your divine body needs rest," said Grand Secretary Xu.

"Your robust health will be a tremendous source of comfort for the people of our country."

"I agree with Grand Secretary Xu," Lu Fang chimed in. "Even though the Heavenly God is guarding Your Majesty, you should also take care of your divine body."

"Do you all really think I'm ill?" asked Emperor Jiajing, who suddenly turned hostile. "How can I be ill?"

Since he had fallen ill, Emperor Jiajing had become more capricious. Lu Fang and Grand Secretary Xu had been frequently subjected to similar impulsive outbursts, which bordered on insanity. Fatigued by such torment, they simply knelt on the floor with their heads down. Neither of them said a word.

Emperor Jiajing stopped questioning them and struggled to get up from his recliner.

"Your Majesty, watch out!" warned Lu Fang, who sprang to his feet and held the emperor's arm.

Emperor Jiajing brushed off Lu Fang's hands as he wobbled towards his prayer mat. Lu Fang followed him. When Emperor Jiajing sat down and crossed his legs, the chief eunuch stood behind him, ready to help if needed. Grand Secretary Xu also rose from his pouf and watched the emperor nervously. He was prepared to jump in and assist if the emperor were to collapse.

"When a person falls ill, does the Heavenly God know about it?" the emperor murmured before closing his eyes and starting his meditation exercise. A few minutes into his practice, large beads of sweat dripped down from his forehead. The colour drained from his face.

"Your Majesty! Master!" Grand Secretary Xu and Lu Fang called at the same time. Fear spread across their faces as they bent over to help. But Emperor Jiajing tried to straighten his body and sat there stubbornly. "My pills," he muttered through his teeth.

"Let's send for an imperial doctor," Grand Secretary Xu shouted out of desperation.

Lu Fang hesitated for a moment. As he was about to summon a junior eunuch outside the palace, Emperor Jiajing stopped him. "Do you all want me to die? Hand me the pills!" he ordered. By then, he was soaked with sweat and his face was turning blue.

"Please hold His Majesty for me," said Lu Fang. He released his hands and dashed over to the altar, where he removed the lid from a gold-plated box and picked out a red immortality pill. "Master, here is your pill," said Lu Fang as he rushed over with the pill and a cup of water.

Emperor Jiajing opened his mouth slowly. Lu Fang held the emperor's neck and put the pill in his mouth before offering him some water.

Emperor Jiajing swallowed the pill with difficulty. Then he pulled up his body, trying to straighten his back. Grand Secretary Xu helped him up. The pills seemed to have worked miracles. Soon, Emperor Jiajing's energy appeared to be restored. The sweat on his forehead gradually disappeared, and his face was blazing red as blood surged back to his face.

When Emperor Jiajing resumed his practice, Grand Secretary Xu and Lu Fang breathed a sigh of relief. But the emperor's flushed face deepened their gloom and concern.

"Xu Jie," Emperor Jiajing said calmly.

"Yes, Your Majesty," Grand Secretary Xu replied with a heavy heart.

"What were you saying? Did you plan to invite one of those doctors at the Imperial Hospital to examine me?"

"Yes, Your Majesty," replied Grand Secretary Xu, whose eyes had become moistened.

"Lu Fang, is this your idea too?"

"Master," replied the chief eunuch. Having spent decades serving the emperor, Lu Fang felt more emotionally attached to Emperor Jiajing than to Grand Secretary Xu. Regardless of whether Emperor Jiajing would be furious or not, he felt it his responsibility to speak his mind. "As long as a person eats grain, he will get sick one day, regardless of whether he's a deity or a grand master. So, both Grand Secretary Xu and I feel the same way. Can we be bold enough to seek your permission and invite a physician to examine you? If you don't like those doctors at the Imperial Hospital, we can send for a prestigious one from another province."

Emperor Jiajing looked at Lu Fang and then at Grand Secretary Xu. "Come over here," he said tenderly.

Grand Secretary Xu and Lu Fang wiped their tears and moved closer to each other.

"I'm turning sixty very soon," Emperor Jiajing said softly. "For someone who has practised self-cultivation for decades, sixty is a threshold. Once I cross it, I'll achieve the status of immortality. In other words, none of those morons at the Imperial Hospital can help me. Nobody can help me, do you understand?"

Grand Secretary Xu considered himself an upright Confucian scholar. Unlike Yan Song, his predecessor who used to bow to Emperor Jiajing's every whim, he simply lowered his head in silence and did not accept the emperor's words indiscriminately.

As Emperor Jiajing's personal servant, Lu Fang had to obey his master's wish. Sad as he was, he replied: "Your Majesty, I completely understand."

Emperor Jiajing nodded and switched topic. "How is the Prince of Yu?" he said in a near whisper. "Which genius doctor have you invited to Beijing to examine him?"

Lu Fang turned to Grand Secretary Xu.

"Your Majesty, we invited Dr Li Shizhen, who used to be employed at the Imperial Hospital," said Grand Secretary Xu. "The Prince of Yu has taken the medicine Dr Li has prescribed, and his condition has improved dramatically."

The pill reenergised Emperor Jiajing and his eyes became animated. "So, my son's physician is now in Beijing," he said. "I heard that a different kind of doctor has also arrived in Beijing today. He visited Home of Six Necessities and prescribed a dose of medicine that he claimed will cure the ills of our country. Who is that person?"

Neither Grand Secretary Xu nor Lu Fang responded.

Emperor Jiajing gave Grand Secretary Xu a sideways glance. "We normally review government reports in the afternoon," he said. "But you rushed over here in the morning. Are you here to discuss the so-called prescription that a certain person wrote this morning? Lu Fang, bring the writing that Chen Hong delivered to me earlier."

Walking over to a cabinet that contained different types of

government reports, Lu Fang picked out a roll of paper that Chen Hong had delivered, and handed it to Grand Secretary Xu.

"It's supposed to contain all the elements of a good cure. What do you think?" Emperor Jiajing asked.

Grand Secretary Xu unfolded the paper and read it intently. "Your Majesty, please forgive me for my dimwittedness. I just don't see how the writing contains all the elements of a good cure."

"Do you mean to say that you cannot detect the hidden message in these words?" Emperor Jiajing asked with a sarcastic smile. "If you don't see anything wrong with it, why did you hurry over here this morning to clarify the situation? Are you trying to protect the Prince of Yu?"

This was the most challenging part of Grand Secretary Xu's job – the emperor was extremely sensitive, highly suspicious and unabashedly blunt. Grand Secretary Xu had no idea how to reply to him. He bowed his head without speaking.

The emperor shifted his piercing eyes to Lu Fang. "Zhu Qi came to talk with you, didn't he?" he asked. "What did you two discuss?"

"Your Majesty, Zhu Qi came this morning and reported this incident to me," Lu Fang replied truthfully, as he always did.

"Chen Hong is in charge of the Imperial Investigative Agency, and he was already made aware of the incident. Wasn't that enough? Why did Zhu Qi come to see you? Now that he has consulted with you, tell me what you think of the writing."

"Your Majesty, the person is a low-ranking official who has just been transferred to Beijing," said Lu Fang. "He's one of those people who are full of themselves and have no idea of the immensity of heaven and earth. What he wrote at Home of Six Necessities is worthless. Zhu Qi reported the incident to me because he knew that Your Majesty was feeling a little indisposed. He wanted me to clarify the situation for you, lest you might be upset. He didn't want it to aggravate your illness."

"I'm asking what you think of the writing!"

"Your Majesty, I have seen the writing. I don't think he has broken any taboos. Of course, the writing has nothing to do with the Prince of Yu."

"Nothing to do with the Prince of Yu?" Emperor Jiajing sneered. "Where does this person work? What is his name?"

"Your Majesty, his name appears to be Hai Rui or something," Lu Fang replied.

"What do you mean 'appears to be Hai Rui or something'? Tell me how many imperial officials are called Hai Rui?"

"Your Majesty, that is a good question. If I remember correctly, this Hai Rui used to be the magistrate of Xingguo County in Jiangxi Province."

"He was appointed by the Prince of Yu, wasn't he? Then how dare you say that his writing has nothing to do with the Prince of Yu!"

Lu Fang sank to his knees. So did Grand Secretary Xu.

"I wouldn't dare lie to Your Majesty," Lu Fang explained as he kowtowed to Emperor Jiajing. "This Hai Rui person arrived in Beijing this morning. When he walked past Home of Six Necessities, he dropped in and wrote down those words. The Prince of Yu has been home recovering from his illness for nearly a month now. There is no way he would have known about it."

Emperor Jiajing's face softened. "I believe you. But Hai Rui knew very well that I had urged Yan Song to change the name of the store. Why did he pounce on the word 'necessities' and create a big fuss around it?"

Grand Secretary Xu felt obligated to pipe in: "I will summon him to the Privy Council's duty room today and demand a clear answer from him."

"I'm demanding a clear answer from both of you," Emperor Jiajing insisted. "Why did he 'pick a bone' with me on that word?"

Since Grand Secretary Xu had made it known to the emperor that he wasn't made aware of the incident until later, he chose to keep silent. Lu Fang decided to answer the question. Even though he had rehearsed the words beforehand, he was still nervous. "Master, I couldn't figure it out either," he said. "But Zhu Qi questioned his subordinates who were present. They overheard Hai Rui claiming that he wrote those words to 'set the record straight and stem rumours'. I think that was what he said."

"Hai Rui intended to stem rumours for me?" Emperor Jiajing asked. "It sounds like the plaque has generated a lot of rumours!"

"Your Majesty, King Wen of Zhou was credited for compiling *I Ching* and the Duke of Zhou for the creation of imperial rituals. Their works were misunderstood initially, and the world was full of rumours. When Your Majesty urged Yan Song to write the plaque for Home of Six Necessities, your intention was to unite the people of our Great Ming Empire and promote stability. But when ignorance exists, your divine intentions would inevitably be misconstrued. In May of this year, Your Majesty ordered the execution of Yan Shifan and other members of the Yan Clan, and yet the plaque with Yan Song's inscription still hangs above the door of Home of Six Necessities. Some rumours are bound to spread. Hai Rui must have heard something. I personally think that Hai Rui meant what he stated. He wrote those words to set the record straight and stem those rumours."

Grand Secretary Xu's explanation, sincere and appropriate, convinced Emperor Jiajing of Hai Rui's innocent intention. But some of his suspicions lingered. "We have many senior-ranking officials. None of them came forward to help me dispel rumours. But an auditor at the Ministry of Treasury, with a mere *juren* degree, took upon the task on his first day in Beijing. It sounds like he's a capable person!"

Grand Secretary Xu did not answer for fear that he would be prejudiced in favour of Hai Rui. Emperor Jiajing understood the situation. So he singled out Lu Fang. "I know that Grand Secretary Xu wouldn't give me his honest opinion. Why don't you answer me?"

Lu Fang decided to take a risk and speak his mind. "Master, Hai Rui is a mere grade-six official. I wouldn't overestimate his ability, but it's the thought that counts."

"What thought?"

"The thought of standing up to speak for Your Majesty."

"Is he speaking for me, or are you speaking for him, or are you speaking on behalf of my son?"

Lu Fang raised his head and his eyes were filled with sadness. "Master, if a person thinks of Your Majesty first and sincerely shares your worries, I consider him a man of conscience. I think Hai Rui's writing can truly help Your Majesty clarify the situation and win the public's hearts, but he was just a bit too bold and reckless. I would prefer him over those who submit one censure report after another for the pure sake of showing off their loyalty."

Emperor Jiajing's face was still gloomy but his gaze brightened. "Our Great Ming Empire is not short of bold and fearless individuals, but I haven't encountered many who have a conscience," he said. "As for this Hai Rui person, I have no idea what intention he is harbouring, and neither do I know if he is a man of conscience. Maybe the Prince of Yu does. Since my son hired him, why don't you deliver Hai Rui's writings to him? Let the Prince of Yu copy those words on a separate piece of paper and sign his name. We'll inscribe them on another plaque and send it to Home of Six Necessities. Let's see what kinds of rumours this one generates."

Lu Fang took the paper from Emperor Jiajing.

"You don't need to go. Bring Chen Hong in."

By then, Lu Fang realised that Chen Hong was already waiting outside Yuxi Palace. He walked to the door and poked his head out. "Is Chen Hong here? His Majesty wants to see him."

Chen Hong crept into the main hall like a ghost. When he reached the door of the meditation room, he knelt down. "Your Majesty, your humble servant Chen Hong is here," he announced.

"Why are you kneeling outside? Can't you come in?"

Chen Hong kowtowed before getting to his feet. Then he stepped in with his head bowed like a shy bride.

Neither Lu Fang nor Grand Secretary Xu greeted him.

"I have three things for you. First, take Hai Rui's writing to the Prince of Yu. Ask him to copy it, sign his name and have it inscribed on a plaque. Then, deliver the plaque to Home of Six Necessities, ordering them to hang it up."

"Yes, Your Majesty," Chen Hong said in a lower voice. He moved forward, and Lu Fang handed him Hai Rui's paper.

"Second, I want you to stop by the Imperial Investigative Agency and tell those minions there that the agency is under your control. In the future, when something happens, they can only report it to you. If anyone dares to overstep you and complain to others, you know what to do with those offenders."

"Yes, Your Majesty," Chen Hong deliberately answered softly and slowly.

'Louder," Emperor Jiajing ordered him.

"Yes, Your Majesty!" Chen Hong responded in his loud, high-pitched voice.

"As for the third thing, I've already told you. There's no need to repeat it."

"Yes, Your Majesty," Chen Hong replied a little reluctantly.

2

"Greetings, Second Daddy!"

Feng Bao, an imperial caretaker or daban, was carrying the five-year-old prince on his back, and playing hide-and-seek inside a long corridor of wooden pillars in the front yard when he saw Chen Hong stride into the entrance with two junior eunuchs. Placing the young prince down on the ground, Feng Bao gathered his peers and hurried over. They dropped down on their knees and kowtowed to Chen Hong.

"Please rise," said Chen Hong, who gazed at Feng Bao. "Is the Prince of Yu doing well?"

"The last I heard, his health has improved a lot," Feng Bao replied reverentially. "Dr Li is checking his pulse at this moment."

"Take me to his room."

Feng Bao and several young junior eunuchs stood up and led Chen Gong into the Prince of Yu's inner chamber.

"Daban, stop, you can't leave me here!" shouted the young prince, who leapt out from behind a pillar and blocked Feng Bao.

Chen Hong was about to climb a flight of stone steps when he caught sight of the young prince. He immediately fell to his knees. "Aiya, Your Royal Highness," he greeted the boy. The two junior eunuchs who came with Chen Hong also knelt next to the stairs.

"Who is he?" asked the boy, pointing at Chen Hong.

Feng Bao squatted down and hugged the boy. "Your Highness, this is Chen Gonggong," he explained. "He is your grandfather's daban. He's my boss. Your Highness, please ask Chen Gonggong to rise."

Despite his young age, the boy had already started to show the stubborn arrogance of a prince. "Who makes him your boss?" he said, pursing his lips. "When he's here, you only talk to him and don't play with me any more."

Feng Bao pleaded desperately: "Your Royal Highness, please ask Chen Gonggong to rise. He needs to see your father."

"You may rise," the boy ordered. "But you can't take my Daban Feng away."

Chen Hong stood up and laughed awkwardly. "I... I won't take Daban Feng away," he said before turning to Feng Bao. "Why don't you stay here and play with His Royal Highness?"

Feng Bao nodded and said to two of his colleagues at the Prince of Yu's mansion: "Please usher Second Daddy into the backyard."

明

In July, Dr Li Shizhen prescribed the Prince of Yu two courses of medicine to help improve his health and boost his energy. Now, he was on the mend. Since Dr Li asked the maids to open all the windows and the south-facing door to promote indoor air circulation, Chen Hong could see the Prince of Yu when he entered the backyard. The Crown Prince was sitting on a chair near the north wall while Dr Li was taking his pulse.

Chen Hong knew that it was common practice for veteran doctors like Dr Li to close their eyes while checking a patient's pulse. They needed to focus, and no disruption was allowed. Even though he was there to deliver an imperial edict, he decided to wait in the courtyard.

Noticing Chen Hong out of the corner of his eye, the Prince of Yu made to stand up.

"Don't move," Dr Li reminded him with his eyes still closed.

The Prince of Yu remained sitting, but couldn't hold still. "Dr Li, Chen Gonggong from the palace is here."

"Don't move," Dr Li repeated without opening his eyes.

Chen Hong overheard the brief conversation inside. A trace of displeasure flashed across his eyes. He had no choice but to wait.

The Prince of Yu became anxious. Worrying that the delay would cause him trouble, he defied Dr Li's order and rose from his chair. "Dr Li, Chen Gonggong is here to deliver an imperial edict," he explained. "I have to see him."

Dr Li opened his eyes and stood up. Without a word, he walked towards the door.

Pleased that the Prince of Yu had ended his session with Dr Li, Chen Hong urged the other eunuchs to wait outside and stepped into the Prince of Yu's inner chamber alone. At the door, he passed by Dr Li and smiled at him, but Dr Li ignored his greeting.

Chen Hong's face fell, but when the Prince of Yu came up to him, he quickly put on an ingratiating smile. "His Majesty has a verbal edict. Please listen," he stated before his face turned serious. Walking to the middle of the room, he paused to face the prince, who was kneeling towards the south. The *Great Ming Code* dictated that a messenger carrying an imperial edict should be treated just like the emperor himself.

From his breast pocket, Chen Hong pulled out a piece of paper with Hai Rui's writing on it. The paper had now been folded into a square. "Hai Rui, an auditor at the Ministry of Treasury, wrote something on this piece of paper when he visited Home of Six Necessities this morning," he said. "Are you aware of it?"

The Prince of Yu looked surprised when Chen Hong showed him the paper. "Please notify His Majesty that I'm not aware of it," he replied to Chen Hong.

"Hai Rui claimed that his intent was to set the record straight and dispel rumours about His Majesty. Is it true or false?"

It took a while for the Prince of Yu to respond. "Please tell His Majesty that I wouldn't know the answer."

"Regardless of whether his claim is true or not, or whether you know about it nor not, copy the characters onto a separate piece of paper, sign your name, inscribe the writing on a plaque and ask the owner to display it at Home of Six Necessities."

Dumbfounded, the Prince of Yu kowtowed. "I accept His Majesty's edict."

Once Chen Hong had finished with Emperor Jiajing's message, he resumed his servant status and hurried over to help the Prince of Yu to his feet. When the prince sank into his chair, Chen Hong handed him Hai Rui's writing.

"Your humble servant wishes Your Royal Highness a long life," said Chen Hong, dropping to his knees.

"Please rise," said the Prince of Yu, who unfolded the paper and started to read Hai Rui's couplets.

Chen Hong stood up and waited for the prince to finish.

"What is this about?" asked the Prince of Yu, who shot Chen Hong a blank stare. "I don't understand this at all."

"Your Highness, it is not so important. That new appointee at the Ministry of Treasury must have been bored to tears. On the very first day he arrived in Beijing, he showed up at Home of Six Necessities and wrote down these couplets with the ostentatious claim that he was helping set the record straight and dispelling rumours for His Majesty. I can only assume that His Majesty has approved of his words. That's why he asked you to copy them and display the plaque at Home of Six Necessities."

The explanation allayed some of the prince's fears, but he still had some lingering concerns. "I have never even met Hai Rui before," he said. "Why does my father ask me to copy his words?"

Chen Hong lowered his head and replied: "I wouldn't dare speculate His Majesty's intention."

"Could I bother Chen Gonggong to pass a message to my father saying that I have received his edict and will copy the writing today?"

"I will fashion a proper response to His Majesty on your behalf."

"I'll leave that to you then," said the Prince of Yu as he struggled to get up from his chair. "I truly appreciate your help."

Chen Hong rushed over and tried to assist the Prince of Yu by holding his arm. "Your Highness, please don't say that," he said. "Now, I'm embarrassed."

The Prince of Yu felt repulsed by Chen Hong's touch, but he refrained from acting out. Instead, he feigned an appreciative smile. Untying a small, gold-coloured silk pouch that contained a Hotian jade pendant from his belt, he gave it to Chen Hong. "I've carried this with me for years," said the prince. "I want you to have it as a gift."

Chen Hong dropped to his knees. "Your Royal Highness, your humble servant hasn't done anything to deserve such a valuable gift."

"Well, you attend to my father with the utmost care. That in itself is a tremendous deed. I'm grateful to you. Take the gift."

Chen Hong was well aware that the jade pendant was a rare treasure. The Prince of Yu was obviously bribing him, attempting to win him over. Filled with secret delight, he kowtowed three times. "Thank Your Highness for the gift." On rising from the floor, he folded his hands in front of his chest and gave the Prince of Yu another deep bow.

"Since you're His Majesty's envoy today, I won't invite you to stay for dinner," said the prince. "I know you have to leave and deliver my response to His Majesty."

But Chen Hong showed no intention of leaving. He stood there with a hesitant expression on his face.

Like his father, the Prince of Yu was a sensitive person. Chen Hong's odd behaviour made him suspicious. "Is there anything else you want to discuss with me?" he asked.

Chen Hong assumed an air of reluctance and sadness. "Your Highness, since you're still recovering from your illness, I find it extremely difficult to bring up the matter. But I have to do so because it is His Majesty's order."

The Prince of Yu became visibly nervous. "What is it?" he asked. "Tell me."

"His Majesty is upset with one of your servants here," Chen Hong said in a low voice. "I have been ordered to send this person to Chaotian Temple, where he'll start working as a floor sweeper."

"Who?"

"Feng Bao."

The Prince of Yu looked stunned.

Chen Hong stood there silently.

"Why would my father issue such an order?"

Princess Li, who was obviously listening in on the conversation from inside the bedroom, suddenly shouted: "Who has badmouthed us in front of His Majesty?"

Her angry voice took Chen Hong and the Prince of Yu by surprise.

"Stop it!" interrupted the Prince of Yu.

"Your Highness, I will not remain silent," said Princess Li, who was still inside the bedroom. Her voice became more agitated. "His Majesty has only one grandson. Only Feng Bao knows how to take care of him. Whoever has urged His Majesty to do this is out to ruin our family!"

"You stop it! Stop it! Stop it!" the Prince of Yu shouted. His face was turning white. Soon, he was gasping for breath.

Worrying that the Prince of Yu might collapse, Chen Hong held him by the arm and walked him to a chair.

"Your Highness, are you all right?" cried Princess Li, who darted out of the bedroom. When the prince sat down, she held his head and stroked his chest. "Where is Dr Li?" she shouted. "Send for Dr Li!"

Several palace maids ran in with panic in their eyes. They stood around without knowing what to do.

Sweat appeared on Princess Li's face. "What are you doing here? Go find Dr Li!"

The palace maids swarmed out.

Soon, Dr Li hurried in. "Move aside please!" he said to Chen Hong who was still holding the Prince of Yu's right arm. Chen Hong stepped aside reluctantly.

The Prince of Yu's eyes were closed. He clenched his teeth and his face looked as white as a sheet of paper.

Princess Li, who was still holding the Prince of Yu's neck, pleaded with Dr Li to save her husband. Tears welled up in her eyes.

"Don't panic," said Dr Li as he took out a small needle pouch from inside a satchel that was strapped around his waist. "I need fire."

"Fire," Princess Li shouted to the palace maids outside.

Two maids rushed in. One grabbed a candlestick from a side tea table nearby while the other tried to kindle a fire with a tinder box. Since her hands were shaking, she couldn't manage it.

"Give the tinder box to me," Chen Hong said, seizing it from the palace maid and striking the flint. The tinder was ignited. Chen Hong lit the candle and handed it to Dr Li.

Dr Li pulled out a long silver needle from inside his pouch and held it over the flame. Next, he wiped the needle with a cotton ball coated with an antibacterial herbal drug before piercing the needle into an acupoint above the Prince of Yu's upper lip on the midline. Lastly, Dr Li brought out a roll of mugwort from his satchel and lit it on the candle flame. When it started burning, Dr Li blew out the open flames. Unbuttoning the Prince of Yu's shirt, he held the glowing end of the smouldering mugwort close to a pressure point on his chest.

Gradually, the Prince of Yu unclenched his jaw and let out a long, audible breath.

"Your Highness," cried Princess Li, who cupped his face with her hands.

The Prince of Yu opened his eyes, which were filled with sadness. "Release Feng Bao and let him go with Chen Gonggong," he said.

"I will release him," Princess Li sobbed. "I promise."

The Prince of Yu closed his eyes again.

Dr Li pulled out the needle from the acupoint above the prince's upper lip and said to the others in the room: "We don't need so many people here. Please step out."

Princess Li shot a baleful glance at Chen Hong. "Why are you still here?" she said. "Take him away."

Chen Hong dropped down on his knees. "Your Royal Highness and Princess Li, please don't get me wrong. I have no idea why His Majesty has issued this edict. I'm a mere messenger. I... I'm stuck in the middle..."

As Chen Hong was kowtowing on the floor, the Prince of Yu came to his rescue. "Nobody is blaming you," he said. "It's not your fault... Please deliver my response to Yuxi Palace."

'Your Highness, please take care of your health," Chen Hong said before exiting. "Princess Li, please take it easy."

Princess Li turned to Dr Li. "While you attend to His Highness, I need to check up on my son," she said anxiously.

"His Highness is out of danger," Dr Li consoled Princess Li. "Call someone to carry him to his room and lay him across the bed. You can go and look after your son now."

Princess Li extricated herself and rushed over to the door. "Carry His Royal Highness to his room and lay him across the bed," she said to two eunuchs outside.

Lifting her skirt, she leapt over the threshold and walked to the front yard. Several palace maids followed her.

Feng Bao had never imagined that his stairway to power, which he had painstakingly built for himself over the past five years, could collapse with a light poke of someone's little finger.

At this moment, he was playing hide-and-seek with the young prince. Blindfolded, he wrapped himself around a corridor pillar. "One, two, three, four, five, six and seven!" he counted. "Are you ready? I'm coming to catch you."

The boy and several eunuchs gathered in the yard and shouted excitedly: "Yes, we're all set! Come and get us!"

Feng Bao stretched out his arms and felt his way in the direction of the young prince's voice. The boy suppressed his giggles. Quietly beckoning a junior eunuch over to stand in his spot, he crept away.

Feng Bao could tell that the young prince was tricking him, but he pretended to have lost his bearings and fumbled forwards with both hands. Finally, he zigzagged his way to where the eunuch was standing. Turning around, he seized the eunuch with his arms. "Gotcha!"

"Wrong!" the eunuch declared. "The prince has won the game and gone home!"

The boy giggled on the other side of the yard.

"I'll catch you!" shouted Feng Bao. Pretending to be cross, he turned around and moved towards the boy.

With a piece of cloth wrapped over his eyes, Feng Bao could not see anything, but he was familiar with every brick and every pillar in the yard. As he jumped around nimbly, trying to capture the young prince, he managed to avoid bumping into anything.

At this point, silence suddenly fell. He was under the assumption that the young prince had ordered other eunuchs to squat down at a wall corner or hide behind a corridor pillar. Thus, he avoided those places and felt his way towards the stone steps. His plan was to trip deliberately on the steps, acknowledge defeat and end the game.

Before approaching the steps, he could hear footsteps that sounded like those of an adult. At the same time, the young prince was giggling nearby. Thinking the young prince had sent a junior eunuch to block him, Feng Bao pounced on the person.

"Good catch! Good catch!" the boy shouted and laughed uproariously.

"Hello, Your Highness," said the person whom Feng Bao had seized. The voice belonged to Chen Hong.

Startled, Feng Bao let go of his hands and ripped off his blindfold. "I'm terribly sorry!" Feng Bao sank to his knees and apologised.

Chen Hong gave him a cold stare.

阉

In ancient China, penal castration, known as *'gong xing'*, constituted one of the harshest penalties for imperial officials and prisoners of war, second only to execution. The most famous victim of *gong xing* was Sima Qian (145-86 BCE), a prominent historian during the Han dynasty. After he offended Emperor Wu by defending a disgraced general, Sima Qian was sentenced to death. Since he was a senior official, he was presented with two choices – execution or castration. Sima Qian chose the latter and endured tremendous humiliation. In his remaining years, he left the palace and travelled the country to interview people for his masterpiece, *Records of the Grand Historian*.

At the same time, castration was also a means of gaining

employment in the imperial services. The fact that eunuchs could not have children made them more reliable than the scholar officials because they would not be tempted to seize power and start a dynasty.

Often, families living in destitution donated their sons, hoping that they would enjoy more comfortable and prosperous lives in the palace. Young boys undertook what was known as 'zi gong', or voluntary castration. When selected, they devoted their lives to the Imperial Palace as servants or slaves. Once a eunuch had his reproductive organ removed, he lost the very root of his independence. He was considered less than a man, and attached himself to a master, like a tree to its roots. If his master abandoned him, he withered and died like a tree with a broken root.

Feng Bao was born into a poor family. As a young boy, his parents paid a specialist to remove his genitals. Fortunately, a relative who knew someone at the Imperial Palace secured him a position right after his surgery. As he worked his way up, he was able to serve the emperor directly and became the head of the powerful Criminal Investigative Division of the Imperial Investigative Agency.

On 30 December in the thirty-ninth year of Emperor Jiajing's reign, he supervised the caning of Zhou Yunyi, an imperial astronomer who had criticised Emperor Jiajing and the Imperial Palace for their unrestrained spending and corruption. To ingratiate himself with the emperor, he had Zhou caned to death. Subsequently, when an auspicious snow fell on Beijing following a prolonged dry spell, he attempted to curry favour with the emperor by dashing over to Yuxi Palace and reporting the news of snow to Emperor Jiajing without consulting with Lu Fang. His action enraged other senior eunuchs at the Interior Ministry, who conspired to punish Feng Bao and banish him from the Imperial Palace. As he was about to be uprooted, Lu Fang came to his rescue and imparted the following words:

"One always needs to ponder three things – think about danger, think about retreat and think about change. These three things are connected. If you sense danger, you need to plan your retreat right away and withdraw to a place where you won't be spotted by your enemies. Once you retreat to a safe corner, bide your time and slowly reflect on your mistakes and plan your comeback. This is called 'the contemplation of change'."

To protect Feng Bao, Lu Fang demoted him and sent him to work as an imperial caretaker at the Prince of Yu's mansion, where he quickly took root. After the birth of the young prince, Feng Bao had grasped the true meaning of Lu Fang's advice of 'retreat and the contemplation of change'. He threw his whole self into taking care of the boy. He and the young prince spent days and nights together. They became so inseparable that the young prince saw Feng Bao as a part of himself. Feng Bao had desperately and irredeemably committed the second half of his life to nurturing his young master. He was biding his time. Once his master spread his roots and blossomed, he would flourish accordingly.

As the saying goes, man proposes and the Heavenly God disposes. Who would know that Feng Bao's fate would have been so unpredictable! Even though he kept his former nemeses at a distance, one of them showed up today to uproot him.

Feng Bao knelt before Chen Hong. Initially, he smiled tactfully and put on a look of piety, like a son kneeling at the feet of his father. When he saw Chen Hong's frosty expression, he sensed something ominous and his smile froze.

Several junior eunuchs at the Prince of Yu's mansion lined up behind Feng Bao and dropped to their knees. The young prince was the only person left standing. Without knowing what was happening, the boy became scared. He watched Chen Hong and Feng Bao nervously.

Urgent footsteps sounded in the corridor. Princess Li and the palace maids were dashing out from the backyard.

Chen Hong realised that he could not delay any more. "Listen, Feng Bao, please kneel to accept an imperial edict."

Feng Bao felt a cold shudder. He quickly bowed, touching his head on the ground.

Princess Li, who had arrived at the scene, heard Chen Hong's declaration. She paused under the corridor eaves. The palace maids held their breath and stood behind her.

Knowing that Princess Li was watching, Chen Hong softened his tone and read aloud:

> Feng Bao, when you served in the Imperial Palace, you acted in an unruly fashion, bullying others and frequently swerving from rules and duties. Because Lu Fang begged and pleaded on your behalf, I sent you to the Prince of Yu's mansion, hoping you could modify your behaviour and start a new chapter. But you are incorrigible by nature. During your tenure at the Prince of Yu's mansion, you frequently sneaked into Yuxi Palace and delivered secret messages to sow discord. I have long discerned and endured your ill-intentions. Considering your dedicated services to my grandson, I will spare your life. From today on, you shall be ordered to perform menial chores at Chaotian Temple. Grand Master Lan might be able to use the divine power bestowed upon him by the Grand Supreme Elder Lord to dissolve the malice in your heart. If he can reform you, it is your good fortune. Upon announcing this edict, Chen Hong shall expel this minion from the Prince of Yu's mansion, and deliver him to Chaotian Temple without delay.

Apart from a few formal phrases, the edict was written in colloquial language. Every adult in the courtyard understood it. As Feng Bao lay prostrate on the ground, the other eunuchs knelt behind him silently. The young prince could not comprehend what was said in the edict, but from the grim expressions on the adults' faces, he soon understood the situation. Like a typical five-year-old, he became distressed and stupefied. His face turned pale.

"Are you all right?" asked Princess Li, who rushed over and took him into her arms. "Let's go to the backyard. Your father is waiting for us in his study."

His mother's hug jolted the boy out of his trance. All of a sudden, he pushed his mother's hands away and ran towards Feng Bao. Unprepared for the little boy's sudden burst of strength, Princess Li staggered back. "Prince!" she shouted hysterically and chased after him.

As Emperor Jiajing's envoy, Chen Hong did not kowtow to

Princess Li or the young prince. He simply bowed slightly. "Princess Li, I'm afraid I have to carry out His Majesty's order and take Feng Bao away," he said sternly. "Could you carry His Highness away?"

"I won't allow you to take Daban Feng away," screamed the boy who threw himself onto Chen Hong, grabbing the eunuch's belt and repeatedly jabbing at him. "Help! I need someone to chase this minion out of here!"

Several junior eunuchs stood up, but no one dared help the young prince.

Princess Li caught up with her son. Tears flashed in her eyes. "Stop it," she shouted at the boy. "Don't make trouble!"

The boy grabbed Chen Hong's belt and pressed his whole strength onto his little hands. No matter how hard Princess Li tried, she could not pull him away from Chen Hong.

"Your Royal Highness, I'm here at the order of your grandfather," he said, bending over with a fake smile. "I'm on official business. Your Highness, behave yourself, please! You have to listen to your grandfather's order."

When the young boy refused to release his grip, Chen Hong went ahead to pry the boy's hands from his belt.

The young prince tightened his grasp. When Chen Hong became more forceful, the boy clenched his teeth. His eyes filled up with tears.

Seeing that her son was being treated unfairly, Princess Li lost control and slapped Chen Hong hard across the face.

The smack sent Chen Hong reeling.

The boy, startled by his mother's sudden outburst, let go of his hands.

Everyone in the courtyard was stunned because they had never seen Princess Li act so ferociously before. "You bold slave! How dare you hurt the prince! How dare you tell my son to behave himself! That wasn't part of the imperial edict, was it?"

Chen Hong sank to the ground but held his head high. "Princess Li, please don't be upset," he pleaded. "I didn't harm His Highness. It was His Majesty who urged his grandson to behave himself, and I was merely repeating His Majesty's verbal message. If you don't forgive me, feel free to slap me again."

Incensed at Chen Hong's insolence, Princess Li burst out crying. The young boy came to his senses and flung himself into his mother's lap. "Mother, don't cry! Don't cry!"

As the boy was consoling his mother, he began to weep.

Feng Bao was heartbroken. He raised his head, and his face was wet with tears. "Princess Li and Your Highness, it's all my fault," he pleaded. "You have misunderstood Chen Gonggong. I beg your forgiveness. Please don't feel sad for your humble servant."

As Feng Bao was kowtowing, knocking his head hard on the ground, the boy turned around and seized him. "I don't want you to go!" he shouted. "I won't allow them to take you away!"

Feng Bao stopped kowtowing, but he didn't dare touch the young prince because he was no longer the boy's daban. He lay on the floor sobbing.

The young boy stood up and blocked Feng Bao. Glaring at Chen Hong, who was still kneeling on the ground, he howled: "Get out of here! Get out of here at once!"

Princess Li did not stop her son. She simply stood there, feeling aggrieved. As she was wiping her tears, the two maids rushed over and held her by the arms.

Chen Hong had not expected such chaos. He felt bitter and angry but had no way to vent his frustration. He went off in a fit of pique: "Princess Li, if you think I have done anything wrong, you should punish me. If you don't, I'll punish myself."

As Chen Hong started slapping his face from left and right, the two palace eunuchs, who had accompanied Chen Hong to the Prince of Yu's mansion, recovered their wits and plopped down behind Chen Hong. They also began smacking their own faces.

Appalled, Feng Bao bypassed the young prince and crawled over to Chen Hong. "Second Daddy, Second Daddy, please don't do this to yourself," he begged, grabbing Chen Hong's hands. "It's all my fault. Why don't you just kill me on the spot?"

Chen Hong pushed Feng Bao's hands away and continued hitting his face. Feng Bao seized his hands again and held them to his chest.

"Feng Bao!" Princess Li shouted loudly. "Don't stop him! You know he's not beating up himself. He's beating me. Let him do it. If he still can't be pacified, bring the Prince of Yu out here. Feel free to kill and clean up every single member of the Zhu family! When our family line ends, Chen Hong can have His Majesty all to himself."

Many in the palace knew that the Crown Prince's concubine was a tough and fearless woman. Now, Chen Hong learned about her temperament first-hand. Princess Li's angry accusations petrified him. Trembling in terror, Chen Hong removed his official hat and knocked his head hard on the brick floor. "With His Majesty as my witness, your humble servant wouldn't dare harbour such thoughts," he pleaded. "Princess Li, that was a gross misunderstanding. Please forgive me."

The poor palace eunuchs, who had come with him to deliver the imperial edict, felt obligated to bang their heads vigorously on the ground as well. Meanwhile, since Chen Hong was the deputy interior minister, the other eunuchs and palace maids working for the Prince of Yu also dropped to their knees.

As the fiasco continued, Chen Hong's head-banging slowed down.

Princess Li gritted her teeth and stared at them with a look of disgust. When she made those remarks earlier, she was acting purely out of spite. Once the words were out, she couldn't take them back. Now she had no idea how to end this farce. It looked like the three eunuchs wouldn't cease until she apologised.

Fortunately, the minister of defence Zhang Juzheng happened to be walking in through the gate, holding a stack of *Four Books Annotations* wrapped in silk. He looked at Princess Li and his expression was one of shock and confusion. Princess Li lowered her head to avert his stare. After wiping away her tears, she raised her head and greeted Zhang with the eagerness of a woman who had seen a beloved family member. The gaze warmed his fluttering heart. Composing himself, Zhang bowed: "Greetings to Princess Li and His Highness. May I ask what this is all about?"

Princess Li meant to respond to him, but choked up. "Master Zhang, could I leave the prince with you for a few minutes?" she said, sobbing. Then she walked away. Two palace maids held her arms and left with her.

Zhang's eyes followed Princess Li as she disappeared down the long corridor that led to the backyard. He turned around and noticed that Chen Hong and Feng Bao were still banging their heads on the ground.

"Go over there and hold Chen Gonggong!" he shouted at several junior eunuchs who worked at the Prince of Yu's mansion. When the eunuchs tried to stop Chen Hong and help him to his feet, he refused.

"Your Royal Highness, please tell me what happened," Zhang said, turning to the young prince.

The boy burst out into loud sobs. "That person there wants to take my daban away," he said as he moved over to grasp Feng Bao's collar with one hand and pointed at Chen Hong with the other.

By now, Zhang felt that he had a better grasp of the situation. Realising that the deputy interior minister was still lying on the ground, he shouted to the Prince of Yu's eunuchs again: "Hurry up, help Chen Gonggong. Help him get up."

It took a great effort from the junior eunuchs to lift the half-conscious Chen Hong off the ground. His cheeks were swollen from the slapping. The repeated kowtows left his forehead severely bruised with a big welt in the middle. His eyes resembled a pair of holes in the chipped and weathered face of an outdoor Buddha statue.

Zhang knew that he had just walked into a major political incident. For an important figure like the deputy interior minister, who was the equivalent of the country's deputy grand secretary, enduring such degrading treatment inside the Prince of Yu's mansion was by no means an insignificant matter.

"Chen Gonggong, are you all right?" Zhang asked and then offered him a palm-over-fist salute. "How did you get those bruises on your face? Shall I get some medicine for you?"

Chen Hong opened his eyes. His vision was blurred. He could vaguely see a man standing before him. The voice sounded familiar. Slowly, the man in front of him came into focus. Chen Hong recognised Zhang.

"There's no need for medicine," said Chen Hong, who tried to assume the air of an interior minister. "Mr Zhang, now that you've seen what happened to me, I hope you will serve as a fair witness and explain the situation truthfully to His Majesty and the Prince of Yu. It is His Majesty who issued an edict, ordering me to expel Feng Bao from the Prince of Yu's mansion. I am supposed to deliver Feng Bao to Chaotian Temple so he can reform himself through menial labour. Unfortunately, Princess Li and the young prince vented their anger on me. Of course, when such things happen, the masters are always right. No matter how unjustly I was treated, I wouldn't assert and defend myself. I will wait outside the mansion. Your Highness, please talk with the young prince and make a decision on his behalf as to whether or not he allows me to send Feng Bao to the temple. In this way, I can report the outcome to His Majesty when I return."

Zhang watched helplessly as Chen Hong and his two assistants staggered out of the gate. Obviously, Chen Hong was attempting to pass the buck. Zhang's heart was filled with disgust. He took a deep breath and turned to the young prince. "Your Royal Highness, please come over here."

The boy clung to Feng Bao and stared at Zhang without moving.

Despite his position as minister of defence, Zhang also served as the Prince of Yu's part-time teacher. While lecturing the prince on Confucian classics, he was also tasked with enlightening Emperor Jiajing's grandson. As the teacher of two generations of future monarchs, Zhang was a widely respected and authoritative figure, and the young prince understood it. "Your Highness, come over please," he called out.

The boy reluctantly let go of Feng Bao and tottered over. "Master, don't let them take my daban away," he murmured.

"Listen to me," Zhang told the young prince with a serious look on his face. "Who is the most powerful person in the Great Ming Empire? I taught this to you before."

"My grandfather is the most powerful person," the boy replied somewhat reluctantly.

"Who is your grandfather's favourite boy?"

"I am my grandfather's favourite boy."

"It's good that you understand this. Your grandfather cares a lot about you. He wants to send Daban Feng to Chaotian Temple so he can learn more skills. Once he's finished, he'll come back and keep you company every day. You have to follow your grandfather's order, don't you?"

The boy's lips curled and he was ready to cry again. "But, when... when is he coming back?"

"The sooner you let him go, the sooner he'll come back."

The boy was silent. Tears welled up in his eyes.

Zhang made a prompt decision by hugging the young prince, who pressed his head against his mentor's chest. "Leave now," Zhang signalled to Feng Bao. "I'll ask someone else to send your clothes and personal possessions to the temple."

Feng Bao, who was lying face down on the ground, sprang to his feet and bolted through the gate with his head down. He did not look back.

By the time the young prince had broken free from Zhang's grasp and turned around, Feng Bao was gone. Staring at the empty gate, the boy did not cry. He seemed to be in a daze.

Zhang bent over to console the boy: "Your Highness, I'm teaching you to grow into an intelligent and sensible man. There are things that we are not able to accomplish today, but it doesn't mean that we can't do them tomorrow. Do you understand?"

The boy's eyes still looked dull. "Master, are you in charge of the troops at the Ministry of Defence?" he asked.

Zhang was taken aback. "Yes, all the troops are at the disposal of the Defence Ministry," he replied.

"I want you to kill that person for me," the young boy said through clenched teeth.

Zhang lifted the boy off the ground and carried him in his arms. "Be careful what you say!"

The boy went quiet.

Zhang's piercing eyes swept across the courtyard. "What did the prince say?" he asked the junior eunuchs and maids.

"Your humble servants have heard nothing," they replied collectively, dropping to their knees.

'That's a blessing," he said before walking towards the backyard with the young prince in his arms.

When Grand Secretary Xu dragged his weary body to the Privy Council's duty room, senior officials from the Ministries of Personnel, Treasury, Defence and Public Works rose from their chairs. Four pairs of eyes were immediately drawn to a stack of budget requests in Grand Secretary Xu's hands, like iron filings attracted to a magnet. Those 'magnetic' budget requests involved several million taels of silver.

There were only a few steps from the door to his desk in the middle of the duty room, but Grand Secretary Xu trudged on, as if he had to measure each step before taking it. When he finally reached his destination, he plunked down onto his chair and smacked the stack of papers on his desk.

From Grand Secretary Xu's dejected expression, the ministers had an ominous feeling that Emperor Jiajing had rejected their spending requests.

Gao Gong jumped ahead of Li Chunfang, the deputy grand secretary, and asked: "Grand Secretary, I assume that Lu Gonggong has not signed off on all the spending items, has he?"

As the minister of personnel, Gao Gong was under tremendous pressure because imperial officials had not been paid for months. During the past month, his ministry had been swamped with salary-related grievances.

Deputy Li was known for being a 'wall grass' official who sat on the fence and swayed in the direction of the political wind. The good news was that he seldom put on airs and never regarded himself as a deputy grand secretary. On key issues, he let Grand Secretary Xu make all the decisions. He saw his role as a facilitator who simply collected suggestions from other cabinet members. As the saying goes, he never aimed to distinguish himself in his career, but only hoped to be free from any errors. Therefore, Deputy Li did not mind that Gao Gong spoke first. He simply looked at Gao Gong impassively.

Two non-Privy Council members were invited to the meeting. They stood there silently, waiting for Grand Secretary Xu to brief them. One of them was Zhao Zhenji, the former imperial inspector in Zhejiang Province. Six months ago, Grand Secretary Xu recommended him for the position of treasury minister. Emperor Jiajing approved his promotion, and he was transferred from Hangzhou to Beijing. As Grand Secretary Xu's former student, he strictly observed the teacher-student ritual at cabinet meetings. Out of respect, he seldom looked Grand Secretary Xu in the eye. At this time, he was tempted to read his teacher's eyes and detect clues that would inform him of the status of those spending requests, but he resisted the impulse. The other non-cabinet member was Xu Fan, Grand Secretary Xu's eldest son. Since Grand Secretary Xu headed both the Privy Council and the Ministry of Public Works, Emperor Jiajing specifically appointed Xu Fan as the deputy minister of public works. If anything went wrong at the ministry, the emperor could hold Xu Fan accountable and use the son as a hostage. More important, through Xu Fan, the emperor could lobby Grand Secretary Xu to allocate more funding for palace and Taoist temple repairs. At this particular meeting, Xu Fan observed the father and son etiquette and avoided eye contact with Grand Secretary Xu. He fixed his gaze on the small pile of budget requests on his father's desk.

Even though everyone's circumstance was different, they nevertheless shared Gao Gong's anxiety and concerns. Over the past two months, the Imperial Investigative Agency had raided the homes of several dozen corrupt officials and retrieved a large sum of money. The Privy Council had decided to distribute the confiscated money to different ministries that were in dire need of funding. Before drafting the spending proposals, Grand Secretary Xu had held multiple expanded cabinet meetings to discuss them. Early on, when Grand Secretary Xu visited Yuxi Palace, the four officials in the Privy Council's duty room had hoped that Emperor Jiajing would approve the spending proposals and that Lu Fang, the interior minister, would sign off on all of them. In this way, they could be disbursed immediately. But upon his return, Grand Secretary Xu's defeated expression and his silence made everyone anxious.

The atmosphere in the room tensed up, and when Grand Secretary Xu finally opened his mouth, all he uttered was a soft sigh.

Gao Gong raised his question again: "Grand Secretary Xu, many Imperial Government employees haven't been paid for months. Our troops guarding the borders in the north and fighting the pirates in the south are in dire need of supplies. Several provinces require money to feed their disaster victims. Are these requests approved?"

"Well, His Majesty has approved the requests for government salaries, military provisions, disaster relief and tax refunds," Grand Secretary Xu replied softly.

Eyes sparkled but quickly dimmed as Grand Secretary Xu paused and gazed out of the door, as if he were anticipating someone's arrival. His vacuous facial expression suggested that something had gone awry.

Despite his disarming frankness, Gao Gong was a sensitive person. He quickly figured out the reason for Grand Secretary Xu's unusual reticence. "The Ministry of Public Works has set aside money for His Majesty's palace and temple repairs, and the Ministry of Treasury has allocated funds to cover various palace expenses. Did His Majesty veto these two important items?"

"Yes," Grand Secretary Xu admitted with a sigh.

"Was His Majesty unhappy because the amount of money we have allocated is too small?"

Grand Secretary Xu did not respond, but everyone in the room already knew the answer.

Deputy Li finally spoke up: "If His Majesty refused to sign off on these two items, there is no way we can move ahead with the other approved requests."

The room fell into silence.

A few minutes later, Zhao Zhenji decided to chime in. Looking Grand Secretary Xu in the eye, he asked: "Could it be possible that His Majesty was upset with something else? For example, a few days ago, Hai Rui resorted to innuendo and criticised His Majesty at Home of Six Necessities…"

Zhao had developed quite a dislike for Hai Rui when they worked together in Zhejiang Province. Hai Rui's plain-spoken and pugnacious style had made Zhao so uncomfortable and upset that he was certain that Emperor Jiajing would have reacted similarly in response to what Hai Rui wrote at Home of Six Necessities.

"This is a sensitive topic. Don't make these random speculations," said Grand Secretary Xu.

Xu Fan rose from his chair with his head down. "Father, can I finish the conversation I had with you yesterday?" he asked timidly. "The money we have budgeted for palace repairs is indeed too little. I think that's what is holding up the approval."

Grand Secretary Xu's face fell. "This is a cabinet meeting and we're discussing government business. How many times have I told you not to address me as your father? You're the deputy minister of public works, not my son."

"Yes, Your Highness," Xu Fan apologised and lowered his head. "The Ministry of Public Works initiated several palace repair projects two years ago. So far, we've only finished half because of insufficient funding. At the same time, His Majesty proposed repairing and expanding Chaotian Temple and Xuandu Temple. We laid the groundwork last year, but the construction work was halted due to lack of funding. If we want to resume these projects, we need to order building materials now, and they would have to be shipped to Beijing before the start of winter. It's already July. If we don't get the money and act now, the repair and expansion projects will have to be delayed until next year or the year after. When that happens, His Majesty would no doubt blame the Ministry of Public Works. I don't think the Privy Council can get away with this either. As I mentioned yesterday, we have confiscated nearly ten million taels of silver, and yet you have only allocated one million, six-hundred thousand to the Ministry of Public Works. That's simply not enough. As you know, we are only allowed to use marble and rosewood for building materials. To meet these requirements and deadlines, we need at least one and a half million more. When I brought this up yesterday, you cut me off before I'd even finished. Therefore, I'm not surprised that His Majesty vetoed our spending proposals."

Grand Secretary Xu did not endorse his son's comments even

though he knew they were right on target. He turned to the other three senior officials.

Gao Gong's face was gloomy. Zhao appeared worried. Deputy Li sat there impassively.

Grand Secretary Xu fixed his eyes on Deputy Li. "What do you think of Xu Fan's suggestions?"

Deputy Li disliked being put on the spot, but he had no choice but to reply: "We can certainly revisit the different items and do some recalculations to see if we can squeeze out one and a half million for the Ministry of Public Works."

Given that the budget items involved Emperor Jiajing and that the suggestions were put forward by his teacher's son, Zhao found himself in an impossible position. So he chose not to speak. All eyes were now on Gao Gong.

Gao Gong had always been disdainful of Deputy Li. The deputy grand secretary's indecisive attitude today further incensed him. "There's only this much money here," Gao Gong confronted him. "Where can we extract an additional one and half million taels of silver? Shall we cut the money we have set aside for Imperial Government employees, or shall we reduce the amount allocated for military provisions? What about those disaster victims and vagrants who had fled exorbitant taxes? Are we going to take away their subsidies and let them die of starvation?"

"That's not what I meant. I simply said we can recalculate the numbers carefully and see if we can find some savings."

Gao Gong ignored Deputy Li and turned to Xu Fan. "Why don't you tell us where you want us to cut, and help fund your ministry's projects?"

"Mr Gao, I'm only in charge of palace and temple repairs. It's up to the Privy Council and the Ministry of Treasury to discuss and decide."

Tired of these senseless arguments, Gao Gong sprang to his feet and launched into a diatribe: "What is there to discuss? Our country is in chaos, and yet we are still engaged in this pointless political wrangling. I'm in charge of the Ministry of Personnel. As you all know, Imperial Government officials and clerks in Beijing have not been paid for six months. Many have started to take loans from rice shops, and some are in arrears with their rents. Several grade-six and grade-seven officials are now being chased by their debtors. Every day, I have disgruntled visitors at home. They are in tears when they describe their dire financial circumstances. I can't dodge them, but when I see them, I have nothing to offer them. At the moment, I'm only dealing with petitioners in Beijing. Imagine what is happening to provincial, municipal or county officials! I'm not alone. The Ministry of Defence is experiencing similar challenges. Generals Yu Dayou and Qi Jiguang are waging fierce battles against the pirates in Fujian and Guangdong Provinces. In the north, our troops are facing increasing attacks from the Tartars. Zhang Juzheng has received numerous funding requests for provisions. Deputy Li, you work with Zhang Juzheng at the Ministry of Defence. Have you read any of those reports? And Mr Zhao heads the Ministry of Treasury. We discussed with him yesterday about providing relief to disaster victims and to those who have fled their homes due to high taxes. If we don't provide relief, peasants will revolt against the Imperial Government. Instead of tending to these urgent matters, we rack our brains and try to figure out how to give more money to the Ministry of Public Works so it can repair palaces and temples."

Gao Gong's remarks were met with total silence. He pleaded with Grand Secretary Xu: "As head of the Privy Council, you should stand up to His Majesty and argue with him forcefully about the importance of these proposals. His Majesty has entrusted the country to the Privy Council. We must do what is expected of us. We must be worthy of the Great Ming Empire and the citizens of our country."

Zhao jumped to his teacher's defence: "Mr Gao, I beg to differ. How do you know that Grand Secretary Xu did not argue and fight for our proposals before His Majesty? Speaking of which, we all have the responsibility to remonstrate with His Majesty. In *Spring and Autumn Annals*, the sages were always set up to take the blame. But Grand Secretary Xu alone cannot carry the weight of the Great Ming Empire on his shoulders."

"I agree that we should all share the burden with Grand Secretary Xu," Gao Gong said. "I'll draft a report to His Majesty, requesting him to approve the spending requests. You can also submit a similar report. We can mobilise all the ministerial officials to help us."

Zhao regarded himself as a true inheritor of the neo-Confucian mantle, but having served in the Imperial Government for decades, he became preoccupied with the acquisition of power, rather than the Confucian governing principles. Even so, he always assumed the air of an upright Confucian scholar. Gao Gong detested Zhao's pretentiousness and decided to prick his bubble.

"Didn't you mention Hai Rui just now?" he asked Zhao. "How could you accuse him of defiling His Majesty? He's a mere auditor at the Ministry of Treasury. Upon arriving in Beijing, he was not afraid of speaking the truth and bravely tackled the ills of our country head-on. In comparison, we simply sit here and try to protect ourselves. Hai Rui is putting us to shame. Mr Zhao, here's a calligraphy brush. Would you dare take the lead and draft a report with me now?"

"I understand Mr Gao's noble intent," Zhao said, blushing. "As long as the report helps with our cause, I'll follow your steps."

"This is not the time to spite each other," Grand Secretary Xu interjected. "Nobody is allowed to submit a report to His Majesty at this moment. Nor should anyone even talk about it."

Gao Gong became impassioned and animated. "If it's not for self-preservation, then what is it for?"

"For the future monarchs of the Great Ming Empire," Grand Secretary Xu said with a solemn tone. "Since you brought up the incident at Home of Six Necessities, let me share some details with you. Before I left Yuxi Palace, His Majesty issued an edict, ordering the Prince of Yu to copy Hai Rui's words, inscribe them on a plaque and hang it up at Home of Six Necessities. His Majesty also asserted that only the Prince of Yu knows Hai Rui's true intentions."

Grand Secretary Xu's remarks stunned everyone in the room. He became emotional as he continued: "Do you know that Feng Bao was expelled from the Prince of Yu's mansion earlier? He has been sent to Chaotian Temple to perform menial labour. Why would His Majesty deprive his grandson of his caretaker? The young prince is only five years old! What has he done to deserve this? Gao Gong, you and I are members of the Privy Council. If we are gone someday, we can be easily replaced. But His Majesty has only one son and one grandson. You and I can risk our lives fighting for our causes. But we don't want to rock the foundation of our Great Ming Empire, do we?"

Obviously, Emperor Jiajing had initiated a sweeping crackdown without the slightest regard for the well-being of his son and grandson. Gao Gong stood there silently. His face turned grim.

"This morning His Majesty granted an audience with me for an hour," Grand Secretary Xu mumbled with sadness. "During this short period, he was struck with two bouts of illness and almost passed out during the second bout. His Majesty's heath is getting very worrisome."

Tears ran down Grand Secretary Xu's cheeks. Shocked at the news, Gao Gong became tearful as well.

"Can we discuss the budget another time?" Gao Gong asked while wiping away his tears. "Dr Li Shizhen is at this moment visiting the Prince of Yu. I'm going to see him and take him to see His Majesty right away. I'm sure it will incur His Majesty's wrath. Regardless of how resistant His Majesty is, I will implore with him until he allows Dr Li to treat him."

"Not today," said Grand Secretary Xu. "Even if you go, you won't be able to enter Yuxi Palace."

"I'll seek Lu Gonggong's help. He can invite Dr Li into the palace, can't he? Lu Gonggong should have a better grasp of the situation than we do."

Grand Secretary Xu shook his head emphatically. "Gao Gong, do you know why Feng Bao was expelled from the Prince of Yu's mansion? Haven't you figured it out yet? His Majesty punished Feng Bao because of his close connection with Lu Gonggong!"

It wasn't that Gao Gong didn't understand. His mind had become entangled after hearing the news about Emperor Jiajing's deteriorating health. He just couldn't think clearly. "Is His Majesty suspicious that Lu Fang might be colluding with the Prince of Yu?" Gao Gong murmured.

Grand Secretary Xu nodded.

Sinking into his chair, Gao Gong closed his eyes.

"Regardless of how much we disagree with each other, we all share similar concerns for His Majesty's health and for the well-being of the Great Ming Empire," Grand Secretary Xu concluded. "I want you to notify all ministers and agency heads, urging them to rein in their officials and clerks, and put the interests of our country above everything else. In the next few days, no one is allowed to submit new reports to His Majesty. Neither should anyone criticise or gossip about palace affairs. Zhao Zhenji, come over here."

"Yes, Your Highness," said Zhao, who approached Grand Secretary Xu.

"That Hai Rui person is working for you. He's being closely watched by two imperial agents. If he is allowed to report to work at the ministry tomorrow, summon him to your office and talk with him. As Confucius teaches us, he who is not in charge of governing does not interfere in its business. He's a talented person but he should focus on his assigned duties."

"I couldn't agree with you more. I will talk with him," Zhao promised.

Xu Fan made a last-ditch plea for what he believed was the most important business item. "What about allocating extra money for palace repairs… It's already July," he reminded his father. "When are you going to discuss it?"

"I'm not going to convene another meeting on this," said Grand Secretary Xu. "Go back and take care of your other businesses at the ministry. The Privy Council will decide how to reallocate the funds. Gao Gong, Deputy Li and I will have a discussion later today and revise the spending proposals. Then I'll resubmit them."

"I don't think I'm in the mood to discuss those spending proposals today," said Gao Gong, who now stood up. "I'm going to visit the Prince of Yu. We still need to find Dr Li."

Under normal circumstances, it was considered a violation of protocol for a cabinet member to talk back to the grand secretary and reject his suggestion for a meeting. But given what had happened today, Grand Secretary Xu understood Gao Gong's situation and forgave his brashness. "All right then, we'll discuss these proposals tomorrow," he sighed.

"I agree," Deputy Li said. "Even if we do convene, I doubt we're going to accomplish anything..."

Gao Gong interrupted Deputy Li and bade farewell to Grand Secretary Xu. As he strode towards the door, Zhao shook his head with a look of deep annoyance. "Teacher, how can you tolerate such behaviour?" he complained to Grand Secretary Xu.

"The meeting is adjourned," Grand Secretary Xu announced without responding to Zhao. He and his deputy plodded out of the Privy Council's duty room.

※

The stately south gate of the Prince of Yu's mansion remained shut all year round, like those in the Forbidden City. However, based on the advice of fengshui masters, the two side entrances were left open during the day to absorb the auspicious 'purple air' from the southeast. Eight royal soldiers guarded the gate day and night. Their solemn presence conveyed the supreme authority of the royal family.

Gao Gong's sedan arrived at the mansion's south gate at five o'clock in the afternoon. Surprisingly, the two side entrances were also shut today.

Gao Gong stepped out of his sedan and climbed up the stairs to talk with the guards. "Why is the side entrance closed so early?"

Since he was one of the Crown Prince's teachers, Gao Gong was fairly well known to the guards and eunuchs, and they naturally accorded him with respect. "Mr Gao, the Prince of Yu issued us an order today," reported a guard. "During his time of recovery, he will not see any Imperial Government officials."

"It's a good idea to limit the number of visitors during this time," Gao Gong said. "Open the door for me. I have something important to discuss with His Highness."

"Mr Gao, I just said that from today onwards, His Royal Highness will not see any Imperial Government officials."

"I hear you, but I worked at the mansion as a part-time lecturer,"

Gao Gong said with a hint of irritation in his voice. "In this regard, I'm not here as an Imperial Government official."

"Mr Gao, His Highness has specifically designated Mr Zhang Juzheng as his sole lecturer during this period. Mr Zhang is the only one who is allowed to enter. He said you and Grand Secretary Xu do not need to come."

Why would the Crown Prince choose to sequester himself like this? Gao Gong knew the situation was grim, but he did not expect that the Prince of Yu would take such drastic action. The prince's slight, whether deliberate or unintended, disheartened him. Overwhelmed with feelings of sadness and disappointment, he teared up and stared silently at the red, forbidding gate.

"Please give my regards to His Highness," he said to the guard after a long pause. Then, he walked away.

Before getting into his sedan, he glanced at the Prince of Yu's mansion and noticed that the side entrance door had opened a crack. Soon, Zhang Juzheng slipped out. Gao Gong turned around and waved. Zhang saw Gao Gong and hurried towards him.

"How is the Prince of Yu? Is the young prince all right?" Gao Gong asked.

"They're both doing well," Zhang answered.

"Don't lie to me," said Gao Gong, lowering his voice. "Please tell His Highness to take care of his health. The ills of our country are harder to heal. As the proverb says, as long as the green hills last, there'll always be wood to burn. He's the green hill of our Great Ming Empire."

"As long as Dr Li is around, you and I need not worry," said Zhang.

"I just heard that His Majesty fell ill twice this morning. Juzheng, can you think of a way we can get Dr Li to examine His Majesty in the palace?"

"I don't even know where to start. Chen Gonggong came to deliver an imperial edict this morning. Before he took Feng Bao away, Princess Li lost control and slapped his face. I have no idea how Chen Gonggong will report the incident. Regardless, His Majesty will be angry when he hears about it. A sick person tends to get irritated easily. Anger could aggravate his illness. Brother

Gao, a political storm is brewing. You and I need to be extra cautious and calm."

The news left Gao Gong dumbfounded. A strong-willed and short-tempered man, Gao Gong felt a sudden rush of blood to his head. "If His Majesty is ill like this, it makes it all the more important to bring Dr Li to the palace. Dr Li should be allowed to examine His Majesty and help stabilise his condition. Could you go inside again and invite Dr Li to come out? I'll find a way to take him to see His Majesty."

Zhang shook his head vigorously. "The Prince of Yu and I discussed this option earlier on," he said. "The problem is that Lu Gonggong has been pushed aside and we have no contact with him at all. Chen Hong and his people are adding fuel to the flames. At this moment, it is impossible to take Dr Li into the palace."

"But could you ask Dr Li to come out and meet me?"

"He was here earlier to prescribe some medicine for the Prince of Yu and left soon after."

"Where did he go?" Gao Gong asked earnestly.

"You know Dr Li. He never divulges any information about his whereabouts. We just didn't feel it right to ask."

Gao Gong uttered a long sigh. "Juzheng, would you be able to come and talk with me at home tonight?"

Zhang thought for a few moments before replying: "Since I'm the only one who is allowed to enter his mansion, the Prince of Yu has reminded me repeatedly not to interact or socialise with other officials to avoid the perils of speculation during this special period. Brother Gao, as you can tell, the Prince of Yu is very worried. It's better if I act discreetly. Let's wait patiently and see what happens next."

Gao Gong felt a tightness in his chest. He meant to say something but changed his mind. Waving his hands dismissively, he ordered his porters: "Take me home."

When Zhang's porters carried his sedan over, he didn't get in right away. Instead, he stared at Gao Gong's lone sedan as it gradually disappeared into the sunset.

Emperor Jiajing was the Ming dynasty's eleventh ruler. Throughout its history, there had not been a single case where a eunuch, let alone a deputy interior minister, was beaten up as he delivered an imperial edict. In theory, Chen Hong and other palace eunuchs remained submissive to the Crown Prince and Princess Li, both of whom were considered their masters, but when Chen Hong arrived at the Prince of Yu's mansion with an imperial edict, be it written or verbal, he was required to be treated as a substitute for the emperor. The saying 'to beat a dog is to bully its owner' couldn't have been a more apt description.

The final outcome depended on how Chen Hong would report the incident to Emperor Jiajing, and on whom he wanted to lay the blame. If he made an issue of it, he could cause a major political shake up. At the very least, Princess Li would be dethroned. The future of the Crown Prince could be in jeopardy. Senior imperial officials and palace eunuchs who were favoured by the Prince of Yu would inevitably suffer the consequences.

Chen Hong had entered the palace at the age of ten, and for three decades he had battled fiercely in this deep swamp against all sorts of frogs and alligators. He thrived and became so shrewd that every pore in his body seemed to have turned into a watchful eye, able to detect any danger lurking near him.

One could say that the scuffle at the Prince of Yu's mansion wouldn't have occurred if Princess Li and her son had not felt cornered. In a way, Chen Hong was partially responsible. He had instigated it because of his visceral dislike of Feng Bao. Now that the incident had already happened, like an arrow that had left the bow, there was no way Chen Hong could undo it. He secretly hoped that the arrow would hit Lu Fang in the head. If Emperor Jiajing held Lu Fang culpable for his beating, Chen Hong could seize power from the chief eunuch and take control of the Interior Ministry without putting the Prince of Yu in harm's way. He had to strike a delicate balance. It was a matter of life and death. If the Prince of Yu was censured because of the incident, he would no doubt harbour a grudge against Chen Hong. When the time came, Chen Hong knew that the future emperor would have him executed and feed his body to the wild dogs. In the worst-case scenario, if the Prince of Yu was deposed, senior imperial officials, such as Grand Secretary Xu, Gao Gong and Zhang Juzheng would no doubt retaliate against him.

Upon dropping off Feng Bao at Chaotian Temple, Chen Hong reviewed various possible outcomes in his head. He finally came up with what he believed was the best response and rehearsed it multiple times before visiting the Imperial Hospital. A doctor there put some herbal lotion on a lump in the middle of his forehead and wrapped a piece of white silk around his head. Afterwards, Chen Hong carefully put on his official hat and tipped it back slightly. When he entered Yuxi Palace, his cheeks were still swollen.

"Your Majesty, your humble servant has delivered your edict," announced Chen Hong, who knelt sideways outside the meditation room to hide his bruised face from Emperor Jiajing.

The emperor had just taken an immortality pill, his second dose since the morning. As he was sitting on his prayer mat, he felt more energised. Chen Hong's announcement roused him from his meditation. From Chen Hong's voice, Emperor Jiajing could tell that the eunuch was kneeling in a different spot today. The emperor knitted his long eyebrows quizzically.

Over the past twenty years, whenever Emperor Jiajing meditated, Lu Fang would always sit quietly next to him. Every now and then, the chief eunuch would rise to add sandalwood to the bronze burner, replace incense or candles at the altar or wipe off the dust on the altar or on the floor. He moved around noiselessly like a cat or a kungfu master who could walk on water without causing any ripples. He picked up an object cautiously as if it was a needle. Such 'kungfu moves' pleased Emperor Jiajing, who hated it when his servants disrupted his practice.

But Lu Fang seemed a little rusty these days. When Chen Hong arrived, Lu Fang was holding the lid of the incense burner while adding some sandalwood to the fire. His deputy's voice outside startled him and he dropped the lid to the floor, causing a loud banging sound. Emperor Jiajing had never witnessed such an accident inside his meditation room before. He opened his eyes and gave Lu Fang a side glance.

Lu Fang dropped to his knees.

"This is the third time this month you have disrupted my meditation. Are you nervous? What are you afraid of?"

Lu Fang kowtowed to the emperor. "Master, with you by my side, I have nothing to fear," he said in a trembling voice. "Please don't be upset with me. I'm just getting old."

Emperor Jiajing turned his attention to the door. "Chen Hong, what are you afraid of?"

"Your Majesty, your humble servant is afraid of disrupting your practice," Chen Hong said softly outside.

"No, you're not interrupting me. Nobody can. Come in and answer my questions."

Chen Hong was reluctant to step inside. "Your Majesty, for the sake of your peace and quiet, I can answer your questions from here," he insisted.

Emperor Jiajing could sense that something was awry. "All right then. Go ahead with your report."

"Master, I delivered your edict to the Prince of Yu. He respectfully received it and promised to copy the six sentences that Hai Rui has written. He asked me to tell you that he would inscribe his calligraphy on a plaque and send it over to Home of Six Necessities immediately."

"How did my son react to my order?" Emperor Jiajing asked, closing his eyes. "Was he surprised?"

"Your Majesty, when I announced your decree, the Prince of Yu looked nervous. In fact, he was almost frightened."

"Was he courteous to you?"

"Your Majesty, the Prince of Yu was more than courteous. He was so appreciative that he removed a piece of jade pendant from his belt and gifted it to me. He enquired about your health several times."

"What about Feng Bao? Have you sent him over there?"

"Your Majesty, I delivered Feng Bao to Master Lan's aide at Chaotian Temple."

Emperor Jiajing became withdrawn.

The silence intrigued Chen Hong. He pricked up his ears, trying to figure out what was happening inside.

Lu Fang rose from the floor. Pulling out a white towel from a gold basin, he tiptoed over to Emperor Jiajing. "Master, it's time to wipe your face," he said, handing the towel to the emperor.

Emperor Jiajing waved his right hand, knocking the towel to the floor. "Did anyone give you a hard time?" he shouted to Chen Hong outside. "Did you get beaten up? Crawl inside and show your face. Let me take a look. Your Daddy here is also interested in seeing your face."

Lu Fang froze.

Chen Hong did not respond. He knelt outside, dawdling.

"Daddy, he's afraid of you," Emperor Jiajing said to Lu Fang sarcastically. "Ask him to come in."

Lu Fang quickly dropped to his knees without answering.

"Master, please don't blame Daddy." Chen Hong crawled over the threshold and stopped at about ten feet from Emperor Jiajing. Then, he kowtowed three times. "Your Majesty, nobody scolded me," he said. "I didn't get beaten either. I wouldn't dare lie to my master."

Even though Chen Hong had sewed a long strap to the brim of his hat, and had fastened it tightly to his chin so his hat wouldn't fall off, the white silk bandages around his head gave him away.

Seeing his pathetic look, Emperor Jiajing did not bother to question him further. He simply stared at him, and his eyes flashed with anger.

"Chen Hong, tell His Majesty what happened," said Lu Fang. "Be truthful. Did Feng Bao make a scene and scare the prince? Did you try to punish yourself and take the blame when the young prince started to cry?"

Chen Hong kowtowed to Lu Fang silently.

"Answer!" Emperor Jiajing muttered through his teeth.

"Ah... yes," Chen Hong mumbled ambivalently.

Lu Fang straightened his back and looked at Emperor Jiajing. "I'm shocked that Chen Gonggong got injured when he went out to deliver Your Majesty's decree. This is unprecedented. It is a cardinal crime. Master, I trained Feng Bao for years and I assigned him the job at the Prince of Yu's mansion. Now that he has perpetrated this atrocious crime, I take full responsibility. Master, I'm willing to take whatever you mete out as punishment."

Emperor Jiajing did not address Lu Fang. Instead, he fixed his eyes on Chen Hong's forehead. "Let me ask you one more time. Did you bruise your face and forehead from slapping yourself and knocking your head on the ground? Or did anyone hurt you?"

"Your Majesty, you're an immortal, and nothing escapes your sharp eyes. I wouldn't dare lie to you," Chen Hong said with a panicked voice. "As Lu Gonggong just said, Feng Bao made quite a scene and the young prince started to cry really hard. I was so shocked and frightened! All I could do was to blame and punish myself. I kowtowed and slapped myself in the face because I was worried that the young prince would choke himself when crying."

"What about the Prince of Yu? Where was Princess Li? Didn't they intervene?"

"Your Majesty, the Prince of Yu was resting in bed when I arrived. He crawled out of bed to receive your decree. I encountered Feng Bao in the front yard. The Prince of Yu wasn't aware of the incident. I had to thank Princess Li. She pulled the prince into her arms and enabled me to drag Feng Bao out of the door."

Emperor Jiajing paused. His expression slowly turned from anger to coldness. "It sounds to me that a type of 'fragrant grass' is running rampant," he said scornfully.

'Fragrance', or *fang* in Chinese, referred to Lu Fang, and 'grass' implied Lu Fang's supporters. The allusion couldn't have been more obvious.

"All the twenty-four yamens in Beijing are covered with fragrant grass," Emperor Jiajing rambled. "Our imperial agents are wearing robes with embroidered grass. Even my son's garden is now overgrown with fragrant grass. Our Great Ming Empire is now full of beautiful flowers and fragrant grass!"

Both Lu Fang and Chen Hong lay still on the floor. Emperor Jiajing called Chen Hong's name.

"Yes, Your Majesty," he replied. His heart was thumping with excitement.

"When weeds grow, they choke out crops. Do you understand what I'm saying?"

Of course, Chen Hong knew what Emperor Jiajing meant, but

he feigned ignorance. Lifting his head slowly, he gave the emperor a confused look.

"I issued an edict this morning, ordering you to address members of the Imperial Investigative Agency. Have you done it yet?"

"Your Majesty, I've just returned from the Prince of Yu's mansion and haven't had the time yet," said Chen Hong. "I'm going there now."

"A junior official at the Ministry of Treasury criticised me on the very first day he arrived in Beijing. Among the 'Thirteen Warriors', two stepped out to defend him. I wonder how they became so bold. Where were you when this was happening? I want you to deliver my decree right away. I want you to eradicate the grass. Let's start with the Imperial Investigative Agency."

"Yes, Your Majesty," Chen Hong replied and kowtowed three times.

明

Beijing was a large city, but gossip travelled faster here than in a small town. In the morning, Hai Rui stopped by Home of Six Necessities and wrote six lines on a piece of paper. By noon, the Imperial Investigative Agency placed secret agents outside Hai Rui's house in Qianliang Alley to monitor him. A few hours later, Emperor Jiajing ordered the Prince of Yu to copy Hai Rui's writing and had them inscribed on a plaque. By evening, the whole city knew about it, from officials at the six ministries to patrons of restaurants and teahouses. Even some street vendors and sedan carriers heard a thing or two.

When a horse-drawn carriage approached Qianliang Alley where Hai Rui had rented a courtyard house, the coachman stopped and refused to go inside.

Dr Li emerged from the carriage with two medical bags on his shoulders. The coachman put a small bench on the ground, and held Dr Li's arm as he stepped out. After tipping the coachman five strings of copper coins, the doctor walked into the alley.

At sunset in the summer, families living inside alleys normally opened their courtyard doors, and splashed water outside to alleviate the heat. With their doors open, they would sit around in their yards, eating dinner or drinking tea. As Dr Li strolled in, he was surprised to see that all the doors remained tightly shut. He quickly understood the reason – four plainclothes imperial agents were loitering in the alley, two at each end. Except for a few sparrows that occasionally flew over the houses, no resident was out.

Dr Li made a beeline for two imperial agents who were slightly taken aback by the stranger's audacity.

"Excuse me, do you happen to know which one is Mr Hai's house? He's with the Ministry of Treasury and just moved in today."

"Who are you?" the younger agent asked. "What's your name? What are you here for?"

"I'm his friend, Li Shizhen. I'm here because I haven't seen him for a long time. Could you tell me which house is his?"

The young agent eyed him suspiciously. His colleague, a middle-aged man, noticed the medical bags on Dr Li's shoulders. "Sir, wait, are you the imperial doctor who is in town to examine and treat the Prince of Yu?" he asked.

"Yes, the Prince of Yu is my patient, but I'm no longer an imperial doctor."

The middle-aged imperial agent nodded at Dr Li with awe and saluted him on one knee. "Dr Li, please accept my apology."

The young agent looked baffled.

"He is the magic doctor who used to work at the Imperial Hospital," the middle-aged agent explained. "Shen Lian used to head our agency. Yan Shifan put him in jail. They tortured Shen Lian and broke his legs. Dr Li performed surgery on Shen Lian and healed him. He's a magic doctor who has saved the lives of countless people…"

Dr Li waved his hands, urging him to stop.

"Dr Li, I'll make an exception for you and let you pass," the middle-aged agent said in a low voice. "But you understand the situation. I apologise that I won't be able to take you there in person. Mr Hai lives there, the fifth house on the left. You take care of yourself."

"Thank you," said Dr Li, who gave the middle-aged agent a palm-over-fist salute before walking towards Hai Rui's house.

At this time, the two imperial agents at the opposite end of the alley went up to Dr Li, trying to block him. The middle-aged agent quickly raised his hand and waved a 'let him pass' gesture. The agents turned around and stepped away.

Dr Li stopped outside Hai Rui's house and laughed at the fact that Hai Rui had deliberately left the courtyard door wide open in defiance of the imperial agents' intimidation. He poked his head inside and saw his friend turning the soil with a hoe in a small garden next to the well.

Dr Li made a coughing sound.

Hai Rui didn't hear him and continued digging.

Dr Li made another coughing sound.

Hai Rui continued digging. "If you need me on official business, I will go with you after I finish this," he said without lifting his head. "If you want some water, go get it from the well yourself."

Dr Li ambled inside and caught sight of a table with two stools under a locust tree on the west side of the yard. He stepped over, put his medical bags on the table and sat down. Pouring himself a cup of tea from a porcelain teapot on the table, he started drinking slowly.

"My wife is resting in the bedroom," Hai Rui said irritably without looking at Dr Li. "After you finish your tea, please leave."

"Why don't you invite your wife to step out and let me examine her?" Dr Li asked.

Hai Rui stopped. He tilted his head and his eyes lit up. For a moment, he was too stunned to speak.

Seeing that Hai Rui was sweating profusely, Dr Li poured Hai Rui a cup of tea and rose from his stool. Dr Li recited a Tang poem as he handed the cup to Hai Rui: "'Hoeing the soil under the noonday sun, his sweat drips on the ground beneath the seedling.' Mr Hai, it's already sunset. What are you digging there?"

"Dr Li," Hai Rui shouted in excitement. Throwing his hoe on the ground, he bowed before taking the cup from Dr Li's hands. "It's rather expensive to live in the capital city," Hai Rui said, quoting a famous line from another Tang poet. "It's a waste to let this small garden lie fallow. I'm planning to plant some spring onions and cabbages. Wang Yongji told me that you're in town. We were planning to visit you tomorrow. I didn't expect to see you here."

"Well, it's better that I come to you," Dr Li said matter-of-factly. "You're like one of these people described in this poem: 'When you stir, you cause turbulent waves like a gale. When you lie still, you resemble an intimidating mountain.' Oh well, where is your mother? Take me to her."

"She's in the north room. Let's go into the guest room first. I'll get her for you."

Amu stepped out of her bedroom. Her heart had welled up with a confluence of mixed emotions at the sight of Dr Li. "You're our saviour!" she remarked. "I can't tell you how pleased I am to see you. Please come in."

Dr Li bowed to Amu but did not follow her into the guest room. "Hai Rui, please bring me a bucket of water," he requested.

"Dr Li, you don't have to remove your shoes," Amu quickly explained.

"I seldom pay attention to other people's home etiquette, but I can't break Amu's rule," Dr Li insisted as he took off his shoes. "Hai Rui, please get me some water so I can wash my feet."

Hai Rui turned around and hurried over to the well. Fortunately, a bucket of water was there. Grabbing a wooden ladle, he carried the bucket to the guest room door. Dr Li pulled up his right trouser leg and stretched out his foot. Hai Rui scooped out some water from the bucket and rinsed it. Then, Dr Li put his clean foot inside the room before pulling up his left trouser leg.

Once his feet were cleansed, Dr Li said to Amu: "Please sit there in the middle and accept my official greetings."

"Dr Li, please sit down."

Dr Li held Amu's arms and helped her sit on a chair in the middle of the room. Taking a step back, he dropped to his knees.

Amu stood up. "Hai Rui, please hurry and return the courtesy."

Without time to wash his own feet, Hai Rui ran into the room and knelt opposite Dr Li.

When Dr Li kowtowed to his mother, Hai Rui kowtowed to Dr Li.

Dr Li rose from the floor and helped Hai Rui to his feet.

Amu sat down on her chair. Dr Li took a seat on her right. Hai Rui sat opposite Dr Li.

In a daze, Amu stared at Dr Li and reached out her right hand to him. Dr Li held her hand with both of his. She broke down in tears.

"Dr Li, throughout my life I've never begged for favours or bothered anyone with my personal problems," she recounted. "But when our family moved to Xingguo, Jiangxi Province, I wished you had been around to help us. You have no idea how much I have missed you and looked forward to seeing you again."

Hai Rui lowered his head and his eyes moistened.

Dr Li paused for a while before speaking: "Tan Lun wrote me a letter and mentioned your granddaughter's accident and your daughter-in-law's subsequent illness. How did it happen?"

Amu pulled out a handkerchief from her pocket and wiped her tears. "It was in March three years ago," she said. "Xingguo experienced a severe shortage of irrigation water. Some locals told Hai Rui that several big landowners in a nearby region controlled the upper reaches of a river that flowed through the county and had diverted the water to their own land. When the river in the lower reaches dried out, farmers couldn't plant rice seedlings. Hai Rui was so upset that he went on his own to negotiate with those landowners. He was gone for more than a fortnight and succeeded in procuring the irrigation water for local farmers. When the river started to flow again, my granddaughter accidentally fell into the water outside our house. Many people helped with the rescue and retrieved her tiny body at a place about two kilometres away. When they delivered her to us, my daughter-in-law, who was pregnant at the time, passed out on the spot. The grief harmed the baby inside her tummy. We invited a local doctor and he said there was nothing he could do. In the end, we lost both the girl and the baby boy. The night when this happened, I sat next to my daughter-in-law and thought to myself: if only Dr Li had been there, he would have at least saved the unborn baby. It's been three years and my daughter-in-law has never recovered from her illness. Hai Rui earned about thirty taels of silver each year and we spent half of it on her medication. But she's still bedridden. Each time I think about these tragic events, I want to die so I can join Hai Rui's father in the other world. But what am I going to say to his old man when I reunite with him?"

As his mother was weeping, Hai Rui dropped to his knees. "Mother, it was all my fault. I failed you as a son," he said. "But please don't think this way. If anything happens to you, I wouldn't be able to redeem myself if I die a hundred deaths."

Amu wiped her tears again and excoriated Hai Rui. "I don't want to hear such words again. You devote yourself to the Imperial Government. Nothing can distract you. You don't even care if your whole family dies off."

Hai Rui didn't dare talk back. He kowtowed again.

"Dr Li, I've never chastised him in front of his peers," Amu continued. "But you're different. I'm telling you all these things because you are not an imperial official like him, and you have no interest in being one. If a person is dedicated to the Imperial Government and bent on being a reputable and upright official, he shouldn't be married and have children. He shouldn't even have living parents. If they are around, he wouldn't be able to take care of them. Hai Rui is like an unfilial son!"

Shocked by such a harsh rebuke, Dr Li felt obligated to defend Hai Rui, who was still kneeling on the floor. "Amu, I beg to differ," he said. "A loyal and devoted imperial official is, first of all, a filial son. It's deeply unfortunate that the tragedy occurred, but we can't blame Hai Rui for it. He left home to help people in his county."

Amu did not respond to Dr Li. Instead, she pointed at Hai Rui. "My son knows exactly why I'm scolding him in front of you. When you're here, he acts so obediently like a filial son, but he never takes his mother or his family to his heart. Ask what he did earlier today. We spent a whole month on the road. I'm over seventy now, and you can imagine how exhausted I was. The trip proved to be extremely hard for his wife. But he had not the slightest regard for us. The minute he arrived in Beijing, he got himself into trouble. He claimed he acted for the good of the people. We just moved in here and we are now surrounded by imperial agents. He thinks I'm too blind to notice what is happening…"

"Amu, your reproof is totally justified," Dr Li consoled Amu.

Then, he turned to Hai Rui: "Confucius once said, 'those who want to promote great virtue to the world first need to govern their states, and in order to govern their states, they need to first manage their family'. You have a mother who is already at an advanced age, and you're a low-ranking official. Even though I agree with the saying that 'those in a higher position are short-sighted and may not think as deeply as you do', I don't believe you can do much to change that. I understand you're concerned about the Great Ming Empire, but you should worry about your family first."

"Dr Li, thanks for your teaching," Hai Rui replied sincerely.

"I'm not in a position to teach you anything. As a friend, I'm only offering some advice."

Amu opened her eyes and looked at Dr Li with gratitude.

"Amu, don't be upset. I'll examine your daughter-in-law and prescribe her some medication. The Heavenly God always favours the loyal and the filial. I'll try my best to help the Hai family have another heir."

"Dr Li, the Heavenly God must be touched by what Hai Rui has done for ordinary people. That's why He has sent a noble person like you to help us. Words alone are not enough to express my gratitude for your kindness to our family. Hai Rui, please drop to your knees and kowtow to Dr Li on my behalf."

"Please don't, Hai Rui. Take me to see your wife. I'm going to check her pulse."

"Dr Li, I'll wait for you here," Amu said as she rose from her chair.

"We'll catch up when I've finished," Dr Li replied.

After Hai Rui and Dr Li stepped out of the room, Amu went into her room. A few minutes later she emerged with a small bag in her hand and walked towards the door.

Four imperial agents at both ends of the alley glanced at Amu.

Amu beckoned to the agents whom Dr Li had encountered earlier and shouted in her energetic voice: "Can one of you come over here?"

The middle-aged agent came up to her.

"Would you do me a favour?"

The agent was taken aback. "What do you need?" he asked.

Amu brought out a string of copper coins from her bag and said: "I have a guest tonight. He's a physician. Would you be able to buy me some liquor and cold cuts with this money?"

The middle-aged man looked hesitant. After considering the matter for a few moments, he said: "Madam, I'll go and buy them. You can wait for me inside."

It was already dark outside. The middle-aged agent took the money and strode towards the alley entrance.

3

Giant lanterns under the eaves of the Interior Ministry's duty room illuminated the entire courtyard. Four deputy ministers sat outside in front of the door. Chen Hong took the seat in the middle but moved his chair slightly back in the shadow to hide the bruises on his cheeks.

About two dozen people congregated in the courtyard and the lights shone directly on their faces. Donning black uniforms, they occupied the yard like gigantic crows. Members of the Criminal Investigative Division waited on the left and those with the Imperial Prison on the right. Zhu Qi and Chee Dazhu, who belonged to the latter group, stood in the front row.

Now that everyone had arrived, the two groups saluted Chen Hong and his peers on one knee – imperial agents only knelt on both knees when they had an audience with the emperor. "Greetings to Chen Gonggong, Huang Gonggong, Shi Gonggong and Meng Gonggong!"

Chen Hong slowly rose from his chair. He had summoned the agents at dusk and none of the deputy ministers knew what the gathering was about. They simply looked at Chen Hong.

"I'm here to announce His Majesty's edict. Kneel on both knees," he ordered.

The agents obeyed and dropped to their knees in unison.

Surprised by Chen Hong's announcement, the other three deputies quickly stood up and knelt down opposite Chen Hong.

Wearing his tall hat, Chen Hong towered over his subordinates in the yard. Based on his conjecture, Emperor Jiajing would announce Lu Fang's departure and officially install him as the Interior Minister the next day. Therefore, he decided to use the occasion to establish his authority.

> Members of the Criminal Investigative Division and the Imperial Prison, please listen carefully to His Majesty's holy words, he declared in his shrieking voice. "When Emperor Hongwu first founded the Imperial Investigative Agency, he issued strict rules, and specifically put the first deputy interior minister in charge. However, some members are trying to bypass formal channels of communication. For example, when an incident occurred earlier today, an agent went around Chen Hong and reported it to Lu Fang directly. When did I change the rules? Did Lu Fang tell you to do that? I consider each one of you as members of my family, but some of you are treating me as a monarch in name only. I have raised a group of traitors! This morning, a certain official defiled my name in public. But oddly, when some members got wind of it, they jumped to his defence, attempting to exculpate the offender, rather than expressing outrage at such blatant behaviour. Where does your loyalty lie? This evening, I have authorised Chen Hong to apply our ancestral rules and discipline those who have committed the above offences. I intend this to be a warning to all of you."

In the middle of his reading, Chen Hong paused. There was total silence.

Those in the courtyard were skilled kungfu masters. Even though they were kneeling on the ground with their heads down, they could gauge the reaction of people around them. Their sixth sense told them that Chen Hong was fixing his eyes on two people, Zhu Qi and Chee Dazhu, both of whom would face punishment. But much to their surprise, the deputy interior minister had someone else in mind.

"Bring him in," Chen Hong shouted to people outside the courtyard.

Two eunuchs escorted a man into the yard. He was the middle-aged imperial agent who had taken a string of copper coins from Hai Rui's mother and agreed to buy liquor and food for her.

The man's hands were tied behind his back. The two eunuchs led him to Chen Hong and forced him to kneel.

"Who does this man report to? Step forward!"

The leaders of the Criminal Investigative Division and the Imperial Prison lifted their heads and glanced at the middle-aged agent.

"Do any of you recognise him?" Chen Hong asked them.

"Wait," said Huang Jin, who was kneeling in front of his chair.

Chen Hong looked stunned.

"Chen Gonggong, have you finished reading His Majesty's decree?" asked Huang, who held his head high.

Chen Hong glared at Huang and regarded the question as an undisguised attempt to challenge his authority in public. After their fistfight a few years ago, the hostilities between the two deputy interior ministers had escalated. Chen Hong felt that Huang Jin always picked fights with him whenever an opportunity arose. So he decided to ignore his arch rival.

"Have you reached the end of the decree yet?" Huang asked, again in a raised voice.

"Does it matter if I have finished or not?" Chen Hong retorted fiercely.

Huang sprang to his feet. "If you have finished, why do you still keep us kneeling here? Are we paying respect to His Majesty or to you? If you don't even follow the house rules, how do you expect others to abide by them? I urge everyone here to stand."

"They wouldn't dare!" Chen Hong hooted like an owl.

He was right. Apart for Huang Jin, nobody stood up.

When the owl's hooting subsided, silence reigned upon the yard.

"His Majesty has decreed that..." Chen Hong resumed his declaration, trying to lower his pitch. Huang detected a cunning smile on Chen Hong's face. That subtle facial expression made Huang nervous. Sensing that more bad news was about to be announced, Huang swallowed his anger and dropped to his knees.

Emperor Jiajing was known for packing his edicts with obscure allusions and ambiguous language. His intention was to keep imperial officials on edge while they tried to decipher the meaning of his words. Unfortunately, members of the Imperial Investigative Agency were largely illiterate. Therefore, he granted an exception by allowing eunuchs who delivered his edicts to interpret and paraphrase his messages. At this point, Chen Hong took full advantage of this rule and injected his own words into the decree.

"A type of fragrant grass is running wild in the palace," he said, mimicking Emperor Jiajing's tone and placing special emphasis on 'fragrant'. "The twenty-four yamens in Beijing are now overgrown with fragrant grass. We have spotted grass inside the Imperial Investigative Agency…"

Once again, Chen Hong paused to create an unsettling atmosphere, giving those around him plenty of clues to consider. Naturally, everyone was shocked, especially Huang Jin, who quickly came to the realisation that his beloved Lu Fang had fallen victim to this political shakeup. Chen Hong relished the fear. He continued:

> Look at the gowns you are wearing. Every single one has embroidered flowers on it. But instead of treasuring those flowers, you worship fragrant grass. You people have no idea how much the palace spends on your robes every year. You're getting more generous benefits than me and many senior-ranking imperial officials! Do you know I, Emperor Jiajing, only wear eight sets of gowns all year round? So, have I ever mistreated you? I have created a comfortable environment so you can perfect your kungfu skills, but instead of using those skills to defend me, you protect my attacker. A junior official at the Ministry of Treasury defamed me this morning, but two of our honoured warriors came forward to speak in his favour. I urge these two agents to step out. They owe me an explanation!

Zhu Qi and Chee Dazhu stood up simultaneously. They stepped over to a stone path and knelt in front of Chen Hong.

"Ah, greetings Number Seven and Number Thirteen!" Chen Hong said, feigning an unusually friendly tone. "I didn't realise that His Majesty was referring to you two in his edict."

Straightening his back, Zhu Qi replied: "Chen Gonggong, whichever rule or rules I have broken, I'm willing to accept my punishment."

Ripping off his gown and undershirt, Zhu Qi bared his torso and placed his clothes on the floor. Chee Dazhu followed his example and removed his shirt as well.

Chen Hong's gaze swept across the yard. All the country's top kungfu masters were kneeling on the ground in fear. Realising that he had achieved his intended goal, he decided to wrap up the ceremony. "When Huang Gonggong asked me just now if I had finished, I couldn't answer him," he said in a softened tone. "Now I can say that I have conveyed all of His Majesty's messages to you. If you are supposed to be on your knees, remain kneeling. If you have a chair, sit down. If you don't have a chair, I'm afraid you'll have to pick a spot and sit on the ground."

The other three deputy interior ministers rose from the ground. With a heavy heart, Huang Jin sat on his chair and lowered his head without making any comment. Members of the Criminal Investigative Division and the Imperial Prison sat cross-legged on the ground.

Zhu Qi, Chee Dazhu and the middle-aged agent knelt on the stone path in the middle of the courtyard.

"Liu Er," Chen Hong addressed the middle-aged agent who was still wearing his long gown. "You've been with us more than twenty years. I never expected that a veteran like you would make such a stupid mistake. How could you agree to run an errand for Hai Rui's mother? The family was under your surveillance, weren't they? Put your hand on your chest and do a quick calculation. How much money has His Majesty paid you to support your family over the years? How could you do something so unconscionable? Now, tell me how you should be punished."

Chee Dazhu lifted his head. "Chen Gonggong, Liu Er reports to me," he said. "I instructed him to look after Hai Rui. When he was the magistrate of Chun'an, Hai Rui saved my life. Please spare Liu Er if possible. I should be held responsible."

"What a man!" said Chen Hong. "It is a virtue to repay other people's kindness when you are able. Now, that's a tough decision to make. Zhu Qi, you're Chee Dazhu's boss. Tell me how I should handle this."

Zhu Qi felt obligated to answer. "If His Majesty has not ordered you to behead us, you should apply caning. Based on house rules, Liu Er gets twenty strokes, Chee Dazhu forty and I'll get eighty."

"All right, let's follow house rules," Chen Hong instructed Zhu Qi's superior who was sitting in the front row. "You know how to carry this out. Beat them black and blue. Then I'll send them to Yuxi Palace and let His Majesty take a look. Hopefully, that will placate His Majesty. Understood?"

明

The flickering candles in front of the altar and the glowing lanterns hanging from the ceiling lit up the meditation room. Emperor Jiajing put on the gown embroidered with the texts of Laozi's *Tao Te Ching* and ambled towards the altar. Kneeling on a prayer pillow, he kowtowed three times. Holding his hands before his chest, he started chanting.

Lu Fang was kneeling next to Emperor Jiajing's meditation mat on top of the octagonal platform.

At the end of his chanting, Emperor Jiajing stood up and walked towards his desk. Picking up a calligraphy brush, he dipped it in a bowl of red cinnabar ink and began writing something furiously on a framed piece of yellow paper. Soon, an odd-shaped hierogram appeared.

Putting his calligraphy down on the desk, the emperor examined the hierogram and waited for the ink to dry.

"Lu Fang," he said as he held the yellow paper with both hands. "You've been with me for the better part of your life. Take this with you. It will keep you safe for the remainder of your life."

Lu Fang choked up. Fighting back his tears, he kowtowed.

"Thank you for giving me the opportunity to serve you for forty years," he murmured. "I can die happy now."

"Your protection paper is on my desk," Emperor Jiajing said as he walked towards his dragon bed behind the silk curtains and lay down on his side.

Lu Fang turned around and kowtowed three times towards Emperor Jiajing's bed. Stepping down from the platform, he picked up the hierogram from the desk and tiptoed out of the room with his head down.

Emperor Jiajing's eyes were wide open. As he turned in bed, tears poured from the corner of his eyes. He could hear voices in the main hall.

"Chen Gonggong, from now on, you'll be responsible for taking care of His Majesty," Lu Fang was heard saying. "Please allow me to kowtow and thank you in advance."

Emperor Jiajing sat up.

"Taking care of His Majesty is my duty and honour," Chen Hong replied. "Please don't…"

Then came the sounds of two people thumping their heads on the floor.

After Lu Fang had stepped out, the hall fell silent again.

The emperor stood up, walked over to his prayer mat and sat down cross-legged.

Chen Hong appeared at the door and announced: "Your Majesty, I just want you to know that three minions at the Criminal Investigative Division received their deserved punishment early this evening. I've brought them over here so they can apologise to Your Majesty in person and seek forgiveness."

"Let them enter," Emperor Jiajing ordered.

Chen Hong poked his head outside and instructed them to come in. Zhu Qi, Chee Dazhu and Liu Er, all of whom were shirtless, filed into the meditation room.

Chen Hong kowtowed to Emperor Jiajing, and then he stood up and moved to the side.

The flogging had rendered it extremely painful for the three imperial agents to walk, let alone kneel. Even so, Zhu Qi, Chee Dazhu and Liu Er dropped to their knees. With both hands on the ground, they kowtowed before showing their severely bruised backs and buttocks to Emperor Jiajing.

The Emperor uttered a long sigh, and said: "The *Three Character Classic* admonishes us: 'To feed without teaching is the father's fault, and to teach without discipline is the teacher's laziness.' I am also partially to blame for your wrongdoing."

Chen Hong plopped down on his knees. "Your Majesty, as their leader, I should be blamed for their transgression and receive a caning as well," he said.

"You should reflect on your negligence of duty. In my edict, I simply ordered you to chastise them verbally. Why did you beat them like this?"

Chen Hong raised his hand and started slapping his already swollen face.

"All right, stop!" Emperor Jiajing said with contempt.

Chen Hong dropped to his knees and thanked His Majesty.

Having served Emperor Jiajing for decades, Zhu Qi knew that the master and his eunuch were playing a double act.

"Zhu Xi once said that everything happens for a reason," Emperor Jiajing continued. "Do you know how Chee Dazhu ended up in the palace as an imperial agent? It is because Hai Rui saved his life a few years ago. He did nothing wrong by greeting Hai Rui and expressing his gratitude. It shows Chee Dazhu is loyal. We need loyal people to serve the Great Ming Empire."

"Your Majesty, thank you for your benevolence," said Chee Dazhu, who kowtowed with his back towards the emperor.

"I want you to visit Hai Rui at home and welcome him to Beijing."

"Yes, Your Majesty..."

"Nothing escapes my celestial eyes. I can see that Li Shizhen, the Prince of Yu's physician, is visiting Hai Rui at the moment. Why don't you go there and have him give you some medicine to treat the bruises on your back. If the medicine works, bring some back for your teacher, Zhu Qi and your subordinate Liu Er."

"Your Majesty, I will..." Chee Dazhu said, trying to fight back his tears.

Emperor Jiajing turned to Chen Hong. "Hai Rui is a mere

auditor at the Ministry of Treasury. He doesn't even know how to hold a knife. Why do you post four agents near his house? Summon them back."

"Yes, Your Majesty. I will do accordingly," Chen Hong replied, but deep down he remained unconvinced.

※

Dr Li prescribed some herbs for Hai Rui's wife after examining her and went out to a herbal store to buy the medicine himself. Upon returning, he instructed Hai Rui to boil the herbs in a clay pot.

At this moment, he was chatting with Hai Rui and Amu in the guest room. The steaming medicine pot was bubbling on a small, white charcoal stove in a corner of the room.

"Weaken the fire a little bit," Dr Li suggested.

Hai Rui rose from his chair and stepped over to the stove. Using a pair of tongs, he removed a few pieces of charcoal from the fire.

"Dr Li, since imperial agents are watching over our house, I doubt you'll be able to leave tonight," Amu said to Dr Li. "I know this is a small place, but you're welcome to sleep on the floor in the study. Hai Rui can keep you company."

Dr Li laughed. "I can't sleep in the same room as him," he said. "His snoring will keep me awake all night long. Those people outside can't stop me from going home. I'll stay for a little longer and then leave."

"Mother, you must be tired," Hai Rui said. "Why don't you go to bed now? I'll entertain Dr Li here. Once the medicine is cooked, I'll see him off."

As Amu was about to leave the room, there was a knock on the courtyard door. Amu looked startled. Hai Rui and Dr Li exchanged quizzical glances.

Hai Rui stepped out into the middle of the yard. "Who is it?" he asked. "Are you here for business or is this a personal visit?"

Dr Li and Amu waited anxiously in the guest room.

"My saviour, it's me, Chee Dazhu. I'm here with my wife."

Hai Rui paused for a few seconds before answering: "I told you earlier that you don't need to come and see me. Let bygones be bygones. It's quite late. My mother and my wife are already in bed. Why don't you leave us alone?"

"Please open the door," Chee Dazhu pleaded.

Hai Rui turned around and walked back into the guest room.

"My saviour, I'm here to visit you by order of His Majesty," said Chee Dazhu, who sounded genuinely excited.

Hai Rui's eyes lit up.

"Open the door and let him in," Amu urged.

Hai Rui walked to the door and pulled open the latch.

A glowing lantern dazzled Hai Rui. He squinted at Chee Dazhu, who had difficulty standing. His wife was holding him by the arm. Next to them was an imperial agent who was carrying the lantern.

Chee Dazhu reached out and placed his hand on the door frame for support while his wife let go of her hands and dropped to her knees. "Greetings," she said, kowtowing to Hai Rui. "You can't imagine how happy I am to see you."

"Please rise," Hai Rui said politely. "Come in."

Chee Dazhu's wife got to her feet and held Chee Dazhu, who was grimacing with pain.

"Did you injure yourself?" asked Hai Rui, who peered at Chee Dazhu sympathetically.

"It's not serious," Chee Dazhu said with his teeth clenched. "Just some bruises on the back."

"Help him inside."

Chee Dazhu struggled to climb the stairs. The imperial agent waited outside the door.

Hai Rui closed the door behind them. "Take it easy," he directed Chee Dazhu and his wife. "This way please."

It was late at night. Grand Secretary Xu had summoned Li Chunfang, Gao Gong, Zhao Zhenji and Xu Fan to his residence for a meeting. Suspecting that an emergency had occurred, they came quickly and gathered at Grand Secretary Xu's study, a rather informal setting. Looking tense, they stood in front of their chairs, and fixed their eyes on Grand Secretary Xu, who was sitting on a chair behind his desk with a grim expression on his face.

"Please sit down," he said calmly.

Deputy Li and Zhao Zhenji sat on the right while Gao Gong and Xu Fan took the seats on the left. Holding a stack of budget proposals on his lap, Grand Secretary Xu announced: "His Majesty has requested that we bring these spending proposals to Yuxi Palace for a discussion tomorrow."

"Has His Majesty agreed to sign off on the requests?" Gao Gong asked.

"If His Majesty has signed off on them, why does he request our presence at Yuxi Palace?"

The room felt silent.

"I have one more piece of news to share with you. Lu Gonggong has been exiled to Nanjing. His new assignment is to guard Emperor Hongwu's mausoleum."

The four ministers looked at Grand Secretary Xu in disbelief.

"Chen Gonggong has taken over Lu Fang's position. He'll be responsible for getting all the budget requests approved tomorrow."

The air in the room felt thick and heavy.

"Let's move fast and review these requests one more time," Grand Secretary Xu continued. "Regardless, we need to find one and a half million taels of silver for the Ministry of Public Works so workers can start ordering materials, and finish repairing and renovating those palace buildings and two Taoist temples."

Deputy Li took the initiative and spoke first. "We can take out five hundred thousand taels from the Ministry of Defence budget. I have issued an order to Generals Yu Dayou and Qi Jiguang, telling them not to launch any new offensives this year. Their priorities are to protect a few strategically important cities from pirate attacks."

Grand Secretary Xu nodded. "Gao Gong, can we hold off some of the salary payments for now?" he asked.

"What else can we do? We have decided to defer this year's salary payments to all ministerial officials in Beijing as well as provincial governors, imperial inspectors and department chiefs. Officials in Beijing who are at grade four or lower will receive half of their salaries this year and those mid- and low-level officials working for provincial governments will be paid their full salaries. If we don't pay those provincial officials, they'll go out to seek bribes with a vengeance."

"How much do you think we can get from these belt-tightening measures?" Grand Secretary Xu asked.

"About four to five hundred thousand taels," Gao Gong replied.

"We're still short of another five to six hundred thousand taels," Grand Secretary Xu mumbled before turning to Zhao Zhenji. "I know it's hard to take money from the disaster relief and tax relief funds. Can you figure out a way to get the money we need?"

"Let me try," said Zhao. "Why don't you take six hundred thousand taels from the relief funds first?"

"Let's act fast and revise all the proposals overnight," said Grand Secretary Xu.

明

In the main hall of Yuxi Palace, two long rosewood desks were laid out in the middle. Members of the Interior Ministry occupied the one on the left. Lu Fang was no longer there. Chen Hong was donning a red robe that had belonged to Lu Fang. Surprisingly, Lu Fang's departure had no adverse impact on Huang Jin, who was seated next to Chen Hong. From the embroidered patterns on his robe, it was clear that he had been promoted to first deputy interior minister. Next to Huang sat Deputy Ministers Shi and Meng. At the far end of the desk, there was a new face. Chen Hong had appointed him to fill the vacancy.

Grand Secretary Xu and his two cabinet members, Deputy Li and Gao Gong, stood behind the right table. The junior eunuchs on duty placed a pouf next to Grand Secretary Xu, but he didn't take it. Zhao Zhenji and Xu Fan attended the meeting as observers.

"Grand Secretary Xu," Chen Hong said in a reverential tone while making a slight bow. "Please submit your spending proposals and briefly summarise each item."

"All right," Grand Secretary Xu replied. "We'll start with the Ministry of Defence."

"Yes, Your Highness," said Deputy Li who picked up the budget report from the desk.

Emperor Jiajing was sitting cross-legged on his prayer mat in the meditation room. The bronze chime was within his grasp. He closed his eyes and pricked up his ears.

"The Ministry of Defence reviewed our budget yesterday. Since we're not going to use up the allocated amount, we have decided to reduce spending by five hundred thousand taels of silver, and give the money to the Ministry of Public Works to repair Longevity Palace and Palace of Eternal Longevity."

Emperor Jiajing opened his eyes and picked up his chime. Then he paused.

Inside the main hall, Chen Hong signalled to his aide sitting at the far end of the desk. The eunuch hurried over to Deputy Li, took the spending proposal from him and presented it to Chen Hong.

Chen Hong held a red pen in his hand and turned his gaze to the meditation room.

Everyone in the main hall was waiting for Emperor Jiajing to chime the bell.

Emperor Jiajing did not disappoint. The bell chimed and the sound echoed in the main hall. Chen Hong quickly signed his name on the Defence Ministry's request.

"Next is the Ministry of Personnel. Please present your budget," Grand Secretary Xu requested.

"All ministerial officials in Beijing and Nanjing have expressed their willingness to accept temporary deferral of salary payments. Some independently wealthy officials at local levels have also agreed to wait until next year to receive their arrears. Therefore, we are able to reduce our spending by four hundred thousand taels of silver and use it towards palace and temple repairs."

The aide came over, took the budget report from Gao Gong and handed it to Chen Hong.

The chiming sounded immediately, but louder this time. Even though cabinet members could not see Emperor Jiajing, they knew he was pleased.

Chen Hong signed his name on Gao Gong's spending proposal.

"Ministry of Treasury," Grand Secretary Xu announced. "Zhao

Zhenji, your budget involves offering tax and disaster relief for farmers and migrants. Have you figured out any feasible solutions?"

"Yes, Your Highness. While we offer our steadfast support for provinces and municipalities that have been struck by natural disasters, we find it equally important to offer relief to those who have been victimised by high taxes. Therefore, we will keep our budget intact."

All eyes were now on Zhao.

Emperor Jiajing's eyes appeared resolute and animatedly alert. He put the bronze chime on his lap. "Since ancient times, governments have always encouraged the haves to help the have-nots. Among the thirteen provinces and two capitals, about half are self-sufficient and prosperous. The Ministry of Treasury has contacted the governments in Jiangsu, Zhejiang, Hunan and Hubei. We have requested that they take out some surplus money from their coffers to support provinces that have been adversely affected by natural disasters and heavy taxes. By doing this, we're able to save six hundred thousand taels of silver and give it to the Ministry of Public Works."

Emperor Jiajing's face was a picture of peace and benevolence. He didn't chime the bell. Instead, he listened to Zhao's clear and melodic voice.

"I second your decision," said Grand Secretary Xu. "It's very wise. Did you run into any opposition from Jiangsu, Zhejiang, Hunan and Hubei?"

"Grand Secretary Xu, I started corresponding with the governors of these provinces a month ago. They have all agreed to help. In their letters, which I received yesterday, they said it is incumbent upon the wealthy provinces to pitch in, helping to ease His Majesty's worries and resolve the plight of disaster victims."

Emperor Jiajing picked up the chime and tapped the bell three times.

Chen Hong looked exuberant when he was signing Zhao's report. But he reminded himself not to appear too eager. So he slowed down and wrote every stroke carefully.

Lastly, it was the turn of the Ministry of Public Works. Chen Hong bypassed Grand Secretary Xu and directly questioned Xu

Fan. "Deputy Minister Xu, based on the reports we have just approved, you'll have an extra four million taels of silver for palace and temple repairs. Is four million enough?"

Xu Fan replied loudly: "Chen Gonggong, as you can see, the whole country is united in their support for His Majesty's initiatives. The Ministry of Public Works will not let them down. We will use the money wisely and complete all renovation projects by the end of this year. By then, we hope that His Majesty can move into his permanent residence."

Without waiting for Emperor Jiajing to chime his bell, Chen Hong announced: "Bring the report over and I will sign off on it."

Anxious to secure Chen Hong's approval, Xu Fan walked over to Chen Hong without waiting for the aide, and presented his spending proposal.

Chen Hong dipped his calligraphy brush in a cinnabar ink bowl and wrote an oversized 'approved' on the report cover.

Now that Emperor Jiajing had granted all the spending proposals, everyone looked to Grand Secretary Xu, waiting for him to adjourn the meeting.

"Our Great Ming Empire has witnessed eleven wise rulers, from Emperor Hongwu to His Majesty," proclaimed Grand Secretary Xu. "Our country has flourished under their rule and they are as virtuous as the legendary Emperor Yao and Emperor Shun. That is why it upset me to hear about an incident yesterday. A new appointee at the Ministry of Treasury even had the audacity to blaspheme against His Majesty. Zhao Zhenji, you're his superior. Have you had a chance to investigate the incident?"

Zhao raised his voice so Emperor Jiajing could hear him. "Grand Secretary, please relay this message to His Majesty. The Ministry of Treasury conducted a roll call today and Hai Rui reported to work. I berated him and questioned his motive. As you are probably aware, he was born and raised in Hainan, a barbarous region in the south. I personally believe that he is simply a straightforward person. During our conversation, he didn't strike me as someone who harbours malicious intent. He admitted having committed a blunder. To punish him for those six blasphemous lines that he wrote, I have decided to dock six months of his salary.

Hai Rui is willing to accept his punishment. Do you think such punitive measures are appropriate and sufficient?"

Grand Secretary Xu did not answer. Everyone was waiting for a response from the man inside the meditation room.

"A good kungfu master knows when to punch and when to show leniency," Emperor Jiajing's voice sounded at the meditation room door.

The ten participants of the meeting dropped to their knees.

Emperor Jiajing strode towards his gold throne in the middle of the hall like a Taoist deity, with his wide sleeves fluttering in the air.

Everyone kowtowed and chanted together: "Your Majesty, long live! Long, long live!"

Emperor Jiajing sat cross-legged on the chair and looked straight at Zhao. "A strict father should learn how to love his son, and a demanding superior should learn how to forgive his subordinates," he advised. "I hear that Hai Rui is quite an honest and upright official. If you deduct one month of his salary for each sentence that he wrote, how do you expect him to feed his family for the next six months?"

Zhao kowtowed again. "Your Majesty embodies the benevolence of heaven, and I have failed to appreciate the immensity of your compassion. I deeply regret my decision. I'm willing to take money out of my own salary and compensate Hai Rui for what I have deducted from his pay."

Emperor Jiajing revealed a rare smile. "Have you heard the story about Su Dongpo, a famous poet during the Song dynasty? One day, at a welcome banquet held by the Imperial Government, a foreign envoy wrote the first half of a couplet. It went like this: 'Three sources of light – the sun, the moon and the stars.' When he asked his Chinese host to come up with the second half, nobody at the banquet could manage it. Eventually, Su Dongpo solved the riddle. Grand Secretary Xu, you know what Su Dongpo wrote, don't you?"

"Yes, Your Majesty. Su Dongpo composed the following: 'Four traits of virtue – honesty, compassion, temperance and loyalty [*zhen*].' Since Emperor Renzong's title contained the character *zhen*, Su Dongpo deleted it from the couplet. So, the couplet now reads:

'Three sources of light – the sun, the moon and the stars. Three traits of virtue – honesty, compassion and temperance.'"

"You're a true Hanlin scholar," complimented Emperor Jiajing. "Not many people know about this couplet and its corresponding story. As grand secretary, you only have two cabinet members, Deputy Li and Gao Gong. I assume you are probably stretched too thin. Why don't you add the character *zhen* that Su Dongpo had deleted from the couplet?"

Many in the room looked baffled by Emperor Jiajing's literary allusion. Zhao Zhenji understood right away. He knelt on the floor with his head down. Droplets of sweat appeared on his forehead.

"Your Majesty, please forgive my ignorance. Are you asking me to add another member to the Privy Council? Is that member in this room?"

"Grand secretary, you're truly an intelligent person. His name contains the character 'loyalty', or *zhen*."

"Your Majesty, I accept your recommendation," Grand Secretary Xu proclaimed loudly. "Zhao Zhenji, minister of treasury, is joining the Privy Council today."

Zhao kowtowed three times to Emperor Jiajing. "Thank you for your benevolence," he said. "I will do my best. In this time of crisis, I won't hesitate to sacrifice my life for the Great Ming Empire."

It was noon. The July sun was beating down on the country's oldest courier road, which was built at the beginning of the Yuan dynasty (1279-1368). Some old trees spread their leathery, leafy arms over the trail, offering welcome shade on a day like this. The deafening sounds of cicada buzzing drowned out the rumbling of a lone horse-drawn carriage, which had just departed the capital city. As the carriage drove past a clear stream that was flowing to the side of the path, Lu Fang asked the coachman to stop.

"Can we get some water from the stream?" he asked.

The coachman tugged on the reins and the horse stopped. He jumped off the carriage, pulled out a step bench and lifted the curtain. Lu Fang got off the carriage slowly. He had changed into a blue cloth gown and tied his hair at the back. His face looked rested and calm. Peering at the trees and the gurgling stream, he let out a long sigh of relief. "Why don't you step out as well?" Lu Fang said to someone inside the carriage. "We'll get some water together."

The person inside did not respond. The coachman simply stood there hesitantly. He was too afraid to lift the curtain and help the man inside.

"Why don't you leave us alone?" Lu Fang suggested to the coachman. "Go drink some water and wash your face to cool off."

As the coachman strolled towards the stream, Lu Fang tapped on the carriage door. "Come out."

The curtain opened a crack and a man with a head of unkempt grey hair poked his head out. It was Yang Jinshui. His face looked impassive.

"Come out," Lu Fang said gently. "Step down here."

Yang crawled out of the carriage and looked around furtively.

"Do you know where we are?" Lu Fang asked.

Yang shook his head and started hopping around the carriage like a child.

Lu Fang found a rock under a tree and sat down. "Stop it," he said. "Come over."

Yang ignored him and kept trotting around in circles.

"Come over," Lu Fang repeated in a stern, low voice.

Yang stopped suddenly and moved towards Lu Fang with a frightened look on his face.

Lu Fang reached out his hand. Haltingly, Yang did the same. Lu Fang grabbed Yang's hand and pulled him close. Yang squatted down next to Lu Fang.

In the distance, the coachman was removing his shirt to bathe in the cool stream.

"Jinshui, from now on, you don't have to pretend any more," Lu Fang whispered. "We're safe."

Yang stared at Lu Fang in a daze.

"I know you suffered a lot during the past three years. The hardship is over. You and I are going to guard Emperor Hongwu's mausoleum. Emperor Hongwu cannot even speak. He'll never be mad with us. We don't have to worry about anyone conspiring against us... You see the stream there? Wash your hair and face. Clean that half-man body of yours. From now on, you and I can live a clean life together."

Tears welled up in Yang's stony eyes, which started to move gradually. Then, all of a sudden, he opened his mouth wide and burst out crying. His body twitched uncontrollably.

"Let go of your tears. Cry out all your sadness, anger and grievances... Then, we'll never have to cry again."

Oddly, the cicadas in the trees stopped buzzing. Yang's sobbing echoed in the air.

"All right," Lu Fang consoled him. "Let's go and wash."

Yang held Lu Fang's arm and they ambled towards the stream.

It was cold and the wind was blowing snow. The Ministry of Treasury's Guangying Vault towered over a large, dense crowd. Several hundred imperial officials in Beijing had congregated here early in the morning, waiting to receive their salaries before the New Year. Their anxious eyes fixed on the gigantic wooden gate, which was supposed to open soon. They imagined that sacks of grain and trunks of silver dollars and copper coins were sitting in storage piles inside the vault.

The end of the year was a time of eager anticipation. Many families worked hard and lived frugally for the whole year. Now, as New Year was approaching, both the old and young waited anxiously for the breadwinners to come home with new clothes for the children, and armfuls of meat and other expensive food items that they couldn't afford to buy at other times of the year. For poor families, the end of the year was a time of dread. The children's longing eyes prompted the adults to go out and take on menial jobs so they could at least purchase some meat. Often, they had to beg for favours or put up with all sorts of insults and derision. For the most destitute who were deeply in debt, the end of the year was a time of humiliating fear. Debt collectors normally showed up at their doors with loud threats. The heads of the households would flee as early as 23 December, the day when families paid tribute to the Kitchen God, leaving their elderly parents, wives and children behind. Debt collectors would show up and hover around, yelling and cursing. Such harassments would normally end on New Year's Eve.

At that time, there was a popular couplet: 'The end of the year is hard, the end of this year is even harder, I take it one day at a time./ Debts are to be paid, all debts have to be paid off this year, I give whatever I have.' This couplet not only depicted the plight of impoverished families but also the dire circumstances of imperial officials in Beijing.

The Ministry of Treasury hadn't paid officials since the previous January. In May, when the Imperial Investigative Agency raided the homes of several hundred corrupt officials and confiscated their assets, many had expected that the government would use some of the money to pay their salaries. But the Ministry of Public Works took most of the funds and used them to repair Emperor Jiajing's palaces and Taoist temples. Only half of the officials ended up getting paid.

In the summer, many provinces were struck by natural disasters and autumn harvests failed. As a result, the Ministry of Treasury was not able to collect enough grain and money from the local governments. Salary payments were delayed again. By the end of the year, the government still owed officials six months of back pay. Whether or not they could live through the holiday depended on what they would receive today. Therefore, despite the heavy snow, people started to arrive at dawn.

The Guangying Vault was the Ministry of Treasury's only strongroom that stored money, grain or silk. The vault had three gates and each was seven metres high and eleven metres wide. Those double egress doors were equipped with groove wheels. When carts loaded with grain or cash entered or exited the vault, clerks opened each set of doors by pushing them to the side or closed them by shoving them towards the middle. Each gate had a wicket on the left side for auditors to use when they checked inventories.

The Chinese word *guangying* means 'spacious and abundant'. The vault was spacious, but at this point, the contents inside were far from being abundant. In fact, the inner chamber was almost empty. A pile of cloth sacks sat on the floor. Each sack contained three subsidy items for the New Year: a bag containing fifteen kilograms of rice, two litres of peppercorn powder and ten strings of copper coins. Zhao Zhenji was a strong believer in the Confucian adage that 'the problems with the Imperial Government lie not in scarcity but in its unequal distribution'. He mandated that all imperial officials, regardless of their rank, would receive the same amount of subsidy.

The lanterns were lit. Before the gates opened, officials set up tables outside the three entrances. Ministry rosters were stacked up neatly on each table. Warehouse workers gathered around piles of cloth sacks, waiting to distribute them.

The Treasury Ministry's division chiefs, who oversaw budget and spending in the country's two capitals and thirteen provinces were summoned here to supervise the distribution. Their presence was meant to make a statement that the Imperial Government was attentive to the needs of its officials. However, for those division chiefs, they knew that the ministry was attempting to make a mountain out of a mole hill and that their publicity stunt could backfire.

It was three days before the New Year. The state coffers had run dry for months, and the Imperial Government had no money to pay its employees. All it could afford were fifteen kilograms of rice, two litres of peppercorn powder and ten strings of copper coins. One could imagine the disappointment and outrage once the door opened. The division chiefs were tasked with appeasing the angry officials, explaining the difficulties the Imperial Government was facing and urging them to make do with what they had during the New Year's holiday and place the interest of the country first.

Before the door opened, one of the division heads stood on a box to address the treasury staff. Hai Rui was sitting at a table near the far left gate.

"Attention, please," the division leader started with a loud sigh. "We've cleared out the vault, and everyone, regardless of their rank, gets fifteen kilograms of rice, two litres of peppercorn powder and ten strings of copper coins. Nobody can live through the New Year on this, and we know that. But this is all we can offer at the moment. I don't know how people outside are going to react, but like the saying goes, no matter how ugly the bride is, she'll have to face her in-laws eventually. Be more empathetic. Let's open the door now."

At his order, officials opened the wicket gates and moved the tables to block the side entrances to prevent the masses from charging in and seizing the sacks.

People quickly crowded around the three wickets.

Hai Rui staffed the table that served officials from the Audit and Inspection Commission, Hanlin Academy, the Education Commission and the Imperial Post Office. These four agencies were packed with members of the Clear Stream, scholar-officials who were known for being fearless, outspoken and outright picky. Many from the Audit and Inspection Commission had just taken part in the impeachment proceedings against Yan Song and Yan Shifan. Zhao Zhenji specifically assigned Hai Rui to this group. It was Zhao's unspoken intention to give Hai Rui the opportunity to see how difficult it was to handle like-minded peers. He also wanted Hai Rui to understand that he was not the only one who claimed to truly care about the future of the Great Ming Empire.

"May I ask which agency you work for?" Hai Rui asked the man standing at the head of the queue. "What is your name?"

"Li Qingyuan," the official replied. "I work for the Education Commission."

Hai Rui politely asked Li to wait while he asked his assistant to look up Li's name in the roster. The assistant opened a bound book and located Li Qingyuan's name on page three. He handed the roster to Hai Rui. After confirming the name, Hai Rui put the roster down in front of Li Qingyuan and gave him a calligraphy brush. "Mr Li, please sign here, next to your printed name," he said.

Li took the calligraphy brush and signed his name as instructed.

"Please bring the holiday goody bag to Mr Li," Hai Rui instructed a warehouse worker, who put a sack on the table.

Li looked inside the sack and his eyes widened. "Could you tell me what we are getting and how much?" he asked.

"Fifteen kilograms of rice, two litres of peppercorn powder and ten strings of copper coins," Hai Rui replied.

"Is that it?" Li asked in disbelief.

"Yes, everything is in the sack."

"The government owes me at least twenty taels of silver," Li said in a raised voice. "What I'm getting today is worth no more than five taels. I have a family of six, plus two servants. How am I going to live on that? How am I supposed to pay off my debt?"

"The items in the sack are for the New Year's holiday, aren't they?" an official who was standing behind Li asked after overhearing the argument. "Do all Imperial Government officials get the same?"

"Ministerial-level officials are not receiving anything this year," Hai Rui explained.

"You make those ministerial officials sound so noble," Li yelled. "Do you really think those ministerial officials need extra for the holiday? They receive all sorts of offerings from provincial governments and their subordinates. His Majesty awards them generous monetary gifts. For low-level officials like us, your ministry has cobbled together these paltry subsidies. Do you and other officials at the Ministry of Treasury also rely on these goody bags for the New Year's holiday?"

Hai Rui did not respond.

Many officials thronged their way to the front and were eager to find out how much money they were receiving. Li turned around and shouted at those behind him. "Attention everyone, all we get this year are fifteen kilograms of rice, two litres of peppercorn powder and ten strings of copper coins."

The crowd behind Li erupted in rage and began yelling at Hai Rui. "You people at the Ministry of Treasury are dishonest and corrupt!" accused one person.

"Are you getting the same stuff as us?" shouted another. "I doubt it."

"Where are you hiding our tax money?" a third one asked.

Hai Rui stared at the angry faces and listened quietly as people spewed out their condemnations.

"Answer us!' the crowd yelled. "Answer us. Drag him out!"

Hai Rui sat there quietly.

Someone threw a huge snowball at Hai Rui and struck his official hat. Hai Rui remained motionless.

Meanwhile, a similar fracas erupted outside the other two wickets and they quickly escalated into fistfights.

※

All ministerial officials, including Grand Secretary Xu and three of his Privy Council members, were crammed into the Privy Council's duty room. They sat shoulder to shoulder at two large desks, composing *qing ci,* or flattery essays.

On 29 December, the Ministry of Public Works would complete the repairs and renovations of Emperor Jiajing's two palaces and two Taoist temples. Before the rededication ceremony, which was the country's most important pre-New Year's event, Grand Secretary Xu had summoned a dozen ministers and agency heads in Beijing to the Privy Council and urged them to each write a *qing ci* in praise of the Son of Heaven on behalf of the people of the Great Ming Empire. Since everyone's *qing ci* had to be original, officials found it harder than writing the three compulsory articles during the imperial examinations.

A thick cotton-padded curtain hung on the duty room door. Two large braziers sat in the centre of the room. The four Privy Council members sat around the braziers, polishing their essays with their calligraphy brushes. Each essay was written on green paper made of leaves. Despite the heavy snow outside, everyone was sweating. Nothing could distract them from this important literary task.

Two young clerks, wrapped up in cotton-padded coats, were guarding the duty room outside. Every now and then, they stamped their feet to keep warm.

Suddenly, they saw a man stumbling into the yard. When he moved closer, the clerks recognised him as a division chief at the Ministry of Treasury. The brim of his hat was broken and his official gown looked torn. There were scratches on his face.

"What happened to you?" the two clerks asked, stamping their feet.

"A riot has broken out," the division chief gasped. "Several hundred people are protesting in front of the Ministry of Treasury... Where is Mr Zhao? I need to see him right away."

"He's in the middle of a meeting. No one can disturb him. He doesn't care if the sky is falling."

"If Mr Zhao doesn't take care of it, the protesters will soon march over here," the division chief pleaded.

The clerks exchanged glances with each other and began hesitating. One of them lifted up a corner of the door curtain, and said to the division chief: "If you want Mr Zhao to go to the Ministry of Treasury with you, you tell him yourself. We wouldn't dare interrupt him."

Out of desperation, the division chief dashed in through a slit of the curtain.

Inside the duty room, the piteous-looking division chief knelt at the door, but those in the room were too preoccupied with their *qing ci* to take note of him. Both Grand Secretary Xu and Zhao Zhenji caught sight of the division chief. They shot an inquiring glance at him without saying anything. Zhao resumed his writing and finished it in no time. Rising from his chair, he walked over to Grand Secretary Xu and handed his essay to his teacher with both hands. "Grand Secretary Xu, it would appear that people are demanding their unpaid salaries at the Ministry of Treasury. I need to go and handle the mess. Would you mind polishing it for me?"

"Of course," Grand Secretary Xu said. "Please go there immediately. Make sure it doesn't spin out of control and become a major disruption to His Majesty's house-moving ceremony."

"Understood," Zhao said, bowing to his mentor. Then, he glanced at the division chief who was kneeling at the door. The division chief sprang to his feet and followed Zhao out of the room.

The bruises on the division chief's face made Deputy Xu nervous. Suspecting that a riot had already occurred, he signalled to Gao Gong. Their eyes met. As Grand Secretary Xu walked over to the door, Gao Gong put down his pen, rose from his chair and followed Grand Secretary Xu out.

"Have you finished your essay yet?" asked Grand Secretary Xu, who was staring at the snowflakes that were swirling in the roaring wind.

"I'm almost done. Only a couple of lines left."

"Why don't you go over to the Ministry of Treasury as well?" Grand Secretary Xu urged Gao Gong. "I don't think Zhao Zhenji alone can get the situation under control. He's not as established as you are yet."

"To tell you the truth, I don't really know how to pacify them," Gao Gong sighed. "Many are experiencing extreme hardship."

"Try to explain our situation to them. Tell them that we will figure out a way to pay their outstanding salaries after the New Year."

"When your family is hungry, you set your wok on a stove to cook some rice, but you can't cook a promise. I can certainly try to explain to them, but if we make a promise, we have to keep it. Do you have a solid timeline?"

"Next February. I promise to find a way to pay off their outstanding salaries by then."

"I'll go over there after I finish."

"Thank you for taking care of it," said Grand Secretary Xu.

"This is the least I can do. It's cold outside. Let's go in."

The clerks lifted the curtain. Grand Secretary Xu shot Gao Gong an appreciate glance and the two senior ministers stepped inside.

明

The Guangying Vault had slid into chaos before Zhao Zhenji arrived. Officials who had been waiting in the snow had breached all three main gates and entered the vault. They surrounded Hai Rui and other treasury officials, yelling at them or pushing and shoving them. The floor was strewn with sacks that contained rice, peppercorn powder and copper coins.

On the far left side of the vault, a few officials who happened to know Hai Rui retreated to the side and watched in fear. The majority had no idea who he was. They cornered Hai Rui, haranguing him as if he were a core member of the Yan Clan. Their screaming and cursing were so loud that Hai Rui couldn't understand what they were saying. He simply cast his eyes downward without talking back.

Meanwhile, loud scuffles erupted at the other two entrances. Unlike Hai Rui who confronted his angry peers with silence, those who were staffing tables in the middle and on the right side argued back fiercely. Fistfights quickly ensued. Outnumbered by their attackers, several treasury officials ended up fleeing the scene, but the mob chased them down and beat them. Like water splashing into a wok of burning oil, violence quickly spread to the left gate area. "This person here refuses to answer any of our questions!" one person shouted. "Beat him."

"He'll open his mouth if we slap him!" yelled another, who seized Hai Rui by the collar. Another official hit him on the head.

At this moment, Wang Yongji arrived. He pushed his way to Hai Rui's side, trying to block the jostling crowd with his body.

"Stop," he roared and grabbed the arm of Hai Rui's attacker.

Wang's outburst stunned everyone at the scene.

"You're all imperial officials. If you don't care about the law, you should at least know right from wrong," Wang castigated them. "Look at this person you are attacking. Do you know who he is?"

The attacker who struggled to free himself from Wang's grip shouted back: "I don't care who he is. Mr Wang, you're independently wealthy. It doesn't matter if you get paid or not. But we are broke."

Several others started to barrack Wang. "It doesn't matter who he is, nobody at the Treasury Ministry is clean!" said one person.

"People like him don't give a damn about us. Why should we?" said a second person.

"Beat him up!" a third person instigated the crowd. "We'll see what Zhao Zhenji has to say when he arrives!"

A few of the men raised their fists.

"I dare you!" Wang howled, shoving Hai Rui's attackers away. "I know you face financial problems. But at least the government will pay your outstanding salaries after the New Year. This man here won't get any money for the New Year. Neither is he going to get paid after the holiday. At least you get a sack with some rice and copper coins. He gets nothing. Do you know why? Zhao Zhenji has suspended his pay for six months because he criticised the Imperial Palace. How can you be so heartless and attack one of your own?"

Wang's speech had effectively quietened the crowd. They looked at each other awkwardly.

A person who knew Hai Rui spoke up: "This is Hai Rui. He lost six months of salary for writing a couplet at Home of Six Necessities. We shouldn't target him."

Li Qingyuan, who worked at the Education Commission, had heard of Hai Rui. Looking embarrassed, he quickly gave Hai Rui a palm-over-fist salute. "I had no idea it was you," he said. "Please accept my apology. Actually, we are not just angry over our unpaid salaries. We are worried about the future of our Great Ming Empire."

Before Hai Rui had the chance to respond, Li climbed onto a table and shouted to the crowd. "Attention everyone, I want to say a few words."

Those who were tussling with treasury officials at the other gates stopped to listen to Li Qingyuan.

"Yan Song and his son controlled the Imperial Government for more than two decades," Li stated. "Their greed knew no bounds. In May, the Imperial Investigative Agency raided the homes of Yan Shifan and his followers. I've heard that the confiscated assets are worth ten million taels of silver. The money was supposed to be redistributed, but so far, our troops fighting the pirates and the Tartars are not getting paid. Disaster victims and migrants are not getting any help. Our salaries remain unpaid. Where has the money gone? We demand answers from members of the Privy Council. We're protesting here because we can't support our families and because our country is in shambles. The Imperial Investigative Agency can arrest me for my protest here. I have nothing to fear. I'm fighting for a clean government. I'm fighting for the future of our Great Ming Empire. Forget about our New Year subsidies. We'll survive the holiday without them. For the sake of our country, I suggest we march to the Privy Council. Grand Secretary Xu and other cabinet members need to hear our voices."

Li's speech was met with cheers. Hai Rui shot Li an admiring glance.

"Mr Li is right," one person said. "When our nation is in peril, how can we talk about our homes? Let's march to the Privy Council."

"It's meaningless to see the cabinet members and engage them in a debate," said another. "We should draft a censure report against them."

"Censure, censure!" the crowd shouted as they flocked out of the vaults. A few timid, gentle and bookish officials hesitated. But when they realised that everyone had left, they ran out and joined the protest. Even a number of treasury officials followed them out.

Now, the vault was almost empty. Without a leader, warehouse workers stood around, looking lost. They wouldn't dare leave the vault without permission. All they could do was to collect the sacks that lay scattered on the floor.

Hai Rui and Wang Yongji stayed behind. They both looked forlorn and concerned.

"I work for the Audit and Inspector Commission," said Wang. "If anyone intends to draft a censure report, I need to go and help them. Are you planning to go and sign your name?"

"I'm not going. Neither should you," Hai Rui replied. "It's useless."

"That doesn't sound like something you would say," Wang said in disbelief.

"This is what I should say. Our Great Ming Empire has two capital cities and thirteen provinces, and it stretches for thousands of miles. However, there isn't a single inch of clean land. The root cause does not lie in the Privy Council. The disease is beyond cure. It's useless to treat the symptoms without tackling the root cause. As Dr Li says, reforming the nation is like treating a patient. If you want real change, one has to target the root cause. I know and everyone knows what truly ails our nation. It's just nobody dares touch the Son of Heaven. A censure report won't accomplish anything. I won't lend my name to it."

"Watch what you say," warned Wang, looking around furtively. "You have an ailing mother and a pregnant wife at home. What you are doing is like scraping the scales of the dragon. This is not something you should even consider."

"That's exactly what I'm worried about. Let's discuss it after the New Year."

Wang breathed a sigh of relief. "That's good to know. I don't need to join the protest. Let's go and buy some groceries for the New Year's holiday."

"Thank you for the offer, but you don't need to help me. You have your own family to take care of. I'll figure out a way to live through the holiday."

"What way? Eating porridge every day? Your wife is pregnant and needs to eat well. You are like family. Let's go."

"One of these days, I'll have to entrust my family to you," Hai Rui said with an appreciative look. "So, you don't need to worry about us today."

Wang understood what Hai Rui was trying to convey. He shook his head helplessly.

"Listen to me. Don't go and file a censure report with the protesters," said Hai Rui. "Without a longterm view, a random act accomplishes nothing. Let's have a quiet New Year and talk about it afterwards. We have plenty of time."

Wang nodded. He watched silently as Hai Rui strode towards the vault gate.

4

Hai Rui entered Qianliang Alley and approached his house with a heavy heart. With three days until New Year, he had no idea how his family would live though the holiday. In the heavy snow, he caught sight of a woman sitting by the threshold of his closed courtyard gate. Clutching her arms to her body against the snow, she was closely guarding a large bamboo basket, its top covered with a piece of cloth. Hai Rui went up to her and recognised it was Chee Dazhu's wife.

"What are you doing here in the snow?" Hai Rui asked, shifting his gaze from her face to the bamboo basket.

Chee Dazhu's wife rose to her feet. "Chee Dazhu is held up at work today and won't be able to wish you a happy New Year in person," she said. "He asked me to bring you some holiday food and snacks."

Even though Hai Rui was grateful, he did not show his appreciation. "I told the two of you not to visit me and send me gifts," he said in a stern voice. "Why don't you listen to me?"

"I hear you, but it's different today. New Year is around the corner. You should at least allow me to offer some gifts to Amu."

"Thanks for thinking of my mother, but please take your food back. I won't accept it no matter what you say."

Chee Dazhu's wife remained persistent. "Can you open the door and let me see Amu and Mrs Hai briefly?" she pleaded.

"There's no need. I'm sure you have lots of chores to do before New Year. Go home now. I will pass on your regards to my wife and mother."

Chee Dazhu's wife bent over to pick up her basket from the ground. Removing the cloth cover, she revealed a live hen with its legs bound, a dozen eggs and some packets of food. "I know you don't want to accept anything from Dazhu for fear of getting him into trouble, but I raised this hen myself," she explained. "Mrs Hai is pregnant and she needs nutritious food."

Hai Rui paused for a minute before taking four eggs from the basket. "Thank you," he said. "It's cold out here. Go home."

Realising the futility of her plea, Chee Dazhu's wife put the cover back on the basket. With tears in her eyes, she lowered her head and walked away.

Hai Rui watched her disappear in the blowing snow. Holding the four eggs in his left hand, he stood silently in front of his door before he knocked.

"Go home now," Amu's voice came from inside the house. "If you don't leave, I'm going to be upset with you."

"Amu, it's me," Hai Rui said loudly as he put the eggs in his pocket.

Amu opened the door for him. "You're home early. Are you done with work?" she asked.

"Yes, Amu. I'm off work now," Hai Rui replied as he stepped into the courtyard.

"Chee Dazhu's wife came just now," said Amu, shutting the door. "Since she brought gifts, I didn't open the door for her. When you knocked, I thought it was her again. Is she still there?"

"She should have left by now," said Hai Rui, holding Amu's arm.

Inside the guest room, Mrs Hai was sitting in front of a spinning wheel. When she saw Hai Rui at the door, she struggled to get up. Amu stopped her, and Mrs Hai sat back down.

Amu grabbed a small broom hanging outside on the door frame and dusted the snow off Hai Rui's head and coat. Shaking some snowflakes off her own body, Amu took off her shoes and entered the guest room barefoot.

Hai Rui also removed his shoes and socks, and walked barefoot just as his mother did.

A wooden handloom was propped against the east wall. A piece of half-finished cloth was dangling on top of the loom. Hai Rui glanced at the table and noticed a small bolt of cloth on the top. A sense of guilt and sadness washed over him. "Amu is the world's fastest weaver," Hai Rui said with a fake smile. "When I left in the morning, I thought it would take at least another day to finish. I can't believe it's all done."

Amu sat in front of her loom. "Well, I can't brag about anything else, but weaving is what we Hainan natives are famous for. The legendary weaver, Huang Daopo, learned spinning and weaving from the local Li people in Hainan," said Amu. "Anyway, I've heated up some porridge and corn buns for you in the kitchen. After you have eaten, change into your civilian clothes and sell this bolt of fabric to a store in the market. The money will get us through the New Year."

"Yes, Amu."

"I'll get the food for you," said Mrs Hai who stood up.

"Didn't you promise me to sit down there and relax?" Amu's face fell as she chastised Mrs Hai.

"Amu, there's no need to worry," Mrs Hai replied. "It's not even three months yet. Dr Li suggests I walk about often and do some exercises. Besides, the kitchen is not a place for men."

"Amu, let her do it," Hai Rui chimed in. "A little bit of walking is good for her."

"All right then," said Amu as she started spinning. The loom creaked to life.

Hai Rui beckoned to his wife. When she stopped at the door, he walked up to her and gave her the four eggs. "Boil them," he said softly. "Two for you and two for Amu."

Mrs Hai looked at her husband with affection.

"There's snow in the yard," Hai Rui warned, glancing at his wife's stomach. "Be careful."

The heavy snow failed to dampen the spirits of holiday shoppers and sellers. The open-air market sold a wide variety of New Year's food – chicken, duck, fish, pork, packets of dried rice noodles, dried fruits, sweets, New Year posters and firecrackers. Vendors had set up tents on both sides of the street, each swarmed with shoppers who were yelling or haggling over prices.

Wearing a thick hat with earflaps and a cotton padded gown, Hai Rui elbowed his way past the noisy shoppers, keeping his eyes peeled for a fabric booth or store. He was holding an umbrella in one hand and the bolt of cloth that Amu had woven in the other. After walking up and down the street twice, he finally located a small store. A large plaque with the words 'Prosperity Fabric' hung above its door.

By the look of it, Hai Rui could tell that a dozen people who were lined up before the counter were shoppers. He was the only person who intended to sell his fabric to the store. Closing his umbrella and clutching the bolt of cloth to his chest, he stood in the queue without knowing what to expect.

An older shop assistant behind the counter spotted Hai Rui. Glancing at the bolt of fabric Hai Rui was holding, the assistant waved. "Come to this side please," he said.

Hai Rui hurried up to him.

"Are you selling this piece of cloth?" asked the assistant.

"Yes sir," replied Hai Rui as he put the bolt of cloth on the counter. "Could you take a look and see how much it's worth?"

The old man took the cloth and rubbed the fabric between his thumb and forefinger. Then he spread out part of it and stroked its surface with his palm. "The pattern is very smooth and lustrous," he said. "If you'd brought it in last month, you could have received a very good price. But we won't be able to pay you much now."

"Can you tell me why?"

"A month ago, there would have been time to get it dyed," the shop assistant explained. "Nobody wants to buy plain white fabric for New Year."

"Ah, I see. How much are you willing to pay for this?"

"I can see that you're not a businessman. You're probably selling this to help you get through the holidays. I won't take advantage of you. This bolt of cloth could have easily fetched fifteen strings of copper coins last month, but now, the most I can pay is twelve."

"Sir, we spent ten strings of copper coins on the cotton alone. Twelve is too little."

"What about thirteen? That's the most I want to pay."

From spinning the yarn to weaving it, Amu and his wife had spent nearly a fortnight producing this bolt of cloth. Hai Rui had no experience of bargaining, but he knew the price was bad. It hardly covered the labour cost. He rolled up the cloth without talking and was ready to walk away.

"Given the quality of the fabric, I'm willing to offer fourteen strings," the shop assistant said.

"Fifteen please. Otherwise I'm going to sell it to someone else."

The shop assistant conceded reluctantly. "Please bring me fifteen strings of copper coin," he instructed one of his young colleagues behind the counter.

Carrying a bag of rice on his shoulder, plus a chicken and a fish in his hands, Hai Rui walked into his alleyway. A few feet from his house, he noticed that the courtyard door was open. Suspecting that something had happened, he rushed inside and saw a messenger from the Ministry of Treasury standing outside his guest room. The messenger came up to him and took the bag of rice from his shoulder. "I'm so glad you're back," said the messenger. "I've been waiting for half an hour now. The ministry has an emergency. They need you to go there immediately."

"What emergency? Are those officials still protesting?" asked Hai Rui.

"No, this one is more serious than the protest," said the messenger as he carried the bag of rice and followed Hai Rui into the kitchen. "Daxing and Wanping Counties outside Beijing were supposed to run soup kitchens for migrants before and during the holiday period, but they have run out of funds. A large number of people are now dying of starvation. We've heard that members of the White Lotus Society, a secret Buddhist sect, are taking advantage of the situation and are instigating an uprising."

Hai Rui looked astounded.

"Since it's now supposed to be a festive period, the Privy Council has decided not to notify His Majesty. But senior ministerial officials are worried to death. They are considering taking some grain from the military supply warehouse in Tongzhou, and shipping it to Daxing and Wanping Counties immediately. Our ministry is supposed to escort the grain carts and help set up soup kitchens there to prevent more deaths. Mr Zhao has designated you as project supervisor. You'll have to travel to Daxing."

"I'll go with you now."

In the short days of winter, it turns dark even earlier when it snows. Right after three o'clock, two junior eunuchs inside Yuxi Palace started lighting lanterns and candles. Huang Jin stepped into the main hall without removing his cloak. The junior eunuchs dropped to their knees to greet him.

"Is Chen Gonggong inside the meditation room?" he asked.

"Yes. Chen Gonggong is waiting for you to begin your shift."

"All right, I don't need you to stay around here," instructed Huang. "You two can wait outside the palace."

The junior eunuchs rose to their feet and quietly left the main hall.

Huang tiptoed to the door of the meditation room and dropped down on his knees. "Your humble servant, Huang Jin, is here to serve Your Majesty."

Chen Hong stepped out of the meditation room. Huang stood up with his cloak on. An object inside one of his coat pockets created a significant bulge, and Huang tried to cover it with his cloak. "How is His Majesty today?" he asked.

"He is doing well," said Chen Hong, glancing at Huang's outfit suspiciously. "Why are you wearing your cloak inside the palace?"

"It's so cold outside and I just forgot to take it off," replied Huang.

"Take it off now."

"I still feel cold. I promise I'll do it later. Don't forget to put on your cloak when you step out. Otherwise, you could catch a cold."

"I'm going to put it on now," said Chen Hong, who removed his cloak from a hanger outside the meditation room and fixed his eyes on Huang's cloak. "Come on, why don't you take yours off?"

"What are you two talking about over there?" Emperor Jiajing's voice came from inside the meditation room. "That's a long chat."

"Your Majesty, Chen Gonggong has a few questions for me."

"Have you finished now?" Emperor Jiajing asked.

"Please go in," Chen Hong urged him.

Huang walked into the meditation room wearing his cloak. Chen Hong looked warily at him, but then turned around and left the main hall.

All the windows on the south side of the meditation room were not allowed to be opened. Incense smoke filled the room. The lanterns and candles emitted yellowish, translucent light.

Dressed in a baggy silk robe, Emperor Jiajing was sitting on his prayer mat.

"Your Majesty, I'm sorry to have kept you waiting," said Huang, who kowtowed with his cloak on. When he rose from the floor, he pulled out from his coat pocket a purple clay medicine pot containing a few packets of herbs. Cautiously, he placed the medicine pot at the foot of the bronze incense burner.

"Is the palace gate closed?" Emperor Jiajing asked.

"I'll go and check," said Huang. Still wearing his cloak, he slid out of the meditation room. The emperor could hear Huang fastening the palace gate with a large metal latch. Taking a deep breath, he closed his eyes.

When Huang came back in, he saw that Emperor Jiajing was wrapped up tightly in his thin gown. Hurrying over to a closet next to the bed, he brought out a thick cotton robe. Holding the robe with both hands, he walked cautiously towards Emperor Jiajing. "Master, please stretch out your arms," he said softly while standing behind the emperor.

Huang lifted the shoulders of the coat while the emperor slipped his hands into the sleeves. After stretching the coat from the back, Huang stepped to the front and knelt down. As he was tying the belt, he touched the emperor's hands. "Your hands are icy cold," he said. "I need to get you a vest."

Emperor Jiajing was not protesting like he usually did. Huang rushed back to the closet, picked out a thick cotton vest and offered it to Emperor Jiajing. As Huang was fastening the vest buttons, tears rolled down his cheeks.

"Why are you crying?" Emperor Jiajing asked. "I'm not sick. This is just a hurdle that a practitioner has to jump over at the age of sixty. It takes forty-nine days. Once I cross it, I'll be invincible. Do you understand?"

"Yes, master, but during these forty-nine days, you have to take medicine to help you jump over the hurdle. You can't take the medicine one day and stop the next."

"You're just as long-winded as Lu Fang."

"Yes, master," Huang said. He stood up and moved to his next task. Lifting the lid off the bronze incense burner, he blew onto the fire. The agarwood inside began to flame brightly. Huang placed the purple clay medicine pot above the flames. "Before I came to work, I cooked the herbs in my room," he said. "All I need is to heat up the broth and you can drink it."

Taking out a small porcelain bowl from a cupboard, he rinsed it in clean water, wiped it dry with a white velvet towel and placed the bowl on the emperor's desk. Then, he went back to the bronze incense burner and touched the medicine pot. "Now, it's all warm and ready to serve," he murmured to himself. Using a pair of tongs, Huang fiddled with the incense ash in the copper burner to cover the open flames. Then, he lifted the medicine pot out with both hands.

"Be careful, don't burn your hands," Emperor Jiajing warned.

"Master, don't worry," Huang said as he carefully poured the herbal broth into the porcelain bowl. "My skin is coarse and thick. It doesn't burn easily."

Emperor Jiajing watched as Huang used a spoon to taste the broth first. "It's the perfect temperature, neither too hot nor too cold," he said, handing the bowl to the emperor. "Your Majesty, please drink it up."

As Emperor Jiajing gulped down the broth, a smile flashed across Huang's face. "That's good," he said excitedly when he took the bowl from Emperor Jiajing. "The medicine will cure the disease. I'm sure my master will fully recover after forty-nine days."

Oddly enough, Huang was the only servant who could say things freely, and Emperor Jiajing seldom threw a temper tantrum at his remarks. In fact, the emperor acted like a child in front of Huang. But the mention of the word 'disease' annoyed Emperor Jiajing.

"Are you deaf?" he scolded Huang. "Didn't I just tell you that I'm not ill?"

Huang did not answer straight away. He rinsed the bowl in a basin of clean water, wiped it dry and poured some warm water from a copper kettle into the bowl. Then, he went back to the emperor. "Your Majesty, I'm not saying that you're ill," he said. "But during this crucial time, when you're trying to overcome this hurdle, I just have to treat you like a patient."

Emperor Jiajing took a sip of the water to cleanse his mouth and spat it out. "Whatever you say," he said helplessly. "You're incorrigible. If you say I'm ill, then I'm ill."

Huang put the bowl away and started wiping Emperor Jiajing's face gently with a warm towel. "It's been only eight days since you started taking the medicine," he cooed. "Your condition has improved dramatically. I'm confident that a few more courses will heal my master's divine body completely. By then, spring will return and the ice in rivers will melt."

"Have you heard anything from Lu Fang?"

"Your Majesty, not yet," Huang replied, lowering his eyes.

"He has forgotten all about us."

"Master, I'm not trying to defend Daddy, but I know for sure that he will never forget Your Majesty's benevolence. He'll wear his gratitude like a cloak. He's not like some of those people around you. They work for the Imperial Palace, but their loyalties lie with someone else."

"That's true," Emperor Jiajing said, gazing out of the door. "My parents passed away when I was young. I succeeded to the throne at the age of fourteen. I had neither sibling nor confidante. Lu Fang is one of the few people to whom I feel very close. He treated me well. Now that he's gone, I have you. He's trained you well. In this respect, Lu Fang is worthy of me."

Deeply touched by Emperor Jiajing's praise of Lu Fang, Huang put the towel back in the gold basin and walked to the door. Sitting down on the threshold, he started sobbing.

"Hey, why are you crying?" Emperor Jiajing said, looking at him reproachfully. "Aren't you afraid that your subordinates will hear you?"

"Your Majesty, I've hidden something from you. Regardless of how you might punish me, I have to tell you the truth…"

"All right, if you want to tell me, come over and sit up in front of me. Rub the soles of my feet while you talk."

"Yes, Your Majesty," said Huang, wiping away his tears and standing up. Pulling up a small wooden bench, he sat in front of the emperor and placed his master's feet on his lap. "I hope I'm not making you upset by bringing up Lu Fang," he said, rubbing Emperor Jiajing's right foot. "He's a truly loyal and thoughtful person. The medicine I have brought you was prescribed by Dr Li Shizhen. The Prince of Yu and Lu Fang secretly invited him to Beijing after you fell ill. Before Daddy left for Nanjing, he specifically instructed me not to bring up Dr Li. So I lied to you and said some other doctor had prescribed the herbs. Now that I've told you the truth, please don't blame the Prince of Yu or Daddy. It's all my fault."

Emperor Jiajing looked at him, feeling both lonely and comforted. "I absolve you of guilt," he said. "You are truly a simpleton and need to learn how to be a better liar. I knew it was Li Shizhen's prescription when you had me take the first dose. I just couldn't bear to prick the bubble. All this time, you naively believed that you had deceived me."

"Master, how did you know?" Huang asked in disbelief.

"Before Lu Fang left, he begged me and requested permission for Li Shizhen to come to Beijing and prescribe some medicine for me. I granted his request and asked him to give the secret assignment to you. You were kept in the dark, but you thought you knew everything."

Huang was elated that Emperor Jiajing still treasured Lu Fang's loyalty. Wearing a foolish grin, he said sheepishly: "Your Majesty, you know I'm not a clever person."

"Oh, I like simpletons," Emperor Jiajing teased. "They're reliable and always take me to their hearts."

"Master, I beg to differ. The Prince of Yu and Lu Fang are not dim-witted like I am, but they care deeply about you. Many of your trustworthy ministers are intelligent people. You can't say that they don't take you to heart. Take Dr Li as an example. When he first served at the Imperial Hospital, he had an argument with Your Majesty and left the palace. Many years have passed and his heart is still with Your Majesty. When he received the Prince of Yu's letter, he stopped work and travelled thousands of miles to Beijing. That's what I call loyalty."

"Your argument is not without merit," Emperor Jiajing said after a brief pause. "In this world, there are two types of people whom I consider to be reliable: the simpletons and the straight talkers. Neither of these two types plays mind games with me. The simpletons don't know how to lie and play mind games. Straight talkers simply don't lie. I never nurse any grudges against these two types of people. Neither do I play mind games with them. For example, you are both a simpleton and a straight talker. So, I trust you. For those well-bred straight talkers, I needle them, but seldom punish them. Do you know who I'm talking about?"

Huang thought for a long time. "Do you count Dr Li as one?" he asked.

"I guess you can. Who else?"

"What about that Hai Rui person who works at the Ministry of Treasury?"

"You aren't a simpleton at all," Emperor Jiajing said with a grin.

"I am stupid, but not that stupid. When you asked me to name those whom you have forgiven for offending you with their blasphemous remarks, these are the only two I can think of," Huang said with another of his idiotic smiles.

Emperor Jiajing was quickly losing interest in exploring this topic with Huang Jin. "The medicine that Li Shizhen has prescribed seems to be efficacious," he said, standing up.

Huang quickly supported Emperor Jiajing's right arm.

The emperor interlaced his fingers, and pushed his palms out as he brought them above his head and took a deep breath. Then, he retracted his arms to his chest and slowly exhaled. "I feel really energised. I want to go out for a walk. Don't try to stop me."

Huang was taken aback. "Where does my master want to go?" he asked.

"The repair work on the palaces and temples is scheduled to be completed the day after tomorrow. I want you to go out with me and take a look without disturbing anyone."

"Your Majesty, I don't think it's a good idea," Huang said with a look of concern. "It's snowing hard outside. I don't want you to catch a cold."

"Just get me a heavy coat," said Emperor Jiajing who waved his hand dismissively. "Remember the fur coat I used to wear? Go find it at the bottom of my wardrobe trunk."

Dressed in a black fur coat and a hat that almost covered his face, Emperor Jiajing sneaked out of the palace without his usual entourage. Huang Jin held a lantern and led the way. The emperor and his eunuch took a narrow path near the edge of Taiyechi Lake, along the walls of the Western Compound and trekked towards some flickering lights in the distance.

Fortunately, the snow had stopped. In the dark evening, the sound of crunching snow under their feet accentuated the quiet.

"Those minions are getting lazy," Huang complained as he paused to check up on the emperor. "They don't even bother to shovel the snow. Master, watch your step."

"I'm glad they haven't shovelled the snow," said Emperor Jiajing, whose voice was filled with excitement. "Stepping on snow can help relieve stress. You know this, don't you?"

"Master, I truly didn't know that," Huang responded as he tried to hold Emperor Jiajing's arm.

"Keep going. I don't need your help," said Emperor Jiajing. Adjusting the lantern, he turned around and resumed walking.

"Who's there?" shouted a eunuch guarding the gate of the Western Compound.

"It's me," Huang answered. "Why are you yelling? I'm here to inspect the construction projects. Go patrol somewhere else and make sure everything is all right."

The guard apologised profusely and added: "Huang Gonggong, please walk carefully."

"I didn't realise a simpleton like you could be so intimidating," the emperor said.

"Master, I wasn't trying to intimidate him. I had to follow the rules."

"I can see that."

As they talked, they strolled around a curved wall and stopped at the edge of Taiyechi Lake. Across the icy water, they could see two patches of flickering lights that were about half a mile away from each other. To the east were Longevity Palace and Palace of Eternal Longevity, and to the west Chaotian Temple and Xuandu Temple. Overnight, workers were putting the finishing touches to the buildings.

"Master, shall we just watch from here?" Huang asked. "If we go further down, we'd have to walk past the gate of the Western Compound."

Emperor Jiajing stared into the distance without answering him.

"Huang Jin," he murmured.

"Yes, Your Majesty," said Huang, moving closer.

"I'll recite a Tang poem for you. Take a guess and tell me what I'm thinking about at this moment."

Buoyed by Emperor Jiajing's happy mood and improved health, Huang replied: "Master, I'm not sure about the answer. Would you tell me if I fail?"

Lifting his head and gazing into the dark sky, Emperor Jiajing chanted softly:

> The Moon of Qin shines over the passes of Han,
> Our men have not returned from the distant frontier.
> If the Flying General were here,
> No Hu horses could ever cross the Yinshan.

"Master, this is easy. The Flying General refers to General Li Guang of the Western Han dynasty."

"You idiot! I didn't ask you to identify the Flying General. When I chant this poem, who am I thinking of?"

Huang detected a sense of melancholy in Emperor Jiajing's tone. "Does this poem make you think of the former governor Hu Zongxian?" he asked tentatively.

"Yan Song and his son failed our country and ruined the careers of many talented and competent leaders like Governor Hu. If he were still around, Generals Yu Dayou and Qi Jiguang would have defeated the pirates in Fujian and Guangdong, and cleared the sea routes for our merchants travelling to the West to sell our tea, china and silk. We wouldn't have to waste several million taels of silver in military spending this year…"

There was a moment of sad silence.

"I have an idea. Once these two palaces and two temples are fully restored, I should probably retire and let the Prince of Yu take over. In this way, I can devote myself to meditation. Among those ministerial officials and provincial governors, who do you think can assist with the Prince of Yu's governance?"

"Your Majesty, I wouldn't dare answer this question. I'd be overstepping my remit."

"I won't hold you culpable if you give the wrong answer," Emperor Jiajing said gently. "Just answer truthfully."

"Your Majesty, it's not that I'm worried about offending you. I really can't figure it out."

Emperor Jiajing sighed. "Well, I don't blame you. I can't make up my mind either. Our Imperial Government has hired thousands of talented officials and warriors, but how many of them are trustworthy enough for my son to employ? Not many. Some people within the Imperial Government have already begun to exploit the

Prince of Yu and even my grandson for their own personal gain. I have to guard against those people."

As Huang was pondering the meaning of these seemingly off-the-cuff remarks, Emperor Jiajing pointed to the lights on the west side. "Let's find a small path to skirt around the gate and climb up the hill so we can watch Chaotian Temple," he said before hurrying towards a hill on the left. "I wonder what Feng Bao is doing there."

Huang held the lantern and followed the emperor up the hill. The top was covered with pine and cypress trees, and there they found an unobtrusive spot with a panoramic view of the courtyard and the front gate area of Chaotian Temple. On turning around, they could see the small path that led to the gate of the Western Compound. The pine and cypress trees provided ample cover and no one could see them from down below.

At Emperor Jiajing's order, Huang blew out the lantern and hung it on a tree branch nearby. Sweeping the snow off a stone bench with some pine twigs, Huang took off his cloak, folded it and placed it on the bench. "Master, please sit down," he offered.

Emperor Jiajing sat on Huang's cloak. From his vantage point, he could observe the courtyard and the archway outside Chaotian Temple. Under the bright lantern lights, a foreman was monitoring a dozen workers who were rushing to finish the archway renovation.

Huang stood behind the emperor.

Even at the age of sixty, Emperor Jiajing had a full head of black hair and his vision remained sharp. This might have been the benefit of taking those immortality pills. At this moment, his piercing eyes were eagerly searching for Feng Bao among a group of workers who were painting the temple gates and grinding the stone steps. He did not see him. Then, as he shifted his gaze towards the archway, he spotted his grandson's former playmate.

The archway, which constituted the last leg of the restoration project, was near completion. The scaffolding had been dismantled. Feng Bao was removing a pile of heavy wooden frames, trying to load them onto a cart. Two workers were seen placing a long wooden pole on his right shoulder. With one hand holding the wooden frame, Feng Bao put the other hand on his waist to straighten his back. Then, he staggered towards a cart. When he reached the vehicle, nobody was there to assist him. Squatting down slowly, Feng Bao unloaded the heavy pole from his shoulder. Fortunately, it landed securely on top of a pile of wooden frames.

There were three more poles for him to carry. Feng Bao uttered a sigh and trudged over, waiting for his colleagues to lift the pole from the ground and put it on his shoulder. But the foreman, who was donning a thick cloak, sent the two workers away. Feng Bao's helpers wiped the dust off their hands and sauntered towards a shed opposite the archway.

Emperor Jiajing watched quietly. Huang widened his eyes.

Except for a few workers who were painting the temple gate, Feng Bao was the only person left to clear away the pile of wooden frames near the archway.

Wiping the sweat from his forehead, Feng Bao stared at those three long, thick wooden poles buried in the snow. There was no way he could lift the pole and place it on his shoulder alone.

"Why are you standing there?" the foreman shouted at Feng Bao. "Waiting for a New Year miracle?"

Feng Bao did not answer. Lifting the thin end of a pole with both hands, he managed to set it on his shoulder. Inch by inch, his body moved to the centre of the pole. When he reached the middle, Feng Bao used both hands, trying to raise the log and balance it on his shoulder, but he failed. As he was staggering, the foreman ran up to him and began lashing him furiously with a whip. Despite the pain, Feng Bao held the log to prevent it from falling off his shoulder.

"I thought you were a powerful man," the foreman sneered at him. "If you can't even move a piece of wood, how do you expect to be the future interior minister? I'll count to three, and if you still can't carry the pole to the cart, I'm going to force you to chew on it. One, two…"

Before the foreman uttered three, Feng Bao exerted his strength and moved his body to the middle of the pole. Grabbing the pole with both hands, he laid it horizontally on his shoulder. Before the foreman could flog him again, Feng Bao swung his body. One end of the log struck his attacker hard on his head. The foreman slumped to the ground.

With a smirk, Feng Bao carried the log and loaded it onto the cart without even squatting down.

"Good job!" Huang couldn't help cheering in a low voice.

Emperor Jiajing turned his head and frowned at him.

Huang bowed apologetically.

Emperor Jiajing shifted his gaze back to the archway outside the temple.

When Feng Bao returned to pick up another wooden pole, the foreman sprang to his feet. Creeping up to Feng Bao from behind, he started whipping him repeatedly.

Angered by what he had witnessed, Huang begged Emperor Jiajing: "Master, I need to go down and intervene."

"For what reason?"

"Feng Bao served the young prince for five years. No matter what crimes he has committed, he doesn't deserve such brutal treatment. That dog there bullies people on the strength of his master."

"Is he one of Chen Hong's people?"

"Yes, Your Majesty."

"If that's the case, don't interfere. You're not Chen Hong's match."

Huang disagreed, but without Emperor Jiajing's permission, he could do nothing. Silently, he swallowed his anger.

"That person, Feng Bao, will one day have the power to kill Chen Hong."

Huang could not believe his ears.

"Watch out when you're around Chen Hong," Emperor Jiajing warned him. "Don't be so impulsive. I'm saying this for your own good."

By then, Huang was so stunned that his mind went blank.

"I think those people have arrived," Emperor Jiajing said, pricking up his ears.

"Who's arrived?" asked Huang, who was having difficulty following the emperor's sudden change of subject.

"Can't you hear them? Turn around and see for yourself," said the emperor, pointing to the gate of the Western Compound on the east side of the hill.

Huang heard nothing. But when he turned his head, he saw flickering lanterns in the distance. They seemed to be gliding in the direction of the Western Compound.

"You're absolutely right," Huang marvelled. He squinted, and as the lanterns moved closer, he could see them clearly. "It seems a large number of Imperial Government officials are converging outside the gate to the Western Compound."

Emperor Jiajing sat motionless. "I'm bringing you over here to show you how ungrateful and treacherous these officials are," said Emperor Jiajing. "I also want you to witness Chen Hong's power and see him in action."

明

Li Qingyuan and about a hundred Imperial Government officials were kneeling in front of the gate to the Western Compound. Each of them was holding a censure report above his head.

The imperial agents guarding the Western Compound were mostly younger folk who had never witnessed such group protest during their tenure, but they had all heard about the 'Great Controversy of Rites'. Thirty-five years before, Emperor Jiajing had engaged in a fierce debate with his ministers when he decided to elevate his parents posthumously to an 'honorary' imperial rank, and requested that an imperial-style mausoleum be built for them. Since Emperor Jiajing had inherited the throne from his cousin, many in the Imperial Government argued that he should honour his cousin's father, Emperor Hongzhi, as his adoptive parent, or at least as the superior overlord. Granting his biological parents the titles of overlord and empress dowager would violate the etiquette of the Great Ming Empire, they maintained.

When Emperor Jiajing rejected their arguments, about two hundred scholars and officials assembled outside Zuoshunmen Gate and petitioned the emperor to reverse his decision. The collective petition enraged Emperor Jiajing. Acting on his order, the imperial agents wielded wooden stakes, killing sixteen officials. More than a hundred and thirty people were imprisoned.

Since then, there had been some sporadic individual petitions but Grand Secretary Yan Song crushed the protests brutally. No group incidents had ever occurred again. Therefore, the young imperial agents had no idea how to handle a major incident like this. Nervously, they brandished their swords and guns, and lined up outside the Western Compound.

The supervisor on duty was a eunuch at the Criminal Investigative Division. He reached the top of the stone steps to address the protesters: "What are you doing here? Are you staging a revolt?"

Li was kneeling in the centre of the front row. Waving his censure report in his hand, he responded: "Our Great Ming Empire has no rebels. We're loyal servants who are here to remonstrate with His Majesty. We want to present our reports to His Majesty directly."

"All censure reports will need to be submitted to the Audit and Inspection Commission. The commissioner will forward them to the Interior Ministry. Don't you know the rules?"

"This has to be delivered to His Majesty directly," shouted an official kneeling next to Li. "We are calling for His Majesty to censure ministerial officials and members of the Privy Council."

"Gonggong, please present our censure reports to His Majesty directly," Li implored.

"We want an audience with His Majesty," the protesters shouted as if they had rehearsed the words beforehand.

The Western Compound, which had served as Emperor Jiajing's residence for more than twenty years, was traditionally a quiet place that brought a solemn awe upon officials who were summoned there for meetings. The protest disturbed the usual tranquillity. The howling by more than a hundred officials reverberated in the early evening darkness through the woods. Birds perched in trees and shrubs on top of the hills startled and fluttered away.

Huang looked alarmed. "Master, let's go back to the palace now," he urged Emperor Jiajing.

"How old are you?" asked Emperor Jiajing who remained sitting.

"Master, I'm going to be forty this year," he answered anxiously. "Your Majesty, I don't want anything bad to happen to you. This is frightening. I need to get you back to the palace as soon as possible."

"Frightening?" The emperor responded with a tinge of coldness in his voice. "This is nothing. You haven't seen anything truly frightening yet. Thirty-five years ago, the number of petitioners and protesters who showed up here was much bigger. Many of them were Hanlin scholars who came to defend the rituals and traditions of the Great Ming Empire. I, alone, dealt with two or three hundred of them. In the end, I defeated those demagogues. Lu Fang was by my side then. Unfortunately, you were too young to witness those events."

The ferocity in Emperor Jiajing's eyes frightened Huang Jin. He now fully understood why Emperor Jiajing had decided to step out alone with him tonight. Chen Hong had obviously notified him of the protest beforehand, and he was anticipating this moment. Huang wasn't sure whether to be fearful, anxious or sad. The emperor was revered by his subjects as their endearing parent. Why would the ruler and parent treat his children and courtiers so ruthlessly?

"Master, but I…"

"Hold your tongue!" said Emperor Jiajing, hardening his tone. "If you utter another word, I'll send you down to Chaotian Temple so you and Feng Bao can carry poles together."

Huang was stunned.

"It's time for Xu Jie and Chen Hong to enter the stage now," Emperor Jiajing continued more softly. "Watch carefully. In the future, when you have to document your time with me, write down truthfully what you see today. I haven't done anything to provoke them. They're here to harangue me and instigate trouble."

"Yes, Your Majesty," Huang mumbled. As the protest unfolded, Emperor Jiajing turned his back on the scene. He gazed at Chaotian Temple while Huang was observing the demonstrators outside the Western Compound.

Supported by Zhao Zhenji under his arm, Grand Secretary Xu stepped out from behind the gate with Deputy Li Chunfang and Gao Gong. They were followed by two lines of imperial agents holding blazing torches. A platform had been set up at the top of the stairs under the eaves of the gate.

When the protesting officials saw the cabinet members, they stopped their chanting. Silently, they knelt on the ground, holding their censure reports above their heads.

Grand Secretary Xu scanned the crowd before speaking. "Our Great Ming Empire is facing straitened circumstances. I admit that the Privy Council has not done a good job in managing our finances. We have failed our ancestors and His Majesty. We have failed you and the people of our country. For this, I apologise. But we are currently working to remedy the situation. Things have to be done step by step. I ask for your patience and understanding. Please do not congregate here. You should not disturb His Majesty before the New Year."

"Grand Secretary Xu," Li Qingyuan responded on behalf of the protesters. "I've heard similar promises many times before. We agree that things need to be done step by step, but when are you actually going to get things done? His Majesty has entrusted you with our country. Has he been made aware of the straitened circumstances we now face? Our troops fighting the Tartars in the north and the pirates in the south are running out of supplies. Disaster victims and migrants are suffering from cold and hunger. Over the past two days, about two thousand people have died of starvation in Daxing and Wanping Counties. If we don't make our voices heard now, when do you think we should? We're…"

"Don't be such an alarmist and exaggerate the situation," Zhao interjected. "Who says we have not allocated funds for our troops? Where have you seen widespread hunger? This morning, the Ministry of Treasury received notice that people in Daxing and Wanping are dying of starvation. We immediately moved carts of grain from a military warehouse in Tongzhou to the region and sent officials to organise relief efforts there. You haven't heard about this? I know the government owes you salaries, but we are trying to compensate you bit by bit. None of us cabinet members has received any salary this year. What have we done to deserve this? I talked to you earlier in the day. Mr Gao also explained the situation to you. We said we would try to pay off the arrears in a lump sum next spring. Why are you creating a disturbance now? You know very well that the repair work on the palaces and temples will be finished soon, and we're preparing for the ribbon-cutting ceremony for His Majesty. Are you trying to ruin this auspicious day for His Majesty. Is that your intent?"

"We are not here to demand salary payment," said the official who was kneeling next to Li Qingyuan. "Without the payment, we'll manage to survive on porridge and cabbage during the New Year. We have gathered here this evening to tell His Majesty the truth about our country. We urge His Majesty to find out what the Privy Council and the six ministries have been doing over the past two years. What are your strategies to save the Great Ming Empire and to better the lives of millions of our citizens?"

"Answer us," the crowd roared together. "Answer us."

明

"Where is Chen Hong?" Emperor Jiajing suddenly asked.

Huang Jin craned his neck to get a better view of the situation outside the Western Compound. Inside the gate, he spotted members of the Criminal Investigative Division and the Imperial Prison. They were all holding torches. Some wielded wooden stakes while others carried long whips. They lined up quietly, waiting for orders.

"Your Majesty," Huang reported to Emperor Jiajing who was sitting with his back to him. "A lot of people from the Criminal Investigative Division and the Imperial Prison are here but I don't see Chen Hong."

"Don't you have any idea where he is?"

"Your Majesty, I wouldn't know."

"He has gone to look for me at Yuxi Palace. He wants to secure my permission to slaughter these agitators."

"I see," Huang murmured.

"We want to have an audience with His Majesty!" the crowd

outside the Western Compound shouted. "We want to present our censure reports to His Majesty!"

The shouting unnerved Huang. "Your Majesty, Grand Secretary Xu has knelt down to plead with the protesters," he reported.

Emperor Jiajing began fidgeting.

"Ah, Chen Hong is here," Huang cried out.

Emperor Jiajing sat still and closed his eyes.

明

Inside the Western Compound, members of the Criminal Investigative Division and the Imperial Prison dropped down on one knee when Chen Hong showed up.

Chen Hong tiptoed towards the gate and peeked out. Grand Secretary Xu, Deputy Li Chunfang, Gao Gong and Zhao Zhenji were kneeling on the stone steps to offer their collective apologies to the protesters, but the condemnation continued unabated.

Chen Hong bit his lip. As he paced up and down anxiously between two lines of imperial agents each kneeling on one knee, there was a savage fierceness in his eyes. "His Majesty is in the middle of his meditation," he mumbled to himself. "It's too late to seek his permission…"

All of a sudden, he stopped. "All rise!" he ordered.

The imperial agents sprang to their feet. Chen Hong raised one hand in the air and shouted: "Go out there and beat up those insurgents."

"Yes sir!"

With a roar, two groups of imperial agents charged out of the gate like flying arrows.

Under the shadows of lanterns, Huang could see the guards brandishing their wooden stakes and whips. Those unarmed civil servants who were on their knees did not see it coming. Before they had time to respond, many were knocked to the ground. Their heads and faces were bleeding.

Gao Gong was the first to recover from the shock. He jumped to his feet and shouted at the imperial agents: "Who ordered you to beat up these people? Please stop, stop."

When Zhao helped Grand Secretary Xu to his feet, the old man's face turned pale. "Chen Gonggong, you can't do this," Grand Secretary Xu pleaded. "Please tell them to stop the violence."

Deputy Li also rose to his feet. "This is getting out of control," he yelled. "Please stop!"

Chen Hong ignored their pleas. Standing on the stairs, he smirked as his army of imperial agents attacked the protesters violently, leaving trails of blood.

"Zhenji, please help me get over there," said Grand Secretary Xu. He plodded his way downstairs. Gao Gong quickly followed him.

"Stop!" Grand Secretary Xu yelled at an imperial agent.

"Stop!" Gao Gong bellowed.

Given that both Grand Secretary Xu and Gao Gong were Privy Council members, their words carried weight. Some imperial agents stopped. But elsewhere, the whipping and flogging continued.

"Chen Hong," Grand Secretary Xu turned around and yelled. "Stop! Why don't you order them to flog me as well?"

Reluctantly, Chen Hong signalled to his subordinate to retreat.

The whipping and flogging ceased.

Those who had been kneeling in the middle of the crowd were spared a beating. The rest were lying on the ground with bloody faces and broken legs. Some had been beaten unconscious.

※

Emperor Jiajing sat quietly on top of the hill. He didn't even bother to turn around and observe the violent confrontation outside the Western Compound.

Huang Jin fell to his knees. "Your Majesty, I request that you censure Chen Hong," he said.

"For what reason?" Emperor Jiajing asked with a look of feigned innocence.

"He gave the order without Your Majesty's permission and overstepped his bounds."

"Why did he beat up those officials?"

"Those officials did nothing wrong," Huang opined boldly. "All they did was express their dissatisfaction with Grand Secretary Xu and other cabinet members. One shouldn't be treated so brutally for submitting a censure report."

"You're too naïve," said Emperor Jiajing who rose to his feet slowly. "On the surface, they are protesting against Grand Secretary Xu and other members of the Privy Council, but in reality, their attacks are directed at me because I have approved funding to repair my palaces and temples. Those agitators wouldn't dare do something like this when Yan Song and Yan Shifan were around. I promoted Chen Hong because he's tough and merciless. If it hadn't been for Chen Hong, the Great Ming Empire would have been toppled by those traitors."

Huang was a veteran at the Interior Ministry. In the past, he had been so overwhelmed doing various menial tasks for the emperor that he seldom paid attention to court politics. He even accepted the fact Emperor Jiajing had brought him here today to witness the riot. Now, the emperor's remarks terrified him. Never had he found his master so cold-hearted. He could feel a chill rising from the soles of his feet to the top of head.

"I never intended to act like this, but I have to," explained Emperor Jiajing. "Now you understand why I sent Lu Fang to Nanjing."

"Your Majesty, I don't understand…" Huang said sheepishly.

"If Lu Fang had been here today, he wouldn't have the tenacity to order the crackdown."

Huang stood in a daze. Emperor Jiajing rose alone and began to descend the hill. Huang ran after him without fetching the lantern or his own cloak. When he caught up with the emperor, he held him by the arm. They took a different route and stumbled their way in the darkness. Even though they could no longer see the gate of the Western Compound, they could hear the echoes of screaming and crying.

"Did you see Hai Rui among the protesters today?" Emperor Jiajing blurted out.

"Your Majesty, the answer is no. Earlier today, there was a report from the Criminal Investigative Division and I forgot to share it with you. The report said that Zhao Zhenji had sent Hai Rui to Daxing County to set up soup kitchens there."

"Even if he was in Beijing, Hai Rui wouldn't have joined that crowd. Now that you are in charge of the Imperial Investigative Agency, tell your people to keep a close eye on him."

While many of his fellow officials were converging outside the Western Compound to petition Emperor Jiajing, Hai Rui was on his way to Daxing County.

As part of Shuntian Prefecture, Daxing was about twenty-five kilometres from Beijing. When Hai Rui reached there, he was incredulous that such a tragedy could be allowed to occur at a place so close to the Son of Heaven. In his previous jobs as magistrate of Chun'an County, Zhejiang Province and then of Xingguo County, Jiangxi Province, he had handled several large-scale disasters, both natural and man-made. But nothing in his past had prepared him for what he saw now.

Under his strict supervision, county workers had set up a dozen tents to serve porridge. Large cauldrons were boiling over open fires, but no migrants queued up for food because they were too weak to even get up. They simply sat or lay on the snow-covered field nearby. Many had already died of cold and hunger, and their bodies lay scattered on the road. The Daxing County yamen had recruited workers to wrap up the bodies in straw mats and cart them away.

When Hai Rui inspected the porridge tents, he became distraught. Inside one of them was the magistrate of Daxing. His eyes flashed anger. Dressed in a thick fur coat, the magistrate was sitting near a cauldron to warm himself by the fire. An aide was standing nearby. His sole job was to carry a chair and follow the magistrate around.

"Go over there and ask the magistrate to come over and see me here," Hai Rui told his assistant at the Ministry of Treasury.

The assistant walked over to the magistrate. "Your Highness, Mr Hai at the Ministry of Treasury wants to talk with you," he said.

The magistrate stood up reluctantly and went up to Hai Rui.

"With so many deaths, how are you going to handle the burials?" Hai Rui asked.

"I'm trying to recruit more helpers. We're planning to dig a mass grave and conduct a collective burial."

"What about the survivors? We can feed them some porridge during the day. But where are they going to sleep at night?"

The magistrate sighed. "That's what I'm worried about. I can't find a place to accommodate so many people."

"So, are you going to let them freeze to death?"

"Who says I want them to freeze to death?" retorted the magistrate who was piqued at the fact that a mere grade-six official like him would make such an accusation.

"You didn't allow us to set up tents inside the county township," Hai Rui castigated him. "If you leave these migrants in the wild on a snowy day like this, none will survive the cold."

"But if we allow them to enter the township, where do you want me to put them?"

"Where are you sleeping tonight? And what about your family? Don't they all live inside the township? If you can provide a warm place for your family, you'll surely be able to find places to accommodate these migrants."

"Mr Hai, what kind of logic is that?"

"What do you expect me to say? The Imperial Palace has entrusted this county to your care. The residents of Daxing are your people. Do you treat your sons and daughters like this? As I told you before, I have brought carts of grain for your county. If you run out, you should not hesitate to notify the Ministry of Treasury. We can ship more supplies over here. But from today onwards, if another person dies of starvation or freezes to death, I'm going to submit a censure report to His Majesty."

The Daxing magistrate said despondently: "Mr Hai, let me ask what you would do if you were in my position."

"Free up some space inside your yamen. Look for empty rooms in county schools and temples. Urge the wealthiest in the county to give up unoccupied houses. Once you have secured these places, move the migrants in there immediately."

"Can we really do that? Are there any rules or precedents?"

"That's what I did when I was a magistrate in Chun'an and Xingguo Counties. Once we finish serving this round of porridge, I'm going to move the tents and set them up inside the township."

"But..." the magistrate stammered.

Hai Rui ignored him and strode out of the tent. "The porridge will be ready soon," Hai Rui said to the migrants who were sitting or lying on the snow-covered field. "Brothers and sisters, if you have the strength to sit up, please do so. If you can stand, rise to your feet. If you continue to lie on the ground, you'll never be able to get up. Come in and take the porridge. Once you eat, we'll move all of you into the township. Your magistrate is arranging housing for you. Listen to me. It's important to get up from the ground. If you can't manage it yourself, ask others to help you."

An old man lying on the ground attempted to stand up, but failed. Hai Rui bent over. Wrapping the old man's arm around his shoulder, Hai Rui pulled him up. Then, he yelled at the magistrate and his aide inside the tent: "Why are you standing there? Do I have to beg in order for you to step out and help these people?"

Reluctantly, the magistrate joined Hai Rui in getting the migrants into the tent.

明

Hai Rui left his wife and mother at home and spent the New Year with famine victims in Daxing County. By the time he returned to Beijing, it was already the fifth day of the lunar new year.

Even though he had been away for a few days, he had lost significant weight. His cheeks and bloodshot eyes began to hollow. The official uniform he was wearing was so dirty that it stank.

"Amu, please forgive your unfilial son for not celebrating the New Year with you at home," he said, before turning to his wife. "Please help Amu sit down. Let's kowtow and wish Amu a belated happy New Year."

His wife hurried over and helped Amu sit on a chair in the centre of the guest room. "There's no need, the New Year is already over," Amu said affectionately. "Go and eat the food while it's warm. Take off your clothes and have a bath."

But instead, Hai Rui dropped down on his knees. Despite her pregnancy, Mrs Hai pressed her hand to her belly and slowly knelt down next to her husband. "Your son and daughter-in-law wish you a belated happy New Year. May you live for a hundred years!"

"All right, please help your wife up from the floor," Amu said.

Hai Rui raised his head. As he was about to get up, he passed out and sank to the floor.

"Hai Rui, Hai Rui!" Amu and his wife screamed.

Hai Rui was unresponsive.

※

After meticulous calculations, the imperial astronomer chose 6.45pm on the fifth day of the lunar new year of 1566 as an auspicious time for Emperor Jiajing to move into the newly restored Longevity Palace and Palace of Eternal Longevity. Unfortunately, the weather refused to cooperate. A heavy snow was causing havoc across Beijing.

On the square outside Yuxi Palace, one hundred and eight lanterns on wooden poles gave out an unsteady and faint light. Only a Taoist practitioner could understand the symbolic meaning of installing this number of lanterns: thirty-six at the front represented the thirty-six heavenly spirits of the Big Dipper, and seventy-two at the back symbolised the seventy-two spirits on Earth.

In the dim light, Emperor Jiajing's majestic dragon sedan could be seen parked in front of the stone steps outside Yuxi Palace. Thirty-two carriers genuflected around the sedan, waiting for Emperor Jiajing to board.

On the left side of the sedan gathered the abbot and a group of priests from Chaotian Temple. Each was holding a prayer book and a musical instrument.

The abbot and a group of priests from Xuandu Temple stood on the right side of the dragon sedan. They each held a musical instrument.

Grand Secretary Xu and other ministerial officials were kneeling under the eaves of Yuxi Palace. Even though junior officials were required only to stand, rather than kneel, they had to wait outside on the stone steps and in the square. Their robes were covered with snow. In their semi-conscious state, they fixed their eyes on the gate of Yuxi Palace, which was wide open.

In the centre of the brightly lit main hall sat a gigantic copper kettle water clock. The silence amplified the sound of water dripping inside the copper kettle.

Eunuchs were posted at all corners of the main hall. Carrying different types of imperial objects, they held their collective breath and waited.

A eunuch in a bright robe was shuffling back and forth in the hall. Despite his smiles, he radiated fear. That person was Chen Hong, the first deputy interior minister who was responsible for orchestrating the ceremony. Every now and then, he tiptoed to the door of the meditation room and listened to the sounds inside. Then, he hurried over to the large copper kettle to observe the carved wooden gauge floating on top of the water. Against the silhouettes of Grand Secretary Xu and other cabinet members who were kneeling outside the gate, Chen Hong cut a towering figure.

As the water clock was approaching 6.45pm, people inside and outside Yuxi Palace became alert. They waited eagerly for Emperor Jiajing to chime the bell inside the meditation room. Concurrently, a large bell outside would strike one hundred and eight times. Priests from Chaotian and Xuandu Temples would play *Music of the Holy Palace*. At the end of the music, members of the Imperial Army would fire the gun salutes loud enough for the whole capital city to hear. Residents would know that the emperor was on his way to his new palaces.

A separate copper kettle clock was also installed inside the meditation room. Huang Jin was standing in front of the clock, staring at the carved wooden gauge. He didn't dare look away for fear he would miss the moment.

Emperor Jiajing had changed into the gown on which Princess Li had embroidered the five-thousand-word *Tao Te Ching*. His hair was tied back with a black silk ribbon. At this moment, he was sitting cross-legged on his prayer mat, reading a congratulatory letter.

On his left side, there was a large flower crown on a small table. On his right, a bronze bell sat on a rosewood shelf. A small table in front of the emperor was stacked with a dozen congratulatory letters that he had just opened. Each time he finished reading one, he tossed it onto the table. Just one unopened letter remained. Emperor Jiajing glanced at it without picking it up. "Are all of the congratulatory letters here?" he asked.

"Your Majesty, they are all there," answered Huang, who had grudgingly turned his eyes away from the water clock.

"No more?" Emperor Jiajing asked, looking glum.

Huang had been dreading this moment. Knowing that Emperor Jiajing would question him on the matter, he had consulted with Grand Secretary Xu, who fed him a line. "Since I've been so swamped preparing for this auspicious occasion, I completely forgot to relay a message from Grand Secretary Xu when he delivered those congratulatory letters earlier," Huang replied calmly. "Grand Secretary Xu is worried that reading too many of them could tire you out. So, he simply invited all cabinet members and a few ministerial officials to send you their celebratory messages. Grand Secretary Xu reckoned that this select group could express their love and loyalty to Your Majesty on behalf of all Imperial Government officials and the people of the Great Ming Empire."

Emperor Jiajing responded with a laugh that unsettled Huang. "Xu Jie wasn't concerned when those demagogues attempted to submit a censure report to me a few days ago," Emperor Jiajing sneered. "Now he's worried I could be exhausted from reading too many congratulatory messages. Do you want me to tell you the real reason I have received only a few letters? Many imperial officials in Beijing hate me. They are unwilling to congratulate me because I have spent their money repairing my palaces and temples, and because some people got beaten up by Chen Hong before the New Year. Grand Secretary Xu tried to pull the wool over my eyes. Are you conspiring with him to deceive me?"

Huang dropped down on his knees. "Master, you're the father of our nation," he said. "When the children hear that their father is moving into a new home, they all feel elated. Your Majesty, today is a day of great joy for all of your courtiers and servants. You're an immortal deity who has descended to Earth to save us. The whole nation is celebrating the occasion."

There wasn't the slightest joy in Emperor Jiajing's eyes. He was tempted to rebuke Huang, but the sincerity in his eunuch's plea touched him. Watching the snow blowing through a window in the south wall, Emperor Jiajing began chanting a poem by Du Fu, a famous Tang dynasty poet.

> *If I had mansions covering ten thousand miles,*
> *I'd house all poor scholars and make them beam with smiles,*
> *In wind and rain these mansions would stand like mountains high.*
> *Alas! Should these houses appear before my eye,*
> *Frozen in my unroofed bed, content I'd die.*

"Master, please don't chant such dark verses on an auspicious day like this," Huang pleaded.

"Hold your tongue!" Emperor Jiajing murmured through his teeth and he closed his eyes.

Huang lowered his head apprehensively. The sound of dripping water echoed in the room.

In the main hall outside, Chen Hong, who had been observing the carved wooden gauge, raised his head. Striding over to the main entrance, he was ready to issue the order to start the ceremony.

Grand Secretary Xu and his peers straightened their backs. The priests raised their musical instruments. All eyes were on Chen Hong, who held his hands in the air, waiting for the bell in the meditation room to chime.

Meanwhile, Huang stared at the wooden gauge. It was now 6.45pm. Wearing a big smile, Huang picked up the pestle, held it above his head and presented it to Emperor Jiajing. "The most auspicious moment has arrived," he said. "Your humble servant beseeches Your Majesty to rise and preside over the ceremony."

Emperor Jiajing opened his eyes. He merely glanced at the pestle without taking it.

The dripping inside the copper kettle sounded louder. Emperor Jiajing remained still. Huang felt as if the cold water inside the kettle was dripping onto his forehead. The water drops turned into beads of cold sweat and streamed down his cheeks.

Slowly, Emperor Jiajing stretched his hand and took the pestle from Huang. Peering at the bronze bell to his right, he raised the pestle in the air and smashed it on the floor. The pestle broke into small pieces. Wooden fragments scattered all over the floor.

Huang could not believe his eyes.

Chen Hong heard the noise. He was about to press his hand down and announce the start of the ceremony when he realised that it was not the chime sound that he had been expecting. He had a look of horror on his face.

Grand Secretary Xu also heard the noise. It sounded like something had been smashed to pieces. Everyone directed their gaze in the direction of the meditation room.

People waiting outside Yuxi Palace sensed that something had gone awry. They looked baffled and shocked.

Yuxi Palace fell silent. Now that the snow flurries had eased, the lanterns seemed brighter.

Nobody knew what sound would come next from the meditation room. They waited nervously.

Inside the meditation room, Emperor Jiajing pulled out an edict that he had drafted earlier and tossed it to Huang Jin who was kneeling in front of him. "Step out and deliver my edict," he ordered.

Huang had no idea when the emperor had written it. He picked up the edict from the ground, kowtowed and stumbled out of the meditation room.

Chen Hong dashed up to Huang. "What's happening?" he whispered.

Huang ignored him and went straight to the palace gate.

All eyes were on Huang as he reached the outside steps. He had never addressed so many people before, let alone senior government officials. To the people who were waiting, Huang towered over them like a mountain and they felt suffocated by his presence.

"I've been entrusted by His Majesty to announce an imperial edict," he proclaimed.

"Long live!" people chanted. Grand Secretary Xu and other senior ministers who had been kneeling prostrated themselves on the ground. Those who had been standing fell to their knees.

Chen Hong, who had expected special attention, was sulking over Huang's slight. He knelt down inside the main hall. The eunuchs who were holding imperial ornamental objects also dropped to their knees.

In a shaking voice, Huang Jin declared:

I have been ruling the nation for forty-five years, during which time I have abided by the rules of heaven and diligently cultivated my moral character in governance. Never have I pursued luxury in the way I live, or in the things I eat and wear. I stayed away from the grand mansions inside the Forbidden City because I cannot live in peace when many of my subjects are still struggling to keep a roof over their heads. I therefore moved to the Western Compound with the sole intention of seeking a secluded place for my cultivation and a secure place to shelter me from wind and rain. Who would have thought that I would endure the slings and arrows of so many outrageous critics?

Among the one hundred officials who petitioned me before the New Year, none has submitted a congratulatory letter. When victims in disaster areas are dying of starvation and when the Imperial Government owes salaries to its employees, the public vents its anger at me, blaming me for my moral failings. I have delegated the governance of millions of people in the thirteen provinces and two capitals to the Privy Council and to senior ministers and agency leaders. Under the previous rule of Yan Song, Yan Shifan and other member of the Yan Clan, corruption flourished, eroding the public's trust in the Imperial Palace and harming the interests of common folk. At present, Grand Secretary Xu and other cabinet members lack initiative. Their indecisiveness is ruining our nation. But if one is to assign blame, that blame lies with me.

Huang Jin was sweating profusely. With a parched throat, he found it hard to continue.

Grand Secretary Xu and other senior ministers lay prostrate in total submission. They were seized with fear.

Huang resumed after taking a deep breath.

The condemnation of a hundred imperial officials troubles me. The rising number of starving victims worries me. With such concerns hovering in my mind, how can I bear to move to Longevity Palace and Palace of Eternal Longevity? I urge Grand Secretary Xu and the Prince of Yu to formulate a feasible plan to restore the vigour of the Great Ming Empire and save our people. As long as the world is in turmoil and my people live in misery, I shall not relocate to the newly restored palaces.

For months, Grand Secretary Xu and other cabinet members had attempted to raise funds for the repair and renovation of Emperor Jiajing's two palaces and two temples. They did so at the expense of many more urgent projects. They robbed the Wang's to pay the Li's, and endured complaints and condemnation from all sides. Now that the palaces had been restored to their previous splendour, Emperor Jiajing was refusing to move in. On top of this, he chastised his cabinet members, condemned his detractors and despite his statement, was actually assigning blame to everyone around him.

The emperor had thrown his temper tantrum for one single reason – more than one hundred imperial officials in Beijing did not send him congratulatory letters in protest after they were beaten up by the imperial agents before the New Year.

According to a popular saying, lightning can strike out of a clear sky. Even though the weather is unpredictable, signs can always be detected beforehand. But this emperor was so capricious there was absolutely no warning.

The snow had stopped and a blustery wind had whipped up.

Upon hearing the decree, Grand Secretary Xu was shivering with both cold and fear.

Everyone was dumbfounded. As head of the Privy Council, Grand Secretary Xu had to issue an official response to the imperial edict. Putting both hands on the ground, he raised his head and pleaded loudly: "As the emperor stated, members of the Privy Council lack initiative. Our indecisiveness has caused significant problems for our nation. As grand secretary, I have failed His Majesty and our nation. I am willing to receive condemnation from the Heavenly God. However, I sincerely entreat Your Majesty to move to Longevity Palace and Palace of Eternal Longevity today, giving us the opportunity to compensate for our errors and redeem our sins. Otherwise, we can never die in peace."

All of a sudden, Grand Secretary Xu became overcome with sadness. All of his grievances poured out in the form a loud howl. Tears streamed down his cheeks.

Grand Secretary Xu's emotional outburst deeply affected those around him. Soon, all the senior ministers started weeping and howling.

Huang Jin, who was standing opposite Grand Secretary Xu and other senior ministers, also sank to his knees and cried loudly.

In response to the chaos, the abbots at Chaotian and Xuandu Temples exchanged glances and began chanting the sutras. Soon, other priests joined them in a loud chorus.

Outside Yuxi Palace, the flickering lanterns seemed to be floating in the howling wind, mixed with a cacophony of loud crying and sutra chanting.

5

Hai Rui had fallen ill and fainted after returning from Daxing County. The episode frightened Amu, who had never seen such a sudden collapse. There were no male adults around to help, so the elderly Amu and Hai Rui's pregnant wife lifted him from the guest room floor, dragged his limp body into the north room and laid him on Amu's bed. Out of desperation, Mrs Hai ran across the alley and banged on a neighbour's door, begging for help. Knowing that Hai Rui was an honest and upright official, the neighbour was sympathetic and sent a youngster to fetch Wang Yongji. Upon hearing the news, Wang went directly to the Prince of Yu's mansion, where he reached Dr Li Shizhen. By the time Wang and Dr Li rushed over to Hai Rui's house, it was already dusk.

Hai Rui was still lying unconscious on Amu's bed. His eyes were tightly shut and his teeth clenched. Dr Li sat at the bedside to check his pulse.

Mrs Hai had jettisoned the usual etiquette of avoiding male guests without her husband's permission. Standing by Hai Rui's bedside, she wept silently. Amu was sitting opposite Dr Li. She wiped her tears while holding her son's hand.

Wang watched to one side with a concerned look on his face.

"Get a few things ready for me," said Dr Li after he had examined Hai Rui.

"What do we need?" asked Wang.

Amu and Mrs Hai looked at Dr Li.

"Gather all the quilts in the house and put them over him," Dr Li instructed. "Move the brazier to this room and build a fire."

"I'll get another quilt for him," said Mrs Hai, scurrying away.

Wang rushed out to the courtyard. "Go inside the kitchen. Get the brazier and some wood and bring them inside," he ordered his aide, who was loitering by the courtyard door.

"He's turning fifty this year and I've never seen him like this before," Amu said to Dr Li with tears in her eyes. "He was perfectly healthy before he left. How did he suddenly become so ill?"

"Amu, there's no need to panic," said Dr Li. "Both you and Hai Rui have warm and sweaty feet. Like I said before, in medicine we call this condition 'the body of extreme yang'. Your ancestors used to live in abject poverty and toiled in the field without coats or shoes to ward off the cold. Then, as time went by, their bodies accumulated an abundance of hot, masculine energy. They passed on these natural endowments to their descendants. Thus, Hai Rui's body has a high tolerance for cold temperatures. But when he stayed outside in the extreme cold for too long without eating or sleeping for days, his body temperature swung from one extreme to the other, allowing the coldness to invade and attack his organs. It's called 'extremes beget extremes'."

"Is it a serious condition?" asked Amu, sounding alarmed.

"Don't worry. I'll see what I can do. Let him sweat it out first. Then, get him a bowl of hot porridge. I'll prescribe some herbs later. It'll take some time to heal."

"We have porridge in the kitchen," said Amu, rising from her chair. "I'll heat it up."

"Amu, sit here and let me do it," said Wang, holding her down.

"It's easier if I go because I know where things are," Amu insisted. "Why don't you keep Dr Li company."

At this moment, Mrs Hai appeared with a thin quilt in her arms. Wang took it from her and put it over Hai Rui.

"One quilt is not enough," Dr Li said. "Bring all your quilts over, the more, the better."

Mrs Hai lowered her head in embarrassment. "That's the only one we have in the house," she mumbled with tears in her eyes.

Dr Li and Wang looked appalled at Mrs Hai's admission. Wang's eyes darted around the house, and he caught sight of his own cape on a chair. "Can I take your cape as well?" he said to Dr Li and put both on top of Hai Rui's quilt. Meanwhile, Wang's aide carried a burning brazier into the room.

"Make the fire bigger and hotter," Wang said to his aide as he unbuttoned his thick winter robe.

The aide squatted down to blow on the fire. Flames shot up from the brazier. Wang covered Hai Rui with his thick cotton robe. All he had on now was a shirt and vest.

"Bring some more firewood and make the fire bigger," demanded Dr Li, who was also removing his own thick cotton gown.

Mrs Hai untied her belt and was about to do the same when Wang stopped her. "No, no, you can't do this," he said. "You're pregnant and can't afford to get sick. It's cold here. Please go to the kitchen and help Amu. Dr Li and I can take care of Hai Rui."

Mrs Hai ignored Wang's warning and started unbuttoning her winter coat.

"Listen to Mr Wang and don't be stubborn," Dr Li interjected. "If you fall ill again and harm the foetus, I wouldn't be able to save the baby. Please go to the kitchen and help Amu with the porridge."

The teary-eyed Mrs Hai lowered her head and left the room.

Wang's aide came in with a few small pieces of firewood in his hands.

"Have we run out of firewood?" Wang asked.

The aide nodded. "I left a few for Amu to heat up the porridge."

Wang and Dr Li sighed. Their eyes filled with sadness and a gloom fell over the room.

"I can't believe that Hai Rui lives in such destitution," said Wang, who was filled with self-reproach. "As a friend, I should have paid more attention to his financial situation."

Before his aide left, Wang pulled him aside. "Please take a carriage and go to my house," he said. "Fetch a bag of rice, some firewood and two more heavy quilts."

"Yes sir," the aide said before bolting for the door.

Dr Li bowed to thank Wang for his generosity.

Embarrassed, Wang switched topic. "How is his condition?" he whispered, pointing at Hai Rui who still had not regained consciousness. "I hope it's not serious."

"At this stage, it's hard to say. Treating his physical illness is relatively easy. I don't know if I will ever be able to heal what ails his mind. When Amu enquired about Hai Rui's health just now, I only explained half of what caused his collapse. I'm afraid the underlying cause lies within him."

"What do you mean?"

"You can ask him when he wakes up," said Dr Li.

About half an hour later, Hai Rui remained unresponsive.

Amu sat next to the brazier with a bowl of porridge in her hands. She held the bowl close to the flames to keep it warm. Mrs Hai stood behind Amu and rested her hands on Amu's shoulders. Wang moved to Hai Rui's bedside. His eyes lit up when he noticed that Hai Rui's forehead was glistening with sweat. He brought out a handkerchief from inside his sleeve pocket, trying to wipe the sweat off.

"Don't touch him," said Dr Li as he reached under the quilt and grabbed Hai Rui's wrist to check his pulse. Taking out a roll of mugwort from his medicine bag, he walked to the brazier to light the herb and then returned to the bed with the smouldering mugwort. Removing the hairpin from Hai Rui's bun, Dr Li pulled his hair away from the top of his head and held the glowing end of the mugwort roll close to an acupoint there until the area reddened.

While Hai Rui was receiving moxibustion, Amu cringed and looked away. The others in the room fixed their eyes on Hai Rui's face. Slowly, he opened his mouth and let out a long breath as if it had risen from the deepest part of his abdomen. Then he released another one, which sounded more like a sigh. Gradually, his eyes opened.

"Dr Li!" said Hai Rui, who was now wide awake. Despite his illness, his voice remained robust.

"You don't have to shout," Dr Li said with a grin before directing Wang to wipe the sweat off Hai Rui's forehead.

"You're here as well," Hai Rui greeted Wang.

Mrs Hai held Amu's arm and the two women rushed over to the bedside. Hai Rui tried to sit up. But when he raised his head, his body refused to cooperate. "Lie still and don't move," Amu said in a doting voice.

Hai Rui laid his head back onto the pillow grudgingly. Seeing traces of tears on Amu's face, he forced a smile from the corner of his mouth and consoled her: "I'm all right, Mother. Don't worry about me."

Amu held the porridge with both hands and sought permission from Dr Li: "Can I feed him now?"

Dr Li stood up, moved his chair to the middle and offered it to Amu. "You can sit here and feed him," he instructed. "Take it slow and a little at a time."

Amu sat down on the bench and spooned a small amount of porridge into Hai Rui's mouth.

"Brother Yongji, could you lend me a hand?" Hai Rui asked Wang after swallowing the spoonful of porridge.

"What do you need?" Wang bent over and asked.

"Could you help me sit up?"

"Just lie still for the moment," Amu said before sending another spoonful to the corner of his mouth.

"Mother, I'm a grown man," Hai Rui said, declining her help. "I can manage myself. All I need is to sit up."

"Amu, let him sit up and eat the porridge himself," Dr Li advised.

Amu gave in. With Wang's help, Hai Rui propped himself up against the back of the bed. When Amu handed him the porridge bowl, his hands trembled slightly. Wang held the bottom of the bowl for him.

Hai Rui brought the bowl to his mouth and gulped the food all down. Everyone watched in amazement.

Hai Rui stretched out his right hand. Amu handed him the spoon, which he used to scrape some rice that was stuck to the bottom of the bowl. "I'm feeling good," Hai Rui declared as he gave the empty bowl to Amu.

"Oh, I'm glad to hear that," Amu said with tears in her eyes.

"Brother Yongji, could you help me get up?"

"Lie down," Dr Li ordered.

"Listen to Dr Li and lie down," Amu said.

Dr Li caught sight of the emotional Mrs Hai who was standing unobtrusively at the back. "Mrs Hai, it's your turn now," he said gently. "Please go over and tuck him in."

Mrs Hai nodded at Dr Li appreciatively. Wiping away her tears, she walked over and tucked the quilt tightly around her husband. Since his wife blocked Amu's view, Hai Rui felt able to stare lovingly at his wife. Looking bashful, she avoided his gaze. Once again, tears welled up in her eyes.

At this moment, loud voices outside caught everyone's attention. "Keep an eye on my carriage and take all the items into the guest room," Wang's aide could be heard saying in the courtyard. It sounded as if he had brought several people with him.

"My aide is back!" Wang cried out.

"Your Highness, everything you ordered is here," the aide came in and reported to Wang.

Amu and Mrs Hai had no idea what was happening. They tilted their heads and peered at the door.

A stranger came in with two thick, fluffy quilts in his arms. Two others followed carrying bundles of firewood and packets of food.

"Put some firewood in the brazier," Wang instructed loudly.

One helper put the firewood down on the floor and added a few logs to the brazier.

The aide took the quilts from one of the helpers and stepped over to Hai Rui's bed.

"Wait there," Wang said to his aide as he picked up Dr Li's coat from the bed. "Put the quilt on that chair. Go and put this coat on Dr Li first. It's cold."

"No, no, I'll do it myself." Dr Li took the winter coat from the aide and slipped an arm into a sleeve.

"Please remove our capes from the bed and spread these quilts over Mr Hai," Wang instructed his aide as he was buttoning up his coat.

The aide picked up the capes and hung them on the headboard.

Shaking the new quilt open, he placed it on top of Hai Rui's old one.

Hai Rui lay on his bed and watched quietly. By then, he realised what his friends had done while he was in a state of unconsciousness. His eyes moistened. For the first time, he had a true grasp of the proverbial phrase about genuine friendship: 'Remove the clothes on your body to dress a friend who is cold, and share the food you are eating with a friend who is hungry.'

Amu was not someone who easily accepted favours or gifts from others. Sitting by the brazier, she was deeply moved.

Mrs Hai was by nature a reticent person and seldom participated in conversations in the presence of her husband's friends or colleagues. But seeing that both her husband and mother-in-law were too overcome with emotion to speak, she held back her tears and bowed deeply to her husband's two best friends. "Mr Wang and Dr Li, thank you for your generosity," she said. "I don't know whether we'll ever be able to repay your kindness…"

"We are friends. There's no need to stand on ceremony," Wang interjected.

"Where do you want me to put the other quilt?" one of the helpers asked Wang.

"Take it to Mrs Hai's room and move the food and firewood to the kitchen," Wang replied.

When all the helpers had left the room, Wang's aide stood there, trying to get his attention about something.

Wang noticed and went up to his aide. "Do you need to talk with me?" he whispered.

"Your Highness, a messenger from the Audit and Inspection Commission came earlier. You need to go and see the commissioner immediately."

"Did the messenger say what the meeting is about?"

"He said that all imperial officials, except for those who are away on business, are required to write a congratulatory letter to His Majesty."

Feeling dispirited, Wang shook his head and looked at Hai Rui and Dr Li.

Hai Rui did not comment. He looked back at Wang impassively.

"You should go right away," Dr Li urged him. "I can take care of him here."

Wang let out a soft sigh. "You can probably get away with it because the Ministry of Treasury doesn't know you're already back," he said to Hai Rui. "Sorry, I won't be able to keep you company."

"You need to go and attend to your duty at the Imperial Palace," Amu said, rising from her chair. "You've already done so much for us."

Wang gave Amu and Dr Li a palm-over-fist salute before leaving. When his aide followed him to the courtyard door, he told them to stay: "You don't have to go with me to the Audit and Inspection Commission. Dr Li might need you for errands."

Amu and Mrs Hai walked Wang to the door.

※

Amu and Mrs Hai deeply respected Dr Li's words. They listened to and obeyed everything he prescribed. That night, in keeping with Dr Li's request, Amu retreated into Hai Rui's bedroom and stayed with Mrs Hai. At the same time, Wang's aide huddled around a brazier in the guest room in case Dr Li or Hai Rui needed him for errands.

Inside Amu's room, Dr Li sat on a chair beside Hai Rui's bedside, with his cape draped over his shoulders. Every now and then, he picked up a pair of tongs and bent over to stoke the fire in the brazier near his feet. He looked, and felt, heavy-hearted.

Hai Rui lay propped against the pillows. He gazed at Dr Li intently.

"Few live as long as a hundred years, but many worry about affairs that'll affect our empire in a thousand years," Dr Li said finally, quoting a proverb. "If you have no fear of imprisonment or death and are intent on criticising His Majesty, I can't stop you. I don't think anybody can stop you."

"Does that mean you agree with me?" Hai Rui asked.

"I didn't say that I completely agree with you," said Dr Li as he put down the metal tongs. "Submitting a censure report is like writing a prescription. As the saying goes, a supreme healer treats a society of its ills, a wise doctor cures a patient of his illness and a mediocre practitioner simply tackles the symptoms. At the moment, our Ming dynasty is terminally ill. Of the three categories, where do you fit?"

Seeing that Dr Li was taking an interest in his position, Hai Rui's eyes lit up. "The nation is ill because our people are ill. Healing a nation involves treating its people and easing their suffering. A nation can only heal itself after its citizens are rid of their diseases."

"You're on the right track and it is important to tackle the symptoms," Dr Li said approvingly. "What is the root cause of the disease?"

"The ruler governs the nation like he runs his family. He monopolises power and robs the world of its wealth. He treats imperial officials like mere decorations and has no regard for the lives of common people. This is what I see as the root cause of the disease."

"That's very insightful," Dr Li said, slapping his knee excitedly. "Please go on."

Despite his weakened constitution, Hai Rui launched into a vigorous diatribe: "When it comes to governance, Confucius taught us that benevolence means to love others. Mencius wrote that the people are to be valued the most, followed by the state and the ruler last of all. These principles of good governance have been tested through the ages and remain an enduring truth. The rulers of the Qin dynasty discarded the doctrines proposed by Confucius and Mencius. Hence, the dynasty only lasted fifteen years. Emperor Wen and his son, Emperor Jing of the Han dynasty, followed the Confucian principles and practised benevolence and thriftiness. They listened to the advice of their wise ministers and showed their commitment by putting the interests of their people at the centre. For the first time in history, our country witnessed a period of general stability and prosperity. Emperor Taizong, who cofounded the Tang dynasty, adopted a similar path. He delegated power to his wise ministers and ushered in a period of peace and prosperity, known in history as the Reign of Zhenguan. Our country was ruled by a succession of different dynasties. During each cycle, when a ruler shared power and put people at the centre of governance, his empire flourished.

"Each time an emperor monopolised power, persecuted his upright and loyal courtiers, and showed reckless disregard for the well-being of his people, the dynasty declined and fell. Take our Great Ming Empire as an example. Emperor Hongwu was born into poverty. When he founded the Ming dynasty, he understood and empathised with the peoples' sorrows and sufferings. He took draconian measures against corruption and reduced the tax burden on farmers. While Emperor Hongwu attracted many talents through his virtues, and his policies benefited ordinary people, he also sowed the seeds of destruction. For instance, he ordered the removal of Mencius's memorial tablets from the nation's Confucian temples because he rejected Mencius's principles of good governance. Emperor Hongwu consolidated control over all aspects of government. He created a cabinet but treated his ministers like servants. He hired imperial officials and treated them as his enemies, beating and killing them at whim. He augmented the power of the eunuchs and relied on his relatives and personal favourites to govern the nation. He treated the two capitals and thirteen provinces of the Great Ming Empire as his family property. Of the eleven emperors who held power since the establishment of the Great Ming Empire, the current ruler, His Majesty, has taken it to the extreme. For two decades, he held no court meetings and spent a great deal of time on alchemy. He ostentatiously claims to practise Taoist meditation, but exercises control and manoeuvres behind the scenes. Externally, he relied on the Yan Clan and internally, he trusted his eunuchs to exploit people and rob them of their wealth. Countless numbers of honest and outspoken scholar officials attempted to remonstrate with His Majesty, but many ended up losing their lives. Those corrupt officials ingratiate themselves with this fatuous ruler and pander to his every whim. The Imperial Palace colludes with officials at all levels of government and feeds on the flesh and blood of ordinary people. As a consequence, the people are suffering. Many are dying of hunger or oppression..."

As Hai Rui began to choke up, Dr Li's eyes darkened with anger.

Hai Rui fought back the tears and continued: "Let me tell you about my trip to Daxing. The county is right outside the capital city. On New Year's Day, people were dying in droves. The snow-covered fields were strewn with bodies. Local officials turned a blind eye to the situation, and senior ministerial officials in Beijing remained indifferent. When news reached the Privy Council, Grand Secretary Xu urged the Ministry of Treasury to ship some grain from a military warehouse to the disaster area. But you could tell they were just going through the motions to prevent a large-scale rebellion. Before I left, Zhao Zhenji told me repeatedly to hide the truth from His Majesty so we wouldn't spoil the joyful occasion of his palace-moving ceremony. If this is allowed to occur in a county right near the capital city, imagine the situation in remote regions. Millions are living in misery. When I was in Daxing over the past week, all I could do was save a few lives. I was surrounded by a group of corrupt and heartless officials. I had no place to vent and cry. Sir, you have devoted your whole life to treating disease and saving lives, but for those like me who work for the Imperial Government, we do nothing but watch people die right in front of our eyes…"

Hai Rui, a person known for being tough and reserved, started weeping. Dr Li's eyes moistened too. They sat there, facing each other silently.

"If you intend to submit a report and censure His Majesty, do it then!" Dr Li said. "Even if you may not have the power to bring the much-needed spring rain after a long drought, you can at least generate a clap of thunder to awaken the hibernating public."

"I still haven't figured out how to initiate the censure," Hai Rui said. "I'd like to hear your insight and advice."

"You already have plenty of insight. If you truly want to go down this path, you should target the root cause of the disease. Previously, many officials attempted to remonstrate with His Majesty but they were too timid. They simply spoke out against the sad state of affairs without holding anyone accountable. They denounced the courtiers but spared the emperor. I think it better if you did not follow their example. You have to target His Majesty's one-man rule. If one intends to remonstrate, one has to advocate for power-sharing between a ruler and his courtiers. A good article might not make the current ruler repent and mend his ways, but it can at least jolt someone else out of complacency, sending him a warning that if we continue with the current one-man rule, the Great Ming Empire will be doomed and people will rise up against the ruler. If you can achieve this, you'll be remembered in history as someone who helped save the empire. Do you know who I'm talking about?"

"The Prince of Yu!"

"That's right. Since you're going to censure His Majesty, you need to take two points into consideration. First, you should guarantee the safety of your mother and your wife. Remember Fang Xiaoru, the famed scholar official who was Emperor Jianwen's teacher? After Emperor Jianwen's uncle, the Prince of Yan, usurped the throne in 1402, he ordered Fang to boost his political legitimacy by writing an inaugural address to praise him. Fang refused out of his loyalty for his former student, and in the end, he was given the punishment of 'extermination of ten degrees of kinship'. In addition to his own execution, nearly nine hundred of his blood relations and their spouses were killed along with all of his students and peers. I personally don't think you should follow his example. You shouldn't do anything to endanger the lives of your mother and your pregnant wife. It's not that I don't want to assist you. You know my biggest wish in life is to finish a comprehensive book on medicinal herbs. To collect herbs, I have been travelling the country, moving from place to place. But what I can do is to take your mother and wife out of Beijing as soon as possible. You'll have to count on Wang Yongji to look after them later. Therefore, before submitting your censure report, you have to sever ties with Wang and make sure you don't implicate him."

Hai Rui nodded vigorously. "Dr Li, what's your second point?"

"I want you to protect the Prince of Yu. I've been friends with him for years. I know that he's honest and benevolent by nature. He honours wise, talented and upright courtiers, and cares about the common people. If we intend to effect change in our country and end one-man rule, the Prince of Yu can make it happen. So, when

His Majesty receives your report, he will automatically assume you have acted under someone else's instigation. Given that you were first recommended by the Prince of Yu, His Majesty might suspect his son is scheming against him. If the Crown Prince is deposed because of your remonstrance, our only hope for change would be ruined. Therefore, before you act, don't connect with anyone who is close to the Prince of Yu. You shouldn't mention the prince or anyone else in your article. You should try to convince His Majesty that you're not aligned with any factions and that you're doing it for the sake of the country."

In awe of Dr Li's wisdom, Hai Rui sat up straight and gave Dr Li a palm-over-fist salute. "I'll take your words to heart."

明

A group of imperial officials in Beijing withheld their congratulations to Emperor Jiajing upon his palace-moving ceremony. Upset by their boycott, the emperor refused to move. The monarch and his courtiers had become antagonistic towards each other. Some compared this incompatible relationship to that of fire and water.

Distraught by the events that had unfolded before the New Year, the Prince of Yu summoned members of the Privy Council on the night of the botched palace-moving ceremony. Together, they visited the Imperial Hospital where officials who had been beaten outside the Western Compound were being treated.

The unexpected visit by the Prince of Yu surprised officials who were lying in their sickbeds. Out of reverence for the Crown Prince, they all tried to get out of bed. Those with broken legs or other severe injuries propped themselves up with pillows. While the majority appeared excited, a few responded glumly to the Prince of Yu's visit.

"Please lie down," urged the Prince of Yu, as he walked to the centre of the room and waved at everyone.

Grand Secretary Xu stepped over to a patient's bed and urged him to lie down. Gao Gong and Zhang Juzheng followed suit and rushed over to different parts of the room and persuaded the patients not to get up.

An imperial doctor brought a chair for the Prince of Yu. When Deputy Li Chunfang invited the prince to sit down, he declined.

"Please move the chair out of the way," Zhang told the imperial doctor.

By now, all the patients had returned to their beds. Most propped themselves up on an elbow and waited for the Prince of Yu to speak.

"His Majesty has sent me here to see everyone," he said. "His Majesty is very concerned about you."

Many in the room knew it was a well-meaning lie, but the Prince of Yu's sincere and conciliatory tone deeply moved them. An official from Hanlin Academy at the far end of the room burst into loud sobs. Soon, others began shedding tears. But Li Qingyuan and a few protest leaders remained insouciant and discouraged.

At this point, the imperial doctor opened the door. The courtyard was now crammed. Many officials who had got wind of the Prince of Yu's visit congregated there to see him.

Seeing their eager faces, the Prince of Yu choked up. Grand Secretary Xu and other cabinet members fell silent.

Zhang, who was standing next to the Prince of Yu, gave him a secret nudge.

The Prince of Yu cleared his throat and collected himself. Tilting his body slightly, he raised his voice to address both the patients in the room and the officials who were watching in the courtyard: "Please listen, I have a few words to say. You're all familiar with the popular saying that parents can do no wrong. It means that parents are always well intentioned, and we children should never feel any resentment towards them. The same doctrine applies to our country. In the early days of our Great Ming Empire, when Emperor Hongwu admonished officials who handled litigation cases, he said that, during a family dispute, if the son sues his father, it is always the son's fault. If two brothers are embroiled in a lawsuit, it is always the younger brother's fault. I'm using the same argument to reason with you today. In our Great Ming Empire, we share one everlasting father who protects and deeply cares about this land and the millions of his subjects. There is one beloved father whom his subjects revere and support. When the great ruler of ours, who safeguards every inch of our land and every swath of our waters, builds a home to rest and recover his body, we should be happy for him. We shouldn't make trouble to ruin the auspicious occasion."

The Prince of Yu sounded preachy, but what he stated was irrefutable. Officials both inside the ward and outside in the courtyard fell silent.

"I'm well aware of the fact that our state coffers are empty and people around the country are suffering from cold and hunger. For this, I should be held accountable. The Privy Council should be held accountable. Officials in charge of the six ministries should be held accountable. But in no way should we blame His Majesty. I've brought along members of the Privy Council. Together, we want to apologise to everyone here. I want to apologise to the people of our country."

The Prince of Yu bowed to officials in the courtyard and then to those who were lying on their sickbeds. Grand Secretary Xu followed the Prince of Yu's example and bowed to officials standing outside and to the patients inside. Officials in the courtyard dropped down on their knees.

Inside the hospital ward, those die-hard protesters who initially responded coldly to the Prince of Yu's visit became emotional. Despite his injuries, Li Qingyuan struggled to get up but fell off the bed. As he knelt towards the Prince of Yu, several others also crawled out of bed and dropped down on their knees.

明

The Prince of Yu's persuasive remarks at the Imperial Hospital deeply moved many disillusioned members of the Clear Stream faction. They changed their minds and promised on the spot to each write a congratulatory letter overnight to pacify Emperor Jiajing. At the same time, at the urging of Grand Secretary Xu, senior ministerial officials ordered all officials in Beijing to report to work and compose their congratulatory letters. All the messages would be delivered to Yuxi Palace on the morning of 6 January.

By the time the Prince of Yu returned to his mansion with

Grand Secretary Xu and Zhang Juzheng, it was already midnight. A cold wind was howling. The temperature had dropped so precipitously that his breath could be seen freezing in midair. Many eunuchs were waiting at the gate with lanterns. When the Prince of Yu stepped out of his sedan, they rushed over. Two eunuchs put a fur cloak on him while another handed him a bronze handwarmer. The Prince of Yu clutched the handwarmer to his chest, but still felt cold. On his way to the backyard, he started coughing violently.

Grand Secretary Xu and Zhang followed him closely with looks of concern on their faces.

When the Prince of Yu entered his study, a wave of warm air greeted him. In the middle of the room, two large bronze braziers shot blue flames. The sudden temperature change made it hard for him to breathe. He began to gasp for air.

"Your Highness, please lean towards the door," said Zhang, who held the prince's arm.

A eunuch opened the door, allowing some fresh air to get in. The Prince of Yu tilted his head towards the door while Zhang stroked his back. Soon, his breathing eased. The eunuch hurried over to remove his fur cloak and the prince plopped into a chair before his desk. Another eunuch handed him a cup of hot tea. The prince took a few sips and his coughing stopped. All of a sudden, he felt exhausted. Suppressing a yawn, he rubbed his forehead. The night was not over yet. Before retiring to bed, he needed to ask Grand Secretary Xu and Zhang to tackle another overarching problem.

"Please sit down," he told his two teachers in a hoarse voice.

Grand Secretary Xu and Zhang sat down. They looked at his tired face sympathetically.

When a eunuch came in to serve tea, the Prince of Yu told him to step out while they were having their discussion. "Close the door behind you," he instructed.

"Do you think all the congratulatory letters can be delivered before daybreak?" the Prince of Yu asked Grand Secretary Xu earnestly.

"Your Highness, you can rest assured that the letters will be delivered by dawn," Grand Secretary Xu said confidently. "I have issued a warning to all ministerial officials. If any agency is late, I will dismiss both the agency head and his superior from their posts."

The Prince of Yu cast his eyes downwards and said apologetically: "Thank you for the trouble you have taken. In spring, we have to make every effort to pay back the salaries we owe to imperial officials, and offer tangible relief to disaster victims and migrants to ensure they don't die on us. Are the cotton cloth merchants here?"

"Your Highness, Grand Secretary Xu and I made the arrangement before you left to visit the Imperial Hospital," replied Zhang. "I just checked with your aide. He said they are already here. One of them is waiting in the reception room. The other is talking with Princess Li."

The Prince of Yu became irritated and his face fell. "Why have you got Princess Li involved in this cotton cloth deal?" he asked in a reproachful tone. "Besides, it's midnight. How can you allow a merchant to enter my inner chamber?"

Grand Secretary Xu shot Zhang a quick glance.

"Your Highness, I'm sorry I didn't make it clear to you," said Zhang. "These two merchants are no strangers to you. Do you remember Gao Hanwen and his wife, Madame Yun?"

"Do you mean to say that Gao Hanwen and his wife are running a cotton cloth business in Nanjing?"

"Yes, Your Highness. After Gao lost his job and left Beijing, his family disowned him because he had married a former courtesan. Fortunately, Madame Yun had some savings. Since she stayed connected with some big businessmen in the textile trade in the cities of Hangzhou and Nanjing, she helped Gao Hanwen start a cotton cloth business. Gao had no luck in politics, but struck it rich by running cotton cloth mills. Within a period of four years, they had control over half of the cotton cloth business in Songjiang. At the moment, Princess Li is talking with Madame Yun in her room because she has a few questions about the couple's business."

The Prince of Yu's displeasure and suspicion dissipated. "How did you manage to find them?" he asked out of curiosity.

"Your Majesty, my brother is a cotton farmer in my hometown

of Songjiang," Grand Secretary Xu replied. "He's been running a cotton cloth business for years and has some dealings with Gao Hanwen. I have proposed to Your Highness a few times before that we expand cotton fields in the Songjiang area and increase the production of cotton cloth. This will be a practical solution to fixing our current dire fiscal straits. The Imperial Palace should designate one or two merchants to monopolise the business. In this way, we can stabilise the price and prevent the usual tax evasions. This line of business will enable us to generate at least five million taels of silver every year. Half of the profits will go to businesses and cotton farmers and the Ministry of Treasury will collect the other half. By doing this, the Imperial Government can increase our tax revenue by three million taels of silver a year. I personally think it is a feasible national policy to pursue. It'll benefit both our country and local cotton farmers."

The family connection made the Prince of Yu wary. "For business deals like these, it's better to keep family members out," he warned Grand Secretary Xu.

"Your Highness is absolutely right," Grand Secretary Xu answered. "I have discussed this issue with Zhang Juzheng. To avoid potential conflicts of interest, I have recommended Gao Hanwen and his wife, rather than my brother for this endeavour."

"There's one more thing I want to add," said Zhang. "I brought up this matter with Your Highness last year, but didn't offer you any details. In fact, Gao Hanwen was the one who proposed this idea in one of his letters."

The Prince of Yu fell silent. "I've just remembered something," he said suddenly. "In the fortieth year of Emperor Jiajing's reign, the Imperial Government under Yan Song rolled out the rice-to-mulberry land conversion policy in Zhejiang. Gao Hanwen put forward a strategy that he claimed would both subsidise flood victims and remedy the government fiscal freeze. It was an untested theory proposed by an insulated scholar with hardly any governance experience. His initiative caused political chaos in Zhejiang. We are not repeating the same error, are we?"

"Times have changed and the situation is now different," Zhang Juzheng reassured the Prince of Yu. "There was nothing wrong with Gao Hanwen's proposal. In those days, the Yan Clan was in power and they promoted the policy relentlessly in pursuit of personal gain. Their greed and corruption jeopardised its implementation. If the Imperial Palace takes direct control of the business and adopts proper measures to ensure that the treasury receives its fair share from the deal, this strategy should work."

The Prince of Yu turned to Grand Secretary Xu.

"In ancient times, the prominent legal scholar Shang Yang advised the ruler of Qin to promulgate a series of reform policies to strengthen the rule of law. The Kingdom of Qin flourished. If we have sound policies in place and if we count on reliable loyalists to enforce them, we can succeed."

"Bring them in, please," the Prince of Yu consented.

明

In ancient China, it was common for a man to grow a beard after the age of thirty as a sign of physical maturity, political power or prominent social status. Having traversed the country and entered the world of business for the past four years, Gao Hanwen had started to sport a long black beard. His thick, soft facial hair accentuated his scholarly demeanour. From a glance, one wouldn't associate him with a mercenary businessman. He looked handsome and distinguished. His eyes, which had witnessed the trials and tribulations of life, exuded confidence. Both the calculating and reticent Grand Secretary Xu, as well as the wise and shrewd Zhang Juzheng, were struck by Gao's sophistication and competence.

Gao sat on a chair against the north wall, next to Xu Fan, Secretary Xu's son. Grand Secretary Xu and Zhang sat near a south-facing window. They could hear and watch him talk. Gao's presence reinvigorated the Prince of Yu. He lowered himself into a chair by his desk and leaned forward on his elbow, listening intently.

"I just discussed the current annual output of cotton cloth, and the increased output will result after the new policy is implemented," Gao said, before moving on to his second topic. "Assuming we can increase cotton cloth production by five hundred thousand bolts a year during the next decade and distribute and sell them at various markets in the country, we can reap at least..."

"Have some tea first," the Prince of Yu suggested, looking impressed with Gao's presentation.

Gao rose from his chair and offered a palm-over-fist salute. Picking up his teacup from a small table next to him, he took a sip and resumed his briefing.

Two women huddled around a large bronze brazier inside the Prince of Yu's inner chamber. One was a princess and the other was a businesswoman, whose legendary life as a former courtesan, and whose association with Yang Jinshui and Shen Yishi, had made her a maligned figure among imperial officials both in Beijing and Zhejiang Province.

Both women were in their mid-twenties, beautiful and intelligent. Sitting together like sisters, they felt a unique connection.

"I was also born into a poor family," said Princess Li, trying to put Madame Yun at ease before they deepened their conversation. "I just have a few questions for you. Tell me truthfully. There's nothing to be worried or embarrassed about."

"Princess Li, please feel free to ask anything. I will answer to the best of my knowledge."

"That's good," Princess Li said with a broad smile. "You look so extraordinarily beautiful. You don't resemble someone who was raised in destitution. Why did your family send you to a brothel?"

Madame Yun lowered her head and became silent. "Princess Li, do you mind if I don't answer that question?"

"Why?"

"Princess, by sharing my family history with you, I'm afraid I might break a palace taboo."

Madame Yun's hesitation piqued Princess Li's curiosity. "There are no taboo topics here," Princess Li reassured her. "Don't worry. Tell me."

"My father used to be an imperial official. Like Gao Hanwen, he served as a researcher at Hanlin Academy in the thirty-first year of Emperor Jiajing's reign."

"What happened to him?"

"In the thirty-seventh year of Emperor Jiajing's reign, four senior officials from Zhejiang Province submitted a censure against Yan Song and called for his impeachment. Yan Song retaliated by throwing them into jail. My father, who was friends with all four of them, was implicated. He was also locked up and eventually died inside the Imperial Prison. The imperial agents ransacked our home and confiscated our assets. My mother and I moved in with my uncle. Six months later, my mother died from grief. To distance himself from my family's political trouble, my uncle, with the help of his wife, sold me to a brothel in Nanjing."

Princess Li stood up from her chair and gazed at Madame Yun with sympathy and respect. "I didn't know you were the daughter of a loyal and upright imperial official," she said, handing her handkerchief to Madame Yun, who started to weep.

"I'm sorry for the tears." Madame Yun stood up and took the handkerchief from Princess Li with both hands. She patted her eyes.

"Please sit down," Princess Li said. The revelation brought the two women closer. Princess Li dropped all formalities and held Madame Yun's hands. Sizing up the elegant young woman in front of her, she continued: "I now understand why a young man like Gao Hanwen, who grew up in a family of scholar bureaucrats and who passed the highest levels of the imperial exams, would turn his back on his parents and his career to marry you."

Madame Yun held back her tears. Princess Li's words were meant as a compliment, but little did she know that she had touched a sore spot with Madame Yun. It was also an issue that caused Madame Yun much concern.

"Princess, I have a request," Madame Yun pleaded as she dropped down on her knees and started crying. "I need your help and advice."

"Tell me what it is. I will help if I can. Please rise and sit on your chair."

Madame Yun remained kneeling. "Princess, my husband is my

only family in this world. I hold him very close to my heart. He came from a prestigious family and has a brilliant mind. Because of me, he lost his job and his family rejected him. I feel greatly indebted to him. Since I cherish him, I'm very worried about what he intends to do. He's here to propose a business plan, which he believes can enrich the Imperial Palace. I know his ultimate goal is to gain honour for his family so they'll accept him and welcome him back to his ancestral home."

"There's no need for you to plead with me," Princess Li said. "We invited him here because the Imperial Palace truly needs his help."

"Princess, that's not what I meant. Actually, what I want is just the opposite. I wonder if you could persuade the Prince of Yu to give the cotton cloth contract to someone else. Doing business with the Imperial Palace and the Imperial Government is more perilous than sailing in turbulent seas. The waves are more treacherous. My husband does not have the ability to navigate this boat and reach shore. Princess Li, I beseech you to choose someone else. I just want to go home with him and continue with our peaceful life. We cannot afford another setback."

Princess Li was stunned by Madame Yun's frank admission. As Madame Yun kowtowed to her, the princess helped her guest to her feet and asked: "What makes you think your husband lacks the ability to accomplish this task?"

Emboldened by the princess's encouraging look, Madame Yun disclosed another of her secrets: "Do you remember the blood scripture I brought to you four years ago?"

Since Grand Master Zhang's relic was deemed a politically sensitive topic, Princess Li chose not to respond. She simply stared at Madame Yun.

"When we first met, I felt as if I had known you all my life. I regarded you as a family member. That's why I don't want to hide anything from you. Before I married Gao Hanwen, I was owned by the biggest silk merchant in Nanjing and Hangzhou. That person was Shen Yishi, who had a contractual business with the South China Textile Bureau. Shen Yishi bequeathed me Grand Master Zhang's blood scripture before he died."

Prince Li's expression changed from a cheerful smile to a solemn frown. She listened attentively.

"Shen Yishi was a shrewd man who had manoeuvred himself into the confidence of high-ranking officials such as Yang Gonggong and Zheng Bichang. In terms of political savvy and political connections, my husband is no match for Shen Yishi. He doesn't even have one tenth of Shen Yishi's political acumen. But look at what happened to Shen Yishi. He set himself on fire and committed suicide. All of the assets he had accumulated were instantly burned to ashes. Just imagine what would happen to my husband and me if we started to follow Shen Yishi's path and operated the cotton cloth business for the Imperial Palace. Do you think my husband would fare better than Shen Yishi? I doubt it. He doesn't have Shen's business skills. Neither does he possess his shrewdness and ruthlessness. He's a mere scholar, someone who possesses lofty aspirations but has no idea how high the sky is. He is just not aware of his limitations. Apart from me, nobody knows that he's digging a hole for himself. If we don't stop him, he would not only imperil himself, but also the interests of the Imperial Palace. I'm baring my heart to you. I hope you understand my concern and grant my wish."

Princess Li looked at Madame Yun's imploring eyes and did not know how to respond. She thought for a moment before finding the right words: "I understand your situation, but I'm not sure if your concerns are warranted."

The light in Madame Yun's eyes dimmed.

"Times have changed and the circumstances are completely different now," continued Princess Li. "In the old days, members of the Yan Clan looted our national coffers and brutally persecuted those who spoke against them. Given the atrocious crimes they committed, it doesn't surprise me that they came to a bad end. So you cannot really compare Gao Hanwen to the mercenary Shen Yishi. Your husband was a talented scholar official. Even though he's running a business now, his heart lies with the Imperial Court. If he's dedicated to our country, his loyalty will be rewarded. I just can't see the rationale for your fear."

The remarks were gracious and Princess Li delivered them

eloquently, but Madame Yun remained unconvinced. She did not argue back. Deep down, she was disappointed.

Having laid out the bigger picture, Princess Li smiled and softened her tone: "In the fortieth year of Emperor Jiajing's reign, you played a crucial role in our fight against the Yan Clan. When you visited me that night to present Grand Master Zhang's blood scriptures, you left me with a deep impression. Now, I'm delighted that you treat me as your confidante. I'm also very touched by Gao Hanwen's ardent devotion to the prince. I understand your concerns, but you can be assured that His Highness and I will look after you and your husband. His Highness is the Crown Prince and one day he will govern the Great Ming Empire. Let's all work hard together. In a few years, when the Imperial Palace has weathered this financial crisis, I will request that the palace reinstitute Gao Hanwen to his position at Hanlin Academy and honour you with the title 'Virtuous Wife'. When you two visit the Gao family, you'll be officially installed as Gao Hanwen's wife. Nobody would dare rebuff you."

Despite her political prudence, Madame Yun found it difficult to resist the offer, especially from a woman who was the Crown Prince's concubine. Her eyes slowly brightened as if she had already seen the rosy picture of her future promised by Princess Li.

Princess Li held Madame Yun's hands again and lowered her voice: "At the beginning of our conversation, I mentioned that I might need your help with something," she said. "I hope you can grant me this favour."

"Please let me know how I can be of any help."

Princess Li let out a soft sigh. "Like I told you, I came from a poor family. The Imperial Palace has very strict rules governing the families of His Majesty or the Prince of Yu's concubines. Even though our parents are granted knighthoods, they can neither get a position within the Imperial Government nor can they run a business. As a consequence, many of the concubines' families live in abject poverty."

"I understand. If your family runs into financial difficulties, I'll respectfully send some cash tomorrow. That's not a problem at all."

"Who do you think I am?" Princess Li chastised Madame Yun. "That's not what I meant."

Madame Yun looked baffled. She quickly bowed to apologise. "Please do not take offence at my offer," she said.

"You're well intentioned and I didn't mean to blame you," Princess Li said with an awkward smile. "I have a younger brother. His Majesty granted him a cavalry captain's title, but he is not allowed to hold a position within the Imperial Palace here. I'm thinking of sending him to Nanjing, where he can take a part-time job as a tax collector. If you and your husband decide to run the cotton cloth business in Songjiang for the Imperial Palace, you can probably hire my little brother as a partner. This would give him some business experience. At the same time, if you run into any issues, he can write to me directly and I'll find a way to assist you from here."

With a visible look of relief, Madame Yun sprang to her feet. "Princess Li, this is by no means a favour," she said. "We are very fortunate to have you as our guardian. If you intend your brother to join us in the south, we'll surely take good care of him, regardless of how long he wants to stay."

Princess Li smiled. "I hope you will never again question your husband's ability to navigate the choppy seas."

Madame Yun forced a smile. Somehow, Princess Li's reference to 'choppy seas' still gave her the chills.

※

Emperor Jiajing's refusal to move to his new palace the night before caused quite a stir in Beijing. Inside Yuxi Palace, Huang Jin, who was on duty that night, hardly slept. After begging and cajoling on his knees, he managed to persuade the emperor to retire to bed. Worried that the emperor's wrath could harm his constitution, making him susceptible to a cold, Huang pulled out a quilt and covered the emperor with it. But a few minutes later, Emperor Jiajing threw off the quilt. Huang picked up the quilt from the floor and handed it back to him. Fortunately, nothing that Huang Jin did ever enraged Emperor Jiajing. After a few back and forths of quilt tossing, Huang prevailed. Tucking in his master, Huang added a few pieces of agarwood to the burner. Vigorously, he blew onto the fire to keep the flames burning. The meditation room quickly warmed up.

At dawn, Huang cooked the herbs in a medicine pot before Chen Hong began his shift. Pouring the broth into a bowl, he brought it over to Emperor Jiajing. "Your Majesty, it's time to take your medicine."

"From today on, I'm going to stop," Emperor Jiajing said with his back towards Huang.

Carrying the bowl with both hands, Huang dropped down on his knees. "Master, I know you are troubled by the unruly behaviour of some imperial officials, but like the saying goes, don't cut off your nose to spite your face. In no way should you refuse medicine and let your health suffer. Once you survive this forty-nine day period, Your Majesty will be invincible and able to do anything you want to those people."

Emperor Jiajing stirred but he didn't turn around. "Lu Fang," he suddenly shouted.

Huang blinked twice to make sure that he wasn't mistaken by what he had heard. "Master, Lu Fang is in Nanjing," he replied.

Emperor Jiajing paused for a few seconds. Even though he realised that he had made a slip of the tongue, he refused to admit it. "If I call you Lu Fang, you just go along with it," he said. "Don't try to mess around with me."

"Yes, master. Your humble servant Lu Fang is here," Huang said.

"Do you think all the congratulatory letters will be delivered here before daybreak?"

"Your Majesty, I'm sure they'll be here."

Emperor Jiajing fell silent momentarily. "I guess so," he sighed. "They agreed to write the letters because the Prince of Yu told them. My son is more popular than I am. Lu Fang, you are in frequent contact with the Prince of Yu, aren't you?"

Huang felt like crying, but controlled his emotion. "Master, all of your servants have broken roots," he said. "The Imperial Palace is our home and we devote our lives to serving you. Since father and son are one, we pledge loyalty both to you and your son. There's nothing wrong with being in frequent contact with the Prince of Yu."

Emperor Jiajing responded with a wry grin. "You are not Lu Fang after all," he said, sitting up to face Huang Jin. "Lu Fang would never be so blunt. All right, you simpleton, I'll drink the broth."

"Long live my master," Huang said, handing the bowl to Emperor Jiajing.

The emperor gulped it down. Huang handed him another bowl of lukewarm water. Emperor Jiajing took a sip, swirled it around his mouth and spat it out into the bowl. Then, he wiped his mouth with the warm towel that Huang offered him.

"What time is it?" the emperor asked.

"Your Majesty, it's almost five-o'clock. Chen Hong will be here shortly with Grand Secretary Xu. They'll have all the congratulatory letters."

"Put away the medicine pot. Open a window to get rid of the foul smell of medicine."

"But master, you should put on a coat first," said Huang, handing him a thick cotton coat before hiding the medicine pot inside a cabinet in an inconspicuous corner. Then he put a lock on the cabinet and walked over to open the window.

A blast of wind made Huang shiver. "It's so cold," he mumbled. "I need to get you the fur coat."

Emperor Jiajing was shivering with cold as well. He clutched his coat tight around him.

"Master, your humble servant Chen Hong has arrived," Chen Hong could be heard saying outside in the main hall. He was fifteen minutes early.

Emperor Jiajing frowned.

"He's always so secretive," Huang couldn't help complaining as he rushed around to close the window and adjust the agarwood in the furnace to heat up the room. Emperor Jiajing removed his fur cloak and tossed it to Huang, who folded it and put it away. With Huang's assistance, Emperor Jiajing slipped on his shoes and ambled over to his prayer mat. When he tried to take off his cotton coat, Huang stopped him.

"You should keep this on," he said.

"No," Emperor Jiajing insisted.

With a sigh of resignation, Huang placed the cotton coat next to his cabinet.

Seeing that Emperor Jiajing was only wearing his silk gown, Huang moved the bronze burner close to the prayer mat.

"Master, your humble servant Chen Hong has arrived," Chen Hong's voice sounded again.

"Open the door for him," ordered Emperor Jiajing, who closed his eyes and started his meditation.

Huang brought a small bundle of agarwood and added it the furnace. When the agarwood sticks started burning, he dropped to his knees and kowtowed to the emperor. "Master, I'm off now," he said.

Chen Hong had been waiting anxiously outside Yuxi Palace. When Huang pulled the latch from the inside, Chen Hong pushed the heavy wooden gate so abruptly that it almost knocked Huang to the floor.

Incensed, Huang was tempted to punch his arch-rival, but when he saw a large pile of congratulatory letters in Chen Hong's arms, his anger dissolved. "Do you have everyone's letter here?" he asked earnestly.

"Of course," said Chen Hong, who appeared eager to go in and claim credit. "That's why I'm here early."

"Where is Grand Secretary Xu," asked Huang, who poked his head through the gate.

"It's none of your business," Chen Hong said dismissively as he crossed the threshold. "Just get out of here. And don't forget to close the palace door."

Huang walked out, sulking.

"What a nosy nuisance," Chen Hong mumbled to himself as he walked towards the meditation room. He held the pile of congratulatory letters cautiously as if he had been bearing the Great Ming Empire in his arms.

Inside the meditation room, Chen Hong laid the letters neatly on the emperor's desk. Then he retrieved a bronze kettle from inside the agarwood burner, poured some warm water into a gold basin, rinsed a face towel in the water and walked over to Emperor Jiajing.

"Master, the congratulatory letters have poured in overnight," he reported with a broad smile. "But first, let me cleanse your face."

Chen Hong spread the towel and gently patted the emperor's face.

"Where is Grand Secretary Xu?" Emperor Jiajing asked with his eyes closed.

"Your Majesty, I didn't invite Grand Secretary Xu to come in," Chen Hong said in a lowered voice even though there was no one else around. "I told him to wait in the Privy Council's duty room because I have something to report to you first."

"What is it?" asked Emperor Jiajing, opening his eyes and looking alert.

"Last night, all the Privy Council members accompanied the Prince of Yu to the Imperial Hospital. I was told that all of the rabble-rousers cried after the Prince of Yu delivered his remarks."

"Is that it?"

"There is something else I want to tell you, something quite odd. Late last night, Grand Secretary Xu and Zhang Juzheng congregated at the Prince of Yu's mansion and met with two mysterious out-of-towners."

"Any more details?"

"Your Majesty, do you know who they are? One is Gao Hanwen and the other his wife, a former courtesan. She used to be the mistress of both Shen Yishi and Yang Jinshui."

"Do you know why they brought them to see the Prince of Yu?"

"I have sent someone to look into it," Chen Hong said.

Emperor Jiajing cast him a dubious glance. "Well, take your time on the investigation then," he said.

"Your Majesty, I will get to the bottom of it. I cannot allow those people to involve the Prince of Yu in some shady deals or scandals. They could sully his reputation."

"That is so considerate of you," Emperor Jiajing said with a hint of sarcasm.

"Master, it is my duty to keep a close eye on things to safeguard the interests of Your Majesty and the Great Ming Empire."

"It's good to be vigilant and thoughtful. But now, I want you to run an errand for me."

"Yes, master."

"I want you to pay a call on Master Lan at Chaotian Temple. Ask him to release Feng Bao and send him back to the Prince of Yu's mansion. Reinstate him in his previous position as my grandson's caretaker."

"But master…" Chen Hong stammered. He could not believe his ears.

"I want you to go there now," ordered Emperor Jiajing before closing his eyes again.

"Yes, Your Majesty," Chen Hong replied, looking mortified. On exiting, he felt a little hazy, as if he was stepping on a floor of cotton.

Having spent the better part of the night speaking with protesters at the Imperial Hospital and meeting with Gao Hanwen and his wife, the Prince of Yu didn't retire to bed until dawn. Since he was still recovering from his illness, he felt both physically and emotionally drained. At daybreak, his aide sent word out that the Prince of Yu needed to rest through the morning and that noise should be kept to a minimum. Except for messengers from Yuxi Palace, nobody should disturb the Prince of Yu until after noon.

It was about seven o'clock in the morning. Several maids who had risen early to do chores tiptoed around in the front yard, and gesticulated at each other when they needed help. The eunuchs who were sweeping snow didn't dare use shovels and brooms. Instead, they squatted down on the ground and scraped the snow onto a stone path with their bare hands.

The sudden sound of firecrackers outside the mansion startled the maids and eunuchs in the front yard. The Prince of Yu's aide ran out of the backyard. "What's happening?" he asked. "Didn't I tell you that His Royal Highness is resting? Who is lighting firecrackers outside?"

Before he had even finished, a guard darted into the courtyard.

"A messenger has arrived with an imperial edict. Open the middle gate!"

The aide composed himself and shouted: "Open the middle gate to receive the imperial edict."

Several junior eunuchs hurried over to the main gate. They removed two wooden door bars and pulled the heavy gate open.

Chen Hong and several palace eunuchs appeared.

The Prince of Yu's aide and several eunuchs dropped down on their knees. "Chen Gonggong, greetings!" shouted the aide.

"Please rise," Chen Hong said, beaming. "Please report to the Prince of Yu, Princess Li and the young prince. I have brought good news for them. Feng Bao is back."

The eunuchs at the Prince of Yu's mansion raised their heads and saw Feng Bao standing behind Chen Hong. He was wearing a new robe.

The aide, who was shocked at first and then pleasantly surprised, quickly invited Chen Hong into the front yard. "Let me go to the inner chamber and notify His Royal Highness of your arrival," he said before bolting away.

Chen Hong held Feng Bao's arm and stepped in through the main gate. Several eunuchs followed them. The entourage now waited in the front yard.

Inside the Prince of Yu's inner chamber, two maids were busy putting the official robe on him. Princess Li rushed out of the bedroom with the young prince. Both the mother and son were fully dressed.

"You and the prince wait here," instructed the Prince of Yu. "I'll go and accept the edict."

The young prince began shouting: "I want to go. I want to see my daban."

"Stop it," the father castigated his son. "Stay here with your mother."

Terrified, the young prince pursed his lips and fell silent. Tears welled up in his eyes.

The Prince of Yu strode out.

"Be patient," Princess Li consoled her son. "Daban Feng will be here shortly."

From a distance, the Prince of Yu spotted Chen Hong and Feng Bao standing in the middle of the front yard. He quickened his step. As he approached them, the Prince of Yu fell to his knees.

"Your Highness," Chen Hong greeted the Prince of Yu and helped him to his feet. "There's no official imperial edict today. His Majesty simply asked me to send Feng Bao back to you. You don't need to kneel down."

After Chen Hong finished his report, he kowtowed to the Prince of Yu. Feng Bao and other eunuchs followed Chen Hong's example and kowtowed three times.

"Please rise," the Prince of Yu said.

Everyone got up, except Feng Bao.

"Thanks to His Majesty's benevolence and thoughtfulness, you're able to return to us," the Prince of Yu said to Feng Bao. "After you offer your thanks to Chen Gonggong, go inside. My son is waiting for you."

Feng Bao turned around and kowtowed to Chen Hong, who pulled him up from the ground. Holding Feng Bao's arm, Chen Hong said to the Prince of Yu: "The reason that His Majesty transferred Feng Bao to Chaotian Temple was to give Daban Feng the opportunity to accumulate some good karma and skills so he could better serve our young master. But when I went to fetch Feng Bao this morning, I learned that some bullies there had subjected him to all sorts of beatings. Your Highness, I sincerely apologise for my negligence. No evil deeds should go unpunished. So I have brought these bullies with me so they can seek your forgiveness. At the same time, please do not stop me when I punish them."

Chen Hong's remarks took the Prince of Yu by surprise. As he was struggling for a proper response, he heard Chen Hong howling at the three eunuchs who came with him, ordering them to kneel down in front of the Prince of Yu.

"Whip them hard," Chen Hong ordered. Obviously, Chen Hong had come fully prepared for this. Three imperial agents unfastened the long leather whips from their waists and began lashing violently at the eunuchs who were kneeling on the ground.

Feng Bao looked like a changed man. Casting his eyes downwards, he stood silently without making any attempt to halt the lashings.

The Prince of Yu knew that Chen Hong had orchestrated this theatrical performance to get him off the hook. He simply watched impassively. After a dozen lashings, he ordered Chen Hong to end the show.

The lashings stopped. Chen Hong urged the eunuchs to thank the Prince of Yu.

"Chen Gonggong, are you in a hurry?" the Prince of Yu asked with a contrived gentleness. "Feel free to come in and have some tea with us."

"Your Highness, I'm afraid I have to go back. Grand Secretary Xu is waiting for me to report to His Majesty about your visit to the Imperial Hospital last night. You did a great service to His Majesty."

"It's not worth mentioning," said the Prince of Yu. "Since Grand Secretary Xu is waiting for you, I won't keep you. You'd better hurry up then."

Chen Hong and his entourage dropped down to their knees and kowtowed to the Prince of Yu before they parted.

The Prince of Yu followed Chen Hong out with his eyes. Then, he turned to Feng Bao. His eyes were filled with sympathy. "Go in and see my son," he said. "He's waiting for you."

The Prince of Yu had hardly finished his sentence when he saw Princess Li appear with the young prince in her arms. "Daban, daban," the boy shouted excitedly.

Feng Bao fell to his knees.

A short while later, a eunuch put a brazier in Feng Bao's bedroom. Feng Bao had removed his shirt and was lying face down on his bed. His back looked badly bruised.

Princess Li, who stood at the bedside with her son, winced at the injuries. The boy started crying: "Daban, tell me who beat you like this. Tell me…"

Feng Bao moaned slightly. Princess Li suddenly seemed to remember something. "Where is Dr Li?" she asked a eunuch in the room. "Go and invite Dr Li to examine him."

"I will go and look for Dr Li right away," replied the eunuch.

明

It was a sunny day in mid-February. In northern China, there is a popular saying among farmers: on the seventy-ninth day after the winter solstice, the ice in lakes and rivers melts. On this day, the willow trees on both sides of the Tonghui River were starting to bud. Cargo and passenger boats, which had been docked here all winter, were getting ready to sail south.

The River and Canal Transportation Control Yamen published a packed departure schedule, which was based on a travel list approved by the Ministry of Defence. Priority was given to senior-ranking officials or ships conducting business for the Imperial Palace or the Imperial Government.

The ship that was scheduled to depart first waited at the dock. On the front mast hung a flag with three characters prominently embroidered on it: 'Ministry of Treasury'. The rear mast displayed the flag of the Ministry of Public Works.

On the pier, a large number of officers and soldiers lined up next to a flight of stone steps. Passengers on other ships and boats watched curiously as two carriages and several sedans pulled up near the dock. Zhang Juzheng stepped out of the first sedan; Xu Fan, the son of Grand Secretary Xu, emerged from the second. From their uniforms and the way they were greeted by the soldiers, onlookers knew they must be senior cabinet members.

The person who got out of the third sedan was Gao Hanwen. A young man dressed in military uniform jumped out of the first carriage. He went up to greet Zhang Juzheng, Xu Fan and Gao Hanwen. Together, the three men moved over to the second carriage and stood there reverentially.

Princess Li and Madame Yun sat inside the carriage.

"Take care of yourself," said Princess Li as she held Madame Yun's hands. "The Imperial Palace counts on you and your husband to bring in the much-needed funds. I hope the cotton cloth business will flourish under your care. When the day comes, I will fulfil my promise to you."

Madame Yun was about to kneel down and kowtow to her

inside the carriage, but Princess Li stopped her. She lifted a corner of the curtain and asked the coachman: "Is Li Qi here?"

"Sister, I'm here," the young man in military uniform replied; Li Qi was Princess Li's younger brother.

"As you can see, Madame Yun is like a younger sister to me," Princess Li told her brother. "You should also treat her like your elder sister. Mr Gao is a very distinguished scholar, and you should respect him like your mentor. I hope you can truly learn something from them, become successful and bring honour to our Li family."

"Sister, I'll follow your advice and do my utmost."

Princess Li turned to Madame Yun. "I've entrusted my little brother to your care," she said.

There were tears in Madame Yun's eyes. "Princess Li, thank you for your benevolence. I promise to look after him as if he were my brother. Besides, he is the future first uncle of the Great Ming Empire. How can I not fulfil my obligations to our country?"

"Now I can sleep better," Princess Li joked. "Since it is not proper for me to step out, I'll have to say goodbye here."

The tearful Madame Yun rose from her seat. Despite his royal status, Li Qi reached out his hands and held Madame Yun's arm when she stepped out. "Big Sister, be careful," he said humbly.

Madame Yun and Li Qi joined the rest of the group. They bowed to Princess Li.

"You can board the ship now," urged Princess Li, lifting a corner of the carriage curtain. "Have a safe trip."

Under the watchful eyes of many onlookers at the pier, the group headed for the ship. As they climbed the steps, the soldiers on both sides saluted them.

※

Under a willow tree on the opposite side of the pier stood two plainclothes eunuchs. One of them was the supervisor who had flogged Feng Bao at Chaotian Temple and then received a dozen lashes at the Prince of Yu's mansion. They watched Zhang Juzheng and Xu Fan, both of whom boarded the ship to bid farewell to Gao Hanwen, Madame Yun and Li Qi. Their attention then turned to the second carriage that was parked near the stone steps.

"Princess Li must be inside that carriage," said the supervisor. "Her brother has just boarded the ship. Let's go back and report this to Chen Gonggong."

By the time Zhang and Xu Fan left the ship and returned to the pier, the two eunuchs had crept away.

The ramp was stowed away, and the ship set sail. Propelled by a long pole, it slowly moved away from the bank.

When the carriages and sedans had left the pier, a navigation official ran up to another ship and shouted: "You're next!"

明

A small, unmarked passenger boat was moored discreetly in a quiet section of the dock. Dr Li Shizhen, Hai Rui, Amu and Mrs Hai were sitting quietly inside the cabin. Loud shouting from boatmen and the sound of oars hitting the water could be heard nearby.

"Brother Hai Rui, didn't you tell me you have a meeting at the Ministry of Treasury this morning?" said Dr Li, breaking the silence. "There's no need to keep us company while we wait for our turn. You don't want to be late for your meeting."

"Don't worry about us," said Amu. "Dr Li will look after me and your wife. We'll see you in Nanjing in two months."

"Let me stay here a little longer," said Hai Rui, choking up. Dr Li turned his head away and gazed outside. His eyes became moist.

He and Dr Li had concocted a lie that he would be transferred to Nanjing soon and persuaded the gullible Amu and his wife to leave Beijing.

"This is not the first time we have had to part," Amu consoled Hai Rui. "Since you agreed to serve in the Imperial Government, you have to get used to such frequent transfers. With Dr Li helping us, it'll be much easier this time. What's the matter with you today? You seem sad like a child."

Hai Rui feigned a smile. "Well, Amu is getting old and my wife is pregnant... I'm just a bit worried, that's all."

Amu became emotional. She turned to her daughter-in-law who

was sitting behind her: "See, my son truly cares about us. Come over here and say a few words to him."

"Don't stand up," Hai Rui said as he moved closer to his wife and held her hands. "Take care of yourself and our baby. You're a kind and virtuous woman. While looking after my mother is your filial obligation, protecting our child, the future of the Hai family, is an even bigger one. Always remember my parting words to you."

Mrs Hai grasped her husband's hands. "I won't let you down," she replied. "Now that you're here alone, mind your health. Amu and I will see you in Nanjing."

Dr Li wiped away his tears and turned around. "You should leave now," he urged Hai Rui. "The navigation official has given us the signal to set sail."

Worrying that his sentimentality could arouse Amu's suspicion, Hai Rui released his wife's hands, stepped over to his mother and fell to his knees. "Mother, please forgive me for not fulfilling my filial obligations," he said as he kowtowed to his mother three times.

Before Amu could respond, Hai Rui sprang to his feet and strode out.

For some unknown reason, Amu was struck with a feeling of apprehension.

"Hai Rui," she called.

Mrs Hai also began to feel anxious. She stepped over and helped Amu to her feet. By the time they reached the deck, Hai Rui had already disembarked.

"Please get in," said Dr Li. "We're departing now."

The boat swayed slightly and then started moving away. Amu and Mrs Hai entered the cabin and sat down.

Hai Rui climbed a flight of stairs and reached the top of the pier. Wiping his tears with his sleeve, he paused and turned around. Dr Li was standing on the bow, waving at him.

As the boat sailed south, Hai Rui bowed deeply to Dr Li in gratitude.

6

The clear evening sky was filled with stars. Inside the well-lit duty room of the Privy Council, all the ministerial officials were congregating again to prepare for Emperor Jiajing's rescheduled palace-moving ceremony.

On the right side of Grand Secretary Xu's desk sat piles of flattering poems and essays that senior imperial officials had composed for the occasion. On the left were congratulatory letters submitted by officials who earlier had staged a protest or happened to be out of town when the first botched ceremony took place.

"The imperial astronomer has chosen eleven o'clock this evening as an auspicious time for His Majesty's palace-moving ceremony. It's already nine o'clock. Please count all the congratulatory letters and poetic essays that your ministry has received. Make sure we are not missing any."

"Grand Secretary Xu, we have collected everyone's letter," officials in the room responded one by one.

Grand Secretary Xu spotted one person sitting quietly in a corner, and he asked him: "Zhao Zhenji, you haven't responded to my question. Is everything all right?"

"Grand Secretary, I'm still short one letter," Zhao admitted. "I have already sent someone to collect it."

"What's the problem?" asked Grand Secretary Xu, sounding troubled by the news. "Why is it taking so long? Whose letter is it?"

"Grand Secretary Xu, we are missing Hai Rui's letter. I have urged him multiple times, and he promised to turn it in before the deadline. But I still haven't seen it."

"You should go and collect the letter yourself. Do it now. We need to have everyone's letter, not a single one short. It is extremely important to get Hai Rui on board with this initiative."

"I'll go there now," Zhao said as he hurried out of the duty room.

"We don't have much time," Grand Secretary Xu reminded everyone in the room. "Let's go and wait outside Yuxi Palace."

明

Emperor Jiajing's second attempt to move to his new palace was set at eleven o'clock on 23 February 1566, a supposedly optimal time chosen by the imperial astronomer upon meticulous recalculation. Unlike the previous occasion, the weather cooperated perfectly. The unseasonably warm February had brought the wild geese back from the south. In the clear evening sky, bright stars twinkled. On the ground, one hundred and eight lanterns illuminated the square outside Yuxi Palace. The stars and the lanterns had created an auspicious atmosphere.

More important, cabinet members and senior imperial officials who attended the ceremony were in a celebratory mood – Gao Hanwen and a group of cotton cloth merchants had signed contracts with the Imperial Palace, and Grand Secretary Xu was able to use their advance deposits to cover the unpaid salaries of all imperial officials. As a result, nearly every official in Beijing, more than a thousand of them, had submitted their congratulatory messages to Emperor Jiajing. Grand Secretary Xu was waiting for Zhao Zhenji. Once his protégé returned with Hai Rui's letter, the preparation would be complete and the celebration could proceed as scheduled.

The setup for the ceremony looked the same as that for the previous one: Emperor Jiajing's majestic dragon sedan, which glittered in the glowing lantern lights, sat in front of the stone steps outside Yuxi Palace. Thirty-two carriers, all of whom were eunuchs at the Interior Ministry, genuflected around the sedan, waiting for Emperor Jiajing to come out and board.

On the left side of the dragon sedan gathered the abbot and a group of priests from Chaotian Temple. Each held a musical instrument or a prayer book. Another abbot and a group of priests from Xuandu Temple stood to the right of the sedan. Each of them also held a musical instrument or a prayer book.

Grand Secretary Xu and other ministerial officials were kneeling in the front row under the eaves of Yuxi Palace. Zhao was conspicuously absent. Other senior officials knelt outside on the stone steps and in the square. All eyes were directed towards the gate of Yuxi Palace.

As before, the main hall of Yuxi Palace was brightly lit. In the centre sat a gigantic copper kettle water clock. The silence amplified the sound of water dripping inside the kettle.

Over the past forty-nine days, Emperor Jiajing had secretly taken a daily dose of herbal broth that Dr Li Shizhen had prescribed. His health had improved dramatically. Besides, the congratulatory letters from imperial officials in Beijing had placated him. He felt buoyant and festive today. Donning a fragrant flower crown and wearing the robe embroidered with the text of *Tao Te Ching*, he sat on his prayer mat with a brand new chime on his lap. When the propitious moment arrived, he would ring the bronze bell and move back to Longevity Palace and the Palace of Eternal Longevity, where he intended to live out his remaining years.

Dressed in a bright red ceremonial robe, Huang Jin was also feeling elated. Like a night watchman sounding the hours throughout the night, he conducted the final countdown by fixing his eyes on a smaller bronze kettle water clock inside the meditation room. "Master, we still have three quarters of an hour," he said reassuringly as he adjusted the flower crown on the emperor's head. "There's no hurry."

"Who's in a hurry?" Emperor Jiajing responded in an unusually good-humoured tone. "Don't be such a nag."

In the main hall, Chen Hong stood out with his red ceremonial robe and a fragrant flower crown. Holding a pile of congratulatory letters and flattering essays that the Privy Council had just submitted, he marched into the meditation room.

"Your Majesty, all of the congratulatory letters and essays are here," he announced with an ingratiating smile.

"*All* of them?" Emperor Jiajing asked.

The question caught Chen Hong off guard. He replied hesitantly: "Nothing escapes my master's celestial eyes. We are missing one letter. I'm told that the person has been away on official business and just returned to Beijing today. He's composing it now. Zhao Zhenji has gone to this person's home to collect the letter. He should be back shortly."

Much to Chen Hong's relief, there was no sign of irritation on Emperor Jiajing's face. "I think I made the correct decision in promoting Zhan Zhenji," said the emperor. "He is proving to be quite competent at his job."

"Your Majesty, since the Prince of Yu has taken a lead on this, the ministerial officials have shown a lot of initiative."

"That's good to know," Emperor Jiajing said in a self-confident tone. In moments like this, the emperor tended to be attentive and finicky. One by one, he checked the names on the envelopes and commented on their calligraphy styles. Once finished, he stared at Chen Hong and asked: "You just told me that we are still missing one because an official just returned to Beijing today. Where did Hai Rui go?"

The mention of Hai Rui's name startled Chen Hong. "Master, I… I just received the briefing from Grand Secretary Xu. I don't really know much about this Hai Rui person. I… I had no idea we were missing his letter."

Emperor Jiajing cast a fierce glance at Chen Hong. "Weren't you the one who reported to me about Hai Rui's activity at Home of Six Necessities? How could you not know about him?"

Chen Hong dropped down on his knees and slapped himself hard on the face. "I apologise for my negligence. I'll go and look into this immediately. I'll make sure we receive Hai Rui's letter in time."

After Chen Hong scurried away, Emperor Jiajing closed his

eyes. The dripping water sound from the bronze kettle in the main hall echoed.

Grand Secretary Xu and his deputy Li Chunfang exchanged anxious glances with each other. Gao Gong, who was kneeling next to them, remained stony-faced.

Chen Hong glided out of the meditation room. Lifting his robe to cross the threshold of the palace gate, he approached Grand Secretary Xu. "Why are we still missing one letter?" he began. "Is Hai Rui aware of the deadline? What is Zhao Zhenji doing? How could he allow this to happen? If Hai Rui's letter doesn't get here in the next few minutes, you and I will be in for a 'big reward'."

Grand Secretary Xu shared Chen Hong's exasperation. Lowering his head, he did not respond.

"Chen Gonggong, you shouldn't talk to Grand Secretary Xu like this," Gao Gong said. "Zhao Zhenji left a while ago to collect the letter from Hai Rui."

Chen Hong stomped his feet in frustration. "I have no time to argue with you," he said to Gao Gong. "If the ceremony is delayed or cancelled because of Hai Rui, our careers and lives will be on the line. I hope you understand why I raised my voice to Grand Secretary Xu."

"He's here!" a eunuch at the far end of the courtyard announced in joy.

Chen Hong looked towards the courtyard.

With everyone staring at him, Zhao ran up the stone steps with Hai Rui's letter in his hand. As he was huffing and puffing, the crowd seemed to let out a collective sigh of relief.

"We're all ready," announced Chen Hong as he hurried into the meditation room with a broad grin and knelt in front of Emperor Jiajing. "Master, Hai Rui has submitted his congratulatory letter. Now the whole world is rejoicing at Your Majesty's palace-moving."

"Amitābha," chanted Huang Jin who was watching the water clock. "We still have ten minutes left."

Emperor Jiajing examined the envelope in his hand. Chen Hong rose from the floor, waiting for the emperor to hand the letter back to him so he could add it to the large pile of other letters on the desk.

Oddly, Emperor Jiajing held onto the letter. Tearing open the envelope, he pulled out a thick stack of papers and started skimming the pages.

The title on the first page, 'My Letter of Remonstrance on Governance', caught the emperor off guard. He felt as if a knife had been plunged into his eyes.

"'In my effort to rectify the conduct of this monarch, define the responsibilities of his courtiers, and bring peace and prosperity to the subjects of the Great Ming Empire, I hereby state my honest opinions on some important issues of the day,'" Emperor Jiajing read.

No one had seen this coming. Nobody had suspected that Hai Rui would have submitted what later generations would call the 'number-one remonstrance' in Chinese history. It was done in the guise of a congratulatory letter.

By the time Emperor Jiajing reached the third page, his face had turned blue and his eyes were bloodshot.

> Your Majesty, when you first ascended the throne, you were determined to make a difference and revive the Great Ming Empire, but it didn't take long for you to stray from your course and became distracted by religious quackery and other unproven theories. You put your energy and wisdom in the wrong place. Your Majesty was under the illusion that human immortality is physically possible and blindly pursued alchemy in the hope of prolonging your life. You have inherited an empire with a vast land rich in resources, but failed to use the resources to enrich your people. In fact, you pay no heed to their wellbeing.
>
> For more than two decades, you neglected imperial duties and refused to grant official audiences, choosing instead to relay your wishes through eunuchs. Your laxity has led to the disintegration of rules and corruption at all levels of government. You indulge in your Taoist pursuits and spend more time with alchemists than with your family. You ignore your own son and mistrust your courtiers. Often, you imprison and slaughter those who speak out

against you. As a consequence, corruption among officials continues unabated in the post-Yan Song era. We have lost our military dominance. Floods and droughts occur frequently, and ordinary people live in misery. Riots have broken out in all parts of the country, and they spread like wildfire.

Discontent and dissent, fuelled by Your Majesty's misbehaviour, have been brewing for years. At the onset of your reign, you displayed traits of irresponsible governance, but the situation has worsened in recent years. You have become unworthy of the throne. The heavy burdens of taxation and conscript labour have driven people out of their homes. The greed of local officials knows no bounds. Your Majesty's unrestrained spending on Taoist pursuits over the past ten years has created huge financial burdens and led to division in our country. It has reached the point when many commoners now associate Your Majesty's name, Jiajing 嘉靖 [peace and prosperity] with the homonym 家净 [an empty, looted house]…

Rather than tearing up Hai Rui's remonstrance, Emperor Jiajing gritted his teeth and managed to finish reading it. For years, he dreaded that history would be unkind to him. Hai Rui's censure seemed to confirm his deepest fear. During his reign, he had devoted himself to the practice of Taoism and held a firm belief that he had achieved the status of a Taoist deity. But now, this junior official at the Ministry of Treasury had knocked him off his pedestal. Hai Rui had written a harsh and unforgiving obituary while he was still alive!

Emperor Jiajing felt his head was exploding. Hai Rui's jarring words buzzed in his ears.

"Evil… vicious…" Emperor Jiajing howled and let out a torrent of curses.

The screams startled Chen Hong, making him jump.

Huang turned his head in fright and froze.

Grand Secretary Xu and other cabinet members looked dumbfounded when they heard Emperor Jiajing's shriek. Silence fell. Everyone waited for Chen Hong to brief them on what was happening inside, but the chief eunuch never stepped out. They stared into the cavernous hall with a sense of impending doom.

Inside the meditation room, Chen Hong and Huang Jin knelt in front of Emperor Jiajing whose hands trembled uncontrollably. There was a cruel glitter in his eyes.

"Master, what's the matter?" Huang asked, sobbing.

Emperor Jiajing ignored him. As he recovered from his rage, he flung Hai Rui's letter to the floor with so much force that Chen Hong thought the emperor was about to lose his balance. "Chen Hong," the emperor shouted.

"Ye... Yes, Your Majesty," Chen Hong replied in a quavering voice.

"I want you to... arrest this person right away. Don't let him run away."

Grand Secretary Xu and Deputy Li Chunfang, who had joined the Imperial Government at the beginning of Emperor Jiajing's reign, were no strangers to political turmoil. They had experienced the brutal crackdown during the Great Rite Controversy, the Renyin Plot when sixteen palace women attempted to assassinate Emperor Jiajing, the fall of Yan Song, and the subsequent executions of Yan Shifan and other prominent members of the Yan Clan. But nothing in their past had prepared them for this moment. Emperor Jiajing roared like a lion and sounded as hysterical as a madman.

For Gao Gong, Zhao Zhenji and other younger ministerial officials, whose familiarity with Emperor Jiajing was limited, it seemed as if Yuxi Palace was about to collapse.

"Chen Gonggong, come back!" Huang Jin's shrill cry could be heard inside the meditation room.

Chen Hong, who had just stepped across the threshold of the meditation room door, paused. Turning his head, he glared at Huang.

Emperor Jiajing, who was still seething, raised his eyes and stared daggers at Huang.

"Master, nothing is more important than your move today," Huang implored, lowering himself to the floor. "You shouldn't allow anyone to sabotage your move. If you refuse or delay the move again, it will create chaos in the country. Hai Rui is a mere junior official. He can't run away, I can assure you of that. Your humble servant entreats you to step out and start the ceremony."

Emperor Jiajing was too distracted to answer. He kept his eyes on Huang's face.

"How do you know that Hai Rui won't escape?" asked Chen Hong.

"I know it," Huang replied without looking at him. He raised his head and gazed at Emperor Jiajing. "Master, Hai Rui sent his family away to the south three days ago. After they left, he bought himself a coffin. He's obviously prepared to die fighting for his cause."

"So, you knew about this beforehand," Emperor Jiajing yelled with a murderous look. "Where did you obtain the information?"

"Master, this is clearly a premeditated action," Chen Hong shouted as he ran back into the meditation room and dropped to his knees. "He did not act alone. Someone else is behind this."

Before Huang had a chance to respond, Chen Hong bellowed: "Answer His Majesty! Hai Rui does not work for the Interior Ministry. He's employed by the Ministry of Treasury. How did you gain such intimate knowledge of Hai Rui's activities there? If you were made aware of Hai Rui's plot, why didn't you report it to His Majesty?"

Chen Hong's words sobered up Emperor Jiajing. Taking a deep breath, he murmured to himself: "It is a premeditated action. Who's behind this? I'm going to ferret out the traitors..."

Huang watched in horror as Emperor Jiajing paused. Flashing a menacing smile, he turned to Huang and asked gently: "Tell me, who instigated Hai Rui to write this? It's not too late to be honest..."

Emperor Jiajing's gentle tone spooked Huang. Stretching his neck, the first deputy interior minister carried his head high and replied firmly: "Master, as far as I know, no one forced Hai Rui to submit this remonstrance."

"I won't investigate and hold you culpable for what's happened," the emperor persisted. "It's not worth covering up for anyone. Tell me!"

"Your humble servant is not covering up for anyone. Master, you can launch an investigation if you want. I'm not afraid because

I have nothing to hide from you. All I know is, he has sent away his family members and bought a coffin. I didn't find out about his letter until today. Now I know why he prepared the coffin."

"If he told you beforehand that he would send his family away and purchase a coffin, why did he keep you in the dark about his remonstrance?" Chen Hong howled at Huang Jin. "Answer me!"

"Hai Rui didn't tell me anything," said Huang, who had succeeded Chen Hong as the first deputy interior minister, reminding Emperor Jiajing that the Imperial Investigative Agency and the Imperial Prison now fell under his control. "As I was reviewing my daily surveillance briefing three days ago, I came across an item about Hai Rui buying a coffin. I didn't think much of it. I was stupid and assumed that Hai Rui might have been suffering from a serious illness and planned his funeral ahead of time. Never did I think he was preparing for this stupid act today. This is a negligence of duty on my part, and I claim full responsibility for it. Your Majesty, I wouldn't even appeal if you decide to slice me into pieces. I deserve whatever punishment you grant. But you can't let a stupid person like Hai Rui delay your move and harm your constitution. The people of our country are waiting for this moment..."

Since the palace gate and several lattice windows in the meditation room were wide open, the senior imperial officials who were kneeling on the stone steps outside could hear everything inside. When Huang thumped his head loudly on the brick floor, the ministers were deeply moved by the eunuch's loyalty and courage. There still seemed to be a glimmer of hope that Emperor Jiajing could acquiesce to Huang's plea and continue with the ceremony. They waited expectantly.

Inside the meditation room, Emperor Jiajing looked upwards and Huang Jin could only see the whites of his eyes. "I'm sure that my subjects have been waiting for this moment for years," he uttered sarcastically. "They've been waiting for people like Hai Rui to step out and force me to abdicate. Officials at the top are colluding with those at the bottom, and people inside the palace are conspiring against me with my enemies outside."

By now, the terror felt by Grand Secretary Xu and other cabinet members was turning into panic. It was more so for Zhao Zhenji. As treasury minister, he was Hai Rui's superior. If the emperor was of the belief that Hai Rui's remonstrance was part of a premeditated plot to force him to abdicate, he would be the first to be investigated. There was no doubt about that. With a gloomy expression, he knelt with both of his hands on the ground to prevent himself from collapsing.

Inside the meditation room, the emperor's remarks about forced abdication appalled Huang Jin. He lifted his head and froze.

Chen Hong glowered at him.

"What did Lu Fang instruct you before he left?" Emperor Jiajing asked Huang. "Did he tell you to plot this with anyone outside the palace? Who was the mastermind? Tell me truthfully, and I'll absolve you of guilt."

Nonplussed by such a preposterous question, Huang did not respond.

"Answer! Answer!" Chen Hong screamed.

Emperor Jiajing's words flew out the windows and struck fear in the panicked officials kneeling outside. It was a moment of despair. Grand Secretary Xu and his cabinet members felt as if they had been pushed onto a cliff's edge with a bottomless abyss below. The realisation that they had no means of retreat actually took the edge off their fear and emboldened them to act. Gao Gong was the first to rise from the ground. Others followed his example. Grand Secretary Xu was the last to stand up. He exchanged glances with each one of his colleagues. Their eyes spoke louder than their words. Grand Secretary Xu knew that his ministers were willing to risk their lives and defend themselves against the emperor's accusations. They wanted him to step up and handle this catastrophe.

彡

A suspicious man by nature, Emperor Jiajing had had a premonition years ago when he first heard about Hai Rui that the magistrate of Chun'an would be his nemesis and that their stars would collide one day. But never would he have expected Hai Rui to denounce him today, in front of several hundred imperial officials who had congregated to celebrate his move to the new palaces. Moreover, Hai Rui had shredded all of the things that Emperor Jiajing considered to be the major achievements of his reign. This brazen act left the emperor angry and incredulous. The first thought that came to mind was that Hai Rui had not acted alone. It was a premeditated, collective attempt to overthrow him. He suspected that Lu Fang, members of the Privy Council and the Prince of Yu were conspiring against him. A political crisis that might threaten the very foundation of the Great Ming Empire was unfolding.

As head of the Privy Council, Grand Secretary Xu felt he could no longer allow the crisis to deteriorate without intervention. With his hands clasped before his chest, he began to pace the room. His colleagues' eyes showed their worry and fear. He nodded at them, silently urging them to control their emotions. Then, turning around, he lifted his robe and crossed the threshold of the palace gate.

Suddenly, Zhao Zhenji stood up and ran after Grand Secretary Xu. He caught up with his teacher and blocked him from entering the meditation room.

"Your Majesty, Zhao Zhenji, the treasury minister, kindly requests an audience with you," he announced as they stood outside the meditation room.

Zhao's action took everyone by surprise. Grand Secretary Xu stared at him. Zhao saluted his teacher silently with a deep bow.

"All right, we finally have someone who is willing to step forward and claim responsibility for this," Emperor Jiajing said to Chen Hong. "Show him in."

"Yes, Your Majesty," Chen Hong replied and ran towards the door. "Zhao Zhenji, you can come in," he shouted.

Zhao walked to the meditation room door and dropped to his knees.

"Ah, the fourth member of the Privy Council," Emperor Jiajing remarked as he glanced at Zhao. "I always believed that the Privy Council needed someone like you, whose middle name means loyalty. I hope I was right about you. Come in and tell me what I need to know."

Zhao kowtowed at the door and stepped in. He knelt on a spot three feet away from Emperor Jiajing.

"Speak," ordered the emperor.

"Your Majesty, may I be so bold as to request that you share with me Hai Rui's congratulatory letter?"

The tenderness in the emperor's gaze vanished and his face hardened. "Congratulatory letter?" Emperor Jiajing scoffed, his tone sounding like a chilly blast of wind coming from a deep cave. "I'm appalled that you still characterise Hai Rui's remonstrance as a congratulatory letter!"

In his short tenure at the Ministry of Treasury, Zhao had never witnessed such ruthlessness in Emperor Jiajing's eyes and voice. But then, he remembered what had prompted him to come in and confront the emperor: if he stared into the face of death, death would blink first. He knew he was gambling with his life. What other choice did he have? Fear deserted him. Gritting his teeth, Zhao glanced at the papers scattered on the floor near Emperor Jiajing's feet and stated loudly: "Your Majesty, may I kindly request that you show me Hai Rui's remonstrance?"

Emperor Jiajing always prided himself on vanquishing demons and devils with the sheer force of his piercing gaze and his powerful voice. Zhao's defiance took him by surprise. As he looked at Zhao, his face softened. "Do you mean to say that you had no prior knowledge of what Hai Rui has written?" he asked.

"Your Majesty, I honestly did not know."

Emperor Jiajing peered at Chen Hong with the suggestion of a knowing smile. "See how shrewd they are? He's quick to clear himself of this. I know he's playing games with me," he said.

Zhao lowered his head.

"Have you heard the saying: 'While the demon climbs a post, the Taoist priest climbs ten'?" Emperor Jiajing continued. "Good will always conquer evil."

"Your Majesty, please forgive my ignorance. I don't know what you mean by that. Could you elucidate?"

"Very well, let me explain. Aren't you in charge of the Ministry of Treasury? Where does Hai Rui work?"

"Your Majesty, Hai Rui is an auditor at the Ministry of Treasury."

"And who brought Hai Rui's letter over here?"

"Your Majesty, I personally went to Hai Rui's home an hour ago and he handed me the letter."

"Who sent you over to Hai Rui's house to pick up his remonstrance?"

Emperor Jiajing's question stumped Zhao. He didn't answer immediately.

"Are you deaf and mute, or are you just afraid to reveal the person who issued you the secret order?"

"Your Majesty, Grand Secretary Xu told me to fetch the congratulatory letter while we were gathering at the Privy Council's duty room. He made the request in front of everyone there."

"You still call Hai Rui's report a congratulatory letter?" Emperor Jiajing said with a look of annoyance. "You're stubborn, aren't you?"

Chen Hong felt obligated to chime in. "Zhao Zhenji, a true hero or a brave man shouldn't be afraid of claiming responsibility. Even a junior official like Hai Rui is gutsy enough to prepare a coffin for himself. You're his superior, but you are nowhere near his equal."

Zhao shot a defiant glance at Chen Hong.

Emperor Jiajing watched as his chief eunuch snarled at the minister of treasury. The battle was on and there was no way to avoid it. The thought energised him. Suppressing his anger, the emperor asked coldly: "Zhao Zhenji, why don't you answer Chen Hong's question?"

Zhao turned to Emperor Jiajing. "Your Majesty, Chen Gonggong's question doesn't merit a response because it borders on blasphemy," he stated calmly.

Chen Hong almost jumped up, and said: "Master, it's obvious that Zhao Zhenji is the one who instigated Hai Rui to submit the remonstrance. As for who is behind Zhao Zhenji, leave that to me to find out. I have ways to make him speak."

Chen Hong was threatening to imprison Zhao Zhenji. If Emperor Jiajing nodded his approval, Zhao would be taken away.

Outside the palace, the imperial officials listened intently to the conversation inside. Many closed their eyes in despair.

Inside the meditation room, Chen Hong waited anxiously for Emperor Jiajing to issue an arrest order, but the emperor seemed in no hurry. Silently, he stared at Zhao who was lying prostrate on the floor, motionless.

"Don't you want to know why Zhao Zhenji accuses you of being blasphemous?" Emperor Jiajing asked Chen Hong with a sly smile.

"Master, ye... yes."

"Tell him!" Emperor Jiajing ordered Zhao.

"Yes, Your Majesty," Zhao said, raising his head. "Hai Rui is my subordinate at the Ministry of Treasury. He deceived, insulted and discredited Your Majesty. As his superior, I should be held culpable and I admit my crime. At the same time, I was the one who personally brought Hai Rui's letter to Your Majesty. The presenter of the remonstrance is equally guilty as its author. So, I take that as my second crime. These two crimes alone are sufficient to convict me of treason. It no longer matters whether I knew in advance or not. Since Hai Rui has prepared his coffin and is willing to accept his punishment, I will do the same. Now, let me answer Chen Gonggong's question. If Hai Rui acted out of malice and his remonstrance is considered treasonous, why did Chen Gonggong call him a hero and a brave man? If Hai Rui is regarded as a villain, I'm supposed to be his accomplice. Why did Chen Gonggong call me a hero and a brave man? That's the reason I called Chen Gonggong's remarks blasphemous. Therefore, I hereby request that Chen Gonggong take back his words."

Huang Jin, who was still lying flat on the floor, raised his head and glanced at Zhao with undisguised respect.

Emperor Jiajing caught sight of Huang's reaction and said: "Is that a look of admiration? Deep down, you truly think Hai Rui is a hero, don't you?"

Huang simply kowtowed to Emperor Jiajing without speaking.

Emperor Jiajing came to Chen Hong's defence. "You're truly insightful," he said to Chen Hong. "Hai Rui is a hero. Zhao Zhenji is also a hero. You're right about them. Absolutely right! Absolutely right!"

Emperor Jiajing's remarks disheartened Zhao. He knelt there, trying hard to control his emotions.

"All my life, I have admired heroes and have great respect for brave men," shouted Emperor Jiajing. "Tell your so-called mentors, supporters or cohorts... if they are heroes or brave men, they should step forward. You know how much I respect them."

"Your Majesty, I'm not a hero. Neither do I have any cohorts," Zhao countered, knowing that his life and the lives of many of his colleagues were at stake. "I passed the imperial examination in the twenty-first year of your reign. I considered myself a disciple of the Son of Heaven. If I had a mentor, it was Your Majesty. In the twenty-fourth year of your reign, I was hired as a researcher at Hanlin Academy. Subsequently, I became an imperial lecturer, an imperial inspector of Zhejiang Province and then minister of treasury. Two months ago, I joined the Privy Council. It was Your Majesty who personally promoted me. If I had a backer, it was Your Majesty. If I had a cohort, I am Your Majesty's cohort. Confucius advises us that a ruler could lose his ministers for his indiscreet and inappropriate language. What Your Majesty just stated is not the proper way a ruler should talk about his minister. I kindly entreat Your Majesty to retract your previous statement."

The cavernous main hall reverberated with Zhao's eloquent response.

Emperor Jiajing was struck with the dreaded feeling that he was going mad. What is the matter with me? he asked himself as he sat on his prayer mat, staring at the glowing lanterns outside the windows.

Meanwhile, the senior officials who were waiting on the stone steps outside Yuxi Palace stood in awe of Zhao's courageous response. There were flickers of excitement in their eyes. Even Gao Gong, who had never held Zhao in high esteem, found his remarks inspiring. He looked at Grand Secretary Xu and was prepared to step inside if needed.

Grand Secretary Xu teared up. Concerns about his protégé's safety enervated him. His legs suddenly gave out. As he was about to fall, Gao Gong stepped forward and held him up. Grand Secretary Xu pushed Gao Gong's hands away and dropped down on his knees. Other officials did the same. As they listened carefully, trying to capture the interrogations inside the meditation room, they were still hopeful that Zhao would be able to convince Emperor Jiajing of his innocence and remedy the situation.

Inside the meditation room, Emperor Jiajing shifted his gaze back to Chen Hong. Never had he felt so isolated and helpless.

"Chen Hong, Zhao Zhenji requested you take back your words. He also asked me to retract my statement. Will you do it?"

"Your Majesty, I will never take back what I stated. What happened today is unheard of in the history of our Great Ming Empire. Zhao Zhenji couched his treacherous intent in sweet and noble words. He's actually a traitor in the guise of a patriot and loyal minister. Your Majesty, don't be deceived by him or by his friends who have plotted the scheme. If we put Hai Rui under immediate arrest, we should arrest Zhao Zhenji as well. We should arrest anyone who has been in contact with Hai Rui. We shall investigate and get to the bottom of this."

"Who should investigate this? Whom shall we investigate?" Emperor Jiajing asked.

"I shall take charge of the investigation. We shall investigate whoever we rightly believe is involved in the scheme."

Emperor Jiajing turned to Zhao. "Do you consider Chen Hong's response reasonable?"

"Your Majesty, if you listen to Chen Gonggong's advice, I will voluntarily turn myself in and go to the Imperial Prison with him now."

"I'm not listening to anyone's advice," Emperor Jiajing said unexpectedly. "I'm not quite ready to lock you behind bars. Didn't you just say that you are a faithful disciple of mine? Didn't you say you were my cohort? I will neither honour your claims nor deny them. But I will recognise you as a brave man, and please do not ask me to retract my words. I will assign you to investigate Hai Rui. Let a hero investigate another hero, and let a brave man investigate another brave man. Chen Hong..."

"Your Majesty, I'm here," replied Chen Hong, who by now was looking slightly alarmed.

Emperor Jiajing became breathless and his vision blurry. "Heroes investigate heroes... brave men investigate brave men...," he murmured to himself. "Chen Hong, I'll appoint you as chief investigator and Zhao Zhenji as your assistant. I also want representatives from the Ministry of Justice, the Audit and Inspection Commission, and the Imperial Judiciary, from the Imperial Investigative Agency, and the Imperial Prison... from Chaotian Temple... and Xuandu Temple... All of you shall be called upon to investigate Hai Rui and ferret out his cohorts."

Appointing priests from Chaotian and Xuandu as investigators? Chen Hong wondered if Emperor Jiajing had lost his mind. Even Zhao Zhenji and Huang Jin noticed Emperor Jiajing was acting strangely. The three of them looked astonished.

"Your Majesty," Chen Hong probed. "Whom... I mean, whom shall we investigate first? Whom shall we arrest first?"

Emperor Jiajing gave Chen Hong a blank stare. "Whom shall we investigate... Whom shall we arrest..." he mumbled.

Chen Hong had no idea if the emperor was talking to him or simply murmuring to himself.

"Lu Fang, you tell me," said Emperor Jiajing, whose empty gaze shifted to Huang.

"Master!" Huang began sobbing. He crawled over on his knees and held Emperor Jiajing's arm.

"Lu Fang... Tell me... whom shall we investigate first... whom shall we arrest first?" he repeated.

Convinced that Emperor Jiajing was becoming delirious, Chen Hong rushed over and held his arm. "Master, he's not Lu Fang. Lu Fang is a traitor. Master, please issue an edict so we can arrest those people."

Emperor Jiajing gritted his teeth and closed his eyes. As he faltered, Huang sprang to his feet and held the emperor firmly around the waist. Zhao also got up and held Emperor Jiajing's arms.

"Master, this is a critical time," Chen Hong continued to plead. "Please make a decision."

"Chen Hong, have you no shred of decency?" Huang said in a tearful voice. "Are you trying to hound His Majesty to death? Why don't you go and investigate whoever needs to be investigated? Oh heavens, help. We need the imperial doctor right away!"

When two junior eunuchs on duty darted out of Yuxi Palace to fetch a doctor for Emperor Jiajing, Grand Secretary Xu slowly got up from the ground.

"Li Chunfang and Gao Gong, let's go inside," he said. Gao Gong held Grand Secretary Xu by the arm as they stepped into the palace. Deputy Li staggered behind them. Without seeking permission, they trotted into the meditation room. Emperor Jiajing was sitting on his prayer mat with his eyes closed. He was propped up by Huang Jin, Zhao Zhenji and Chen Hong.

The three cabinet members approached the prayer mat. As soon as they dropped down on their knees, Emperor Jiajing opened his bloodshot eyes. His face looked flushed. Unbeknownst to those present, he had applied his Taoist self-healing techniques and managed to recover from his lapse of consciousness. Upon realising that three people were holding him, he yelled: "Take your hands off me!"

Chen Hong let go of his hands. Mimicking the emperor's tone, he ordered Zhao: "Take your hands off His Majesty!"

Zhao complied and knelt on the floor.

Huang held Emperor Jiajing by the shoulder.

"Chen Hong, arrest this traitorous minion who is holding my shoulder," Emperor Jiajing said contemptuously.

Chen Hong shouted to his helpers outside the meditation room. "Seize Huang Jin and send him to the Interior Ministry," he ordered.

Huang put a coat over Emperor Jiajing's shoulders and kowtowed to his master before striding out with two junior eunuchs.

"Xu Jie, who has given you permission to come in?" shouted Emperor Jiajing when he noted the presence of Grand Secretary Xu and two other cabinet members. "Are you trying to depose me?"

The trio lay prostrate on the floor.

"If any of you is a supporter of Hai Rui, you still have time to run away," Emperor Jiajing jeered. "Otherwise, go and wait for my order in the Privy Council's duty room. Get out!"

The three cabinet members rose from the floor and walked out. Unsure of what to do, Zhao also got up and followed his colleagues.

"Stop," Emperor Jiajing shouted at Zhao, giving him a cold stare.

"You were such a hero just now. You can't sneak out like this, can you?"

"I'll stay and wait for your decree," muttered Zhao, who knelt down again.

"I have no more orders for you. Chen Hong shall give you instructions on what to do next."

Chen Hong kowtowed to the emperor.

"Take the rubbish written by that cold-blooded brute," Emperor Jiajing told Chen Hong. "You know who I want you to investigate and arrest. Feel free to use whatever means to make them speak."

"I understand," Chen Hong pledged as he picked up the sheets of Hai Rui's remonstrance from the floor. Then he turned to Zhao. "My hero, please follow me."

Zhao kowtowed to Emperor Jiajing before exiting.

It was midnight, but fire torches lit up the alley outside Hai Rui's courtyard. Everyone who congregated here came from the Interior Ministry. There was not a single agent from the Imperial Investigative Agency.

As usual, Hai Rui left the courtyard door wide open. When the eunuch wearing hobnail boots barged in through the door, the ground in the front yard vibrated as if some ironshod hooves of horses had just trampled on it.

The eunuchs divided themselves into three groups. The first group broke into the west room; the second ransacked the east room and the kitchen; and the third, led by a supervisor, targeted the guest room in the middle. Despite the cold February weather, the guest room door was open. The supervisor paused at the threshold. Inside the room, Hai Rui was sitting on a chair in front of a square table. Behind him lay a large white coffin.

"Are you Hai Rui?" the supervisor asked. "Do you work for the Ministry of Treasury?"

"Yes, that's me," said Hai Rui, standing up.

"Put the cuffs on him," the supervisor ordered his subordinates who were standing behind him.

Two eunuchs carrying handcuffs and shackles charged into the room. They put an iron collar around Hai Rui's neck before tightening and clasping it with a brass lock. Then, the eunuchs handcuffed Hai Rui's hands and squatted down to wrap a pair of fetters around his ankles. The leash between his feet was only about five inches long.

Known as the 'tiger and wolf trap', this set of instruments was used by imperial agents and law enforcement agencies to restrain mass murderers, pirates and rebel leaders. No matter what type of kungfu skills a felon possessed, the shackles made it impossible for him to escape. Subsequently, the Imperial Investigative Agency and the Imperial Prison began using these instruments to manacle imperial officials who had incurred the wrath of the emperor. The imperial agents jokingly called this set of instruments 'golden lotus shoes' because offenders whose feet were fettered walked in tiny steps, making loud clanking noises like a bejewelled woman with bound feet. This elegant name was meant to humiliate scholar officials, many of whom were members of the Clear Stream faction and valued honour above all else.

"Take him away," the supervisor ordered.

As the two eunuchs were about to pull the shackles and forcibly drag Hai Rui out of the room, the supervisor stopped them. Pulling one eunuch aside, he whispered: "Don't rough him up yet. We need to check out his background before deciding what to do."

"Yes sir," said the eunuch who loosened the shackles, allowing Hai Rui to totter out of the room himself.

"Search every room thoroughly," the supervisor ordered his subordinates in the yard.

Several eunuchs marched into the guest room and made a beeline for the coffin. Flipping its lid off, they found Hai Rui's neatly folded grade-six official robe and hat. One eunuch grabbed the robe while another took the hat. They shook the coat and hat but nothing fell out. Then, they checked the coffin and it too was empty.

Hai Rui hobbled towards the courtyard door. Since the eunuchs who came to conduct the arrest had been warned not to use excessive force on Hai Rui, they simply followed him patiently. At the courtyard door, the high threshold blocked Hai Rui. He stared at the threshold and glanced down around him. He was surrounded by hobnailed boots, but nobody was willing to lend him a hand. They simply stood there quietly, watching.

Many who had been summoned to Hai Rui's residence were angry with him. It was supposed to be a day of celebration. Emperor Jiajing had promised to issue a bonus to every eunuch after he moved to his new palace. But then, Hai Rui spoiled everything with his remonstrance and they had to come all the way here to arrest him at this late hour. Their annoyance was palpable.

"Kneel down and crawl over," the supervisor shouted from behind him.

Hai Rui ignored the order. Turning around slowly with his back to the door, he grabbed the chains attached to his handcuffs and sat down on the threshold. Then, he lifted his shackled feet and slowly pivoted them outside the door.

As Hai Rui stood up and moved towards the police wagon, the supervisor exchanged an admiring glance with his subordinates.

Two eunuchs flipped the rear wagon door open as Hai Rui approached. Lifting him up, they tossed him inside. The door clanked shut. A eunuch locked the door from the outside.

◆

Once again, lanterns and fire torches illuminated the Interior Ministry's courtyard. Members of the Criminal Investigative Division and the Imperial Prison convened outside the duty room. They lined both sides of the lawn, going down on one knee.

Chen Hong and Zhao Zhenji stood in front of the duty room door. They were flanked by three deputy interior ministers. In line with Emperor Jiajing's request, officials from the Ministry of Justice, the Imperial Judiciary and the Audit and Inspection Commission had been summoned to assist with the investigation. In the pre-dawn hours, the yard fell into dead silence. The fire torches popped and crackled in the early morning breeze.

Chen Hong simply stood there without speaking. Those in the

yard assumed he was waiting for someone, but nobody dared ask. The night seemed endless.

Urgent footsteps sounded outside the courtyard gate. The supervisor who had been dispatched to arrest Hai Rui darted in and knelt in front of Chen Hong. "Daddy, we have captured Hai Rui," he reported. "Everything went as planned. We detained him at the Imperial Prison."

"Good. Accompany Mr Zhao, our hero, to the Imperial Prison so he can interrogate his fellow hero there. Keep a record of every question and every answer. If any of you leak a word to other officials, I'll have you executed on the spot."

"Yes, Daddy," said the supervisor who got up and glanced at Zhao Zhenji. "Mr Zhao, after you."

A gloomy-faced Zhao stepped out.

Chen Hong cleared his throat and started to address the imperial agents: "Listen carefully. An attempted coup has occurred."

The agents raised their heads in disbelief.

"An auditor at the Ministry of Treasury submitted a subversive remonstrance with the intent of forcing His Majesty to abdicate. We shall find out who is behind him and prosecute them to the full extent of the law. Remember, a thief in the family is dangerous because he is harder to detect. Some of these traitors are lurking among us. They are bold enough to conduct treacherous activities in the presence of His Majesty. So, I'm going to start with our group here. Bring the traitor in."

Noises could be heard outside the courtyard. All eyes were on the gate.

Huang Jin appeared, wearing handcuffs and chains. Two eunuchs escorted him to the middle of the courtyard.

The imperial ministers gasped. Huang Gonggong had faithfully served His Majesty for decades. How was it possible for him to turn into a traitor overnight? What prompted him to participate in a scheme to dethrone the emperor? They were incredulous.

A simple-minded person, Huang was stubborn by nature. Even though his hands were shackled, he kept his head high. When Chen Hong ordered him to kneel down, Huang refused.

"Who do you think you are?" Chen Hong scoffed. "You act like you're still the first deputy interior minister. Are you waiting for me to hand you some government reports to sign off?"

Huang averted his eyes.

"Break his legs and get him to kneel down," Chen Hong barked.

Two of Chen Hong's supporters came up and kicked hard behind Huang's knee. The former first deputy interior minister fell to his knees. Despite the excruciating pain, he struggled to straighten his back and continued to hold his head high.

Enraged by Huang's defiance, Chen Hong howled: "Why are you raising your head so high? Are you looking at the stars? Reward him with some hard slaps so he can see more stars."

One eunuch struck Huang on the right cheek while the other hit the left. At the beginning, Huang maintained his posture, but soon he began to see stars. As the slapping continued, he passed out and collapsed on the ground.

The agents who were kneeling in the yard lowered their heads. The three deputy ministers who were standing under the eaves closed their eyes in fear.

"Help him up," Chen Hong ordered.

The eunuchs lifted Huang from the ground, bent his legs and put him in a kneeling position. Huang's head sank to his chest.

"Wake him up with cold water," Chen Hong commanded. "I want him to be awake so he can reveal his fellow schemers."

One eunuch went away and came back with a bucket of icy cold water. A colleague took the bucket from him and poured it over Huang's head. His body jerked. When he came to, Huang could only open his eyes a crack because his face had become swollen from the slapping. All he could see was a line of flickering lights.

"Don't let your pig-headedness and personal loyalty colour your judgment," Chen Hong's fierce voice sounded in his ear. "If you want me to stop, simply confess. Tell me who else plotted with you against His Majesty."

Huang took a deep breath, opened his mouth and spat at Chen Hong. The blood-speckled phlegm landed at Chen Hong's feet. Chen Hong did not immediately retaliate against Huang's public display of insubordination. Closing his eyes to suppress his anger, he said a few prayers and contemplated for a few moments. Then, on opening his eyes, he scanned the courtyard before addressing the crowd.

"I understand that many of you here have fond memories of Lu Fang. Whether you're a veteran or a newcomer, you have probably received certain favours from that Daddy of yours before he left. But there's one thing I want you to think about. If Lu Fang is so benevolent, why did he betray His Majesty like this? For people like us, loyalty to His Majesty comes before personal loyalty to Lu Fang and his cohorts. I've been with the Imperial Palace for decades and never for a moment have I been ambivalent about where my loyalty lies. I want to emphasise again that I value loyalty to His Majesty above all else. But as your Daddy I will try to protect as many of you as possible. After all, Lu Fang took care of you for four decades and you can't help feeling attached to him. I understand that. As long as you follow my orders and renew your loyalty to His Majesty, I will let bygones be bygones. People like Huang Jin, who treasured his friendship with Lu Fang more than his loyalty to His Majesty, will be punished severely. Look at him. He acts like a tough warrior within the brotherhood who honours the law of the word. He forgets that I'm a hundred times tougher. Once again, I want to make it clear to you here. Among all the twenty-four agencies of the Imperial Palace, I shall arrest one person only. That person is Huang Jin. For the rest of you, you need to repent, disavowing your past connections with Lu Fang and renouncing Huang Jin. By the way, there are two people here I won't be able to protect because of their affiliations with Hai Rui."

Zhu Qi and Chee Dazhu, who were kneeling in the front row, stood up.

"Hai Rui is a treacherous person and what he did was unprecedented in history. How did you get involved with him?"

Chee Dazhu was about to explain when Zhu Qi stopped him. "Chen Gonggong, there's no need to question us," he said. "Please put the cuffs on us now."

Chen Hong beckoned to two eunuchs near the courtyard door. They came over with handcuffs, and put them around their wrists.

"Don't beat them. Their bodies are as strong as iron. Torture never works on them. Let them reflect on their transgressions in confinement and examine their consciences. They'll come to their senses eventually."

Zhu Qi and Chee Dazhu were escorted out of the Interior Ministry courtyard.

"It's your turn now," said Chen Hong, addressing the three officials from the Ministry of Justice, the Imperial Judiciary, and the Audit and Inspection Commission. "Grand Secretary Xu and other cabinet members are being confined to the Privy Council's duty room. I want you to go there now and urge them to each draft a statement relating to their individual role in Hai Rui's subversive activity. If they have no contacts with Hai Rui, have them state that clearly. We don't intend to harm the innocent, but at the same time, we won't allow any traitor to slip through the cracks."

The trio appeared hesitant.

"I know the people in the Privy Council's duty room are your superiors, and the assignment will put you in an awkward position," Chen Hong reassured them. "But you're acting on the orders of His Majesty. During the investigation, their titles mean nothing. With the backing of His Majesty, no one will dare retaliate against you and sabotage your careers. If you worry about your future and go soft on them, you won't have a future. Do I make myself clear?"

"Understood," the trio replied with a palm-over-fist salute.

"You can leave now," ordered Chen Hong.

The trio trudged towards the courtyard door with heavy hearts.

Chen Hong turned to his deputies: "Shi Gonggong, Meng Gonggong and Bian Gonggong, I want you to contact the Metropolitan Police Department and impose martial law in Beijing. During the investigation, no imperial official is allowed to leave the city."

明

The Imperial Prison, which fell under the direct control of the emperor, was regarded as the country's number one jail. Inmates were mostly senior imperial officials. The windowless cells with marble ceilings, marble walls and marble floors were about three metres below ground floor level. Despite the dry winter months in

Beijing, it was always damp down under. Thus, even without torture, many inmates who served long sentences barely survived the harsh conditions there.

Carrying lanterns, a jailer and the eunuch from the Criminal Investigative Division, who supervised the arrest of Hai Rui, led Zhao Zhenji down a flight of steep stone stairs. In the dim light from oil lamps secured to the stone walls, Zhao saw a deep passageway ahead of him. As he fumbled his way through the dank, poorly-lit tunnel, his mood turned gloomier.

There is a popular Buddhist saying: a chance encounter between two strangers is fate, while the bond between two neighbours is driven by necessity. The relationship between Hai Rui and Zhao Zhenji had the elements of both fate and necessity. Fate brought them together in Zhejiang Province, where they had been assigned to investigate a major corruption scandal. Zhao was the imperial inspector and Hai Rui, a mere magistrate. Over the course of the investigation, Hai Rui resisted Zhao's orders repeatedly, putting him in an impossible position. Zhao detested Hai Rui, but was powerless to remove his nemesis because Hai came at the recommendation of the Prince of Yu. Subsequently, they were both transferred to Beijing. Zhao became the treasury minister while Hai Rui served under him as a junior auditor. On the first day of Hai Rui's arrival, he caused a scandal at Home of Six Necessities. Barely had Zhao settled the case before Hai Rui created another political incident that had led to a major shakeup in the upper echelon of the Imperial Government. Zhao became Hai Rui's first victim and had almost lost his life. One could just imagine Zhao's fury when he entered the Imperial Prison.

Near the end of the deep, dark hallway, the jailer and the supervisor stopped at a cell with iron bars. There was no lamp inside the cell. The light from the jailer's lantern spilled in, casting long shadows on the walls. Zhao could see Hai Rui wearing shackles and sitting on a thin layer of straw on the floor. He seemed to be resting with his eyes closed.

The sight of Hai Rui filled Zhao with loathing and disgust. "Take him to the torture chamber," he ordered the imperial agent. "I shall conduct a thorough interrogation there."

"I'm sorry we can't do that," the supervisor replied coldly. "We have been instructed not to inflict torture. I'm afraid you'll have to interrogate him here."

"Do you mean to say that I'm only allowed to interrogate him inside this cell?" Zhao snapped.

"We didn't want to do it here either, but we have to comply with the order from above. Mr Zhao, you question him inside and we'll stay outside to monitor and record the session."

Zhao swallowed his anger. "Open the door then," he said.

The jailer opened the cell gate. Soon after Zhao entered, he clanked it shut.

"What are you doing?" Zhao turned around and asked the jailer. "Why are you locking me inside?"

"I'm afraid we have to abide by the rules," the eunuch explained. "After you finish, we'll unlock the door and let you out."

The eunuch's words made Zhao's blood boil. Closing his eyes, he took a deep breath, trying to compose himself. On opening them, he surveyed the cell. There was no chair, so it looked like he had to conduct the interrogation while standing.

As he was about to start, the jailer and the eunuch brought in a low table and a small bench. "Mr Zhao, you can begin now," said the imperial agent who placed a bowl of ink, a calligraphy brush and some papers on the table before leaving.

"Hai Rui!" Zhao shouted, his voice filled with anger and frustration.

Hai Rui had kept his eyes closed while Zhao and the eunuch were arguing. At this moment, he opened his eyes and turned his head towards Zhao. "Yes, I'm here," he replied.

"This is all your doing!" Zhao fumed. "You were supposed to compose a congratulatory letter to His Majesty. What did you end up writing in your remonstrance?"

"Your Highness, you've come all the way to interrogate me about a letter that you have not even read," Hai Rui countered. "Isn't it rather odd that His Majesty didn't even share it with you?"

Hai Rui's rejoinder left Zhao seething with rage. But at the same time, he quickly realised that Hai had provided him with the perfect opportunity to prove his innocence. "The remonstrance you have submitted is treasonous and His Majesty does not believe it deserves our consideration," Zhao said emphatically and paused so the supervisor could record his words.

What Zhao did not know was that Hai Rui shared a common intention. While Zhao desperately attempted to dissociate himself from the controversy, Hai Rui also intended to illustrate to Emperor Jiajing that nobody had instigated him to deliver the remonstrance.

"Mr Zhao, if you have not had the chance to read my letter, how do you know what I've written is treasonous?" Hai Rui proclaimed and paused for the supervisor to record his question.

Zhao was stumped. At the same time, it became clear to him that Hai Rui had no intention of implicating him or anyone else. The thought eased his fear. Shrewd as he was, Zhao decided to start all over and question Hai Rui freely so he could at least extract some useful information for Emperor Jiajing.

"Hai Rui, tell me what prompted you to write this subversive remonstrance?"

"Remonstrating with His Majesty is every official's bounden duty," Hai Rui replied calmly.

"What kinds of treasonous things did you write?"

"His Majesty will judge my words righteously. Feel free to consult with His Majesty."

"I'm asking you," said Zhao, raising his voice again. "Following His Majesty's decree, I'm here to question you."

"I wrote the remonstrance for His Majesty. If His Majesty chooses to make it public, he will grant you access and let you read it. So far, His Majesty hasn't done that. I won't share it with anyone either."

Zhao turned his head, peering at the supervisor outside the cell with a helpless expression. He was sending them a clear signal that the interrogation was going nowhere. The supervisor lowered his head to avert Zhao's gaze.

Realising that he still had to go through with it, Zhao turned back to Hai Rui. "Let me ask again, who instructed you to write and submit this remonstrance?"

The eunuch raised his head with interest. Hai Rui simply closed his eyes without responding.

"Answer my question," Zhao shouted, feigning anger.

"Mr Zhao, do you normally receive instructions from others when you submit a report to His Majesty?"

"What do you mean? Give me a straight answer."

With his hands and legs shackled, Hai Rui sat still like a mountain and replied calmly with his eyes half-closed: "I stated clearly at the beginning that 'Hai Rui, an auditor at the Ministry of Treasury, humbly presents his remonstrance'. What I attempted to convey is that I did it of my own accord and it had nothing to do with anyone else."

Despite his intense dislike for Hai Rui, Zhao could not help but admire the man's courage. A look of awe crept onto his face. He no longer felt the need to continue. When he turned around to consult with the supervisor, he was surprised to see that the jailer was ready to unlock the door and that the supervisor was waiting for him to step out.

Zhao pretended to be in no rush to end the interrogation. "Did you just hear what the suspect said?" he asked the supervisor.

"Yes, I have recorded every single word he uttered."

"Are we ending the session now?" Zhao asked.

"Since you can't extract any sensible answers from him, we don't have much choice, do we?"

The eunuch's waspish comment unnerved Zhao. He looked distracted when he stepped out of the cell. The door clanked shut behind him.

明

Hai Rui's controversial remonstrance sat prominently on the Prince of Yu's desk. Chen Hong stood next to the desk, peering at the Prince of Yu who had just finished reading it. Much to Chen Hong's surprise, the prince, who had always struck him as being weak and indecisive, appeared calm. There was not a trace of panic in his gaze.

"Your Royal Highness," Chen Hong said in a probing tone. "His

Majesty stated in his edict that he is eagerly awaiting your comments."

The Prince of Yu gave him a vacant stare. "Here is my response. Listen carefully, and I want you to report to His Majesty truthfully. I'm shocked at the sheer audacity and impertinence of this person to revile my father, His Majesty, like this. As His Majesty's son, I would definitely kill this person myself."

Chen Hong raised his head, looking relieved. "Your humble servant will truthfully report your statement back to His Majesty."

"I'm not finished yet," the Prince of Yu continued. "As the descendent of the founding father of our Great Ming Empire, I will promote this person if I inherit the throne someday."

The Prince of Yu's words shocked Chen Hong, who dropped down on his knees and pleaded in a trembling voice: "Your Royal Highness, I kindly and urgently request that you retract your last sentence."

"I will not retract my statement, never!" insisted the Prince of Yu, showing the obstinacy he had obviously inherited from his father. "I understand very well that His Majesty suspects I have instigated this person to submit the remonstrance. He might be of the belief that I'm conspiring with others against him, trying to force him to give up the throne. I seriously do not care what he thinks. I can draft a letter to my father, requesting that he strip me of my royal titles and demote me to commoner's status. Or he can order me to commit suicide. Whatever he decides, I will comply with his order and act immediately."

Chen Hong was stunned as the Prince of Yu picked up his pen and started writing furiously on a blank piece of paper.

"Your Highness, please don't," he implored. When the Prince of Yu ignored him, Chen Hong crawled over on his knees and seized the Prince of Yu's wrist. "Your Highness, stop!"

The Prince of Yu gave him an icy look.

"Your Highness, any hasty and reckless action at this time could have serious consequences," Chen Hong pleaded as he held the Prince of Yu's hand. "You could wreck our forefather's empire."

"That wouldn't be necessary since people like you are already wrecking it."

"People like me?" Chen Hong asked with a frightened look.

The Prince of Yu did not respond.

Chen Hong let go of the Prince of Yu's hand. Turning around, he caught sight of a sword perched on a rosewood table nearby. He rose and walked over to the table. Grabbing the sword with both hands, he returned to the Prince of Yu and dropped down on his knees: "Your Royal Highness, if you truly consider me a dynasty wrecker, why don't you grant me the honour to slash my throat with this sword?"

The Prince of Yu scowled when Chen Hong raised the sword above his head. "At the moment, all the ministerial officials and cabinet members are being detained inside the Western Compound," growled the prince. "You put the whole nation in a state of paralysis. Except for His Majesty, you're the most powerful person in the Great Ming Empire. How dare I kill you?"

"Your Highness, I have been unfairly wronged..." Chen Hong said before he put the sword on the floor and burst into loud sobs.

The Prince of Yu looked away and stared into the distance.

Noting that his dramatic display of emotion failed to move the prince, Chen Hong quickly switched tactics. "If Your Royal Highness has such a low opinion of me, I'm doomed," he mumbled. "You might spare my life today or tomorrow, but sooner or later, you will put my head on the chopping block. Now that I'm a condemned person, allow me to say a few words to Your Highness."

"You can choose to say anything you want. No one has the power to stop you."

"All right then," Chen Hong said, wiping away his tears. "Your Highness, you're well aware that His Majesty has a fiery temper. Who could blame him? Throughout history, can you think of a single ruler who would tolerate such fierce condemnation from a courtier like Hai Rui? As the saying goes, the wrath of a ruler leads to the death of thousands. When a horrible incident like this happened tonight, what would you have done if you had been in my position?"

The Prince of Yu softened his hostility and peered at Chen Hong.

"All I could do at first was appease His Majesty's anger. Mollifying His Majesty is the only way we can prevent the situation from getting out of control."

"So you locked up all the cabinet members and key ministerial officials for the sole reason of placating His Majesty?" asked the Prince of Yu.

"Only by placating His Majesty can we dispel His Majesty's suspicions. I have served His Majesty for more than thirty years. I can claim without exaggeration that I'm more familiar with His Majesty's temperament than Your Highness. If we don't make an effort to remove his suspicions, more cabinet members will be implicated. I doubt Your Highness would be spared either. Come to think of it, do you know why I urged His Majesty to send Zhao Zhenji to interrogate Hai Rui? Zhao is Grand Secretary Xu's protégé and Grand Secretary Xu is your teacher. Hai Rui is Zhao's subordinate at the Ministry of Treasury. If we don't give Zhao the opportunity to prove his innocence, His Majesty will accuse you and others of harbouring ulterior motives. Your Highness, can't you see what I'm trying to get at?"

Chen Hong's words touched the Prince of Yu's heart. He sized up the emperor's chief eunuch while trying to decide whether or not to trust him.

"Your Royal Highness just blamed me for confining all cabinet members to the Western Compound. How would I dare? Even if I wished it, I wouldn't have the guts. And even if I did have the guts, I don't have the ability. Besides, why would I want to turn all cabinet members and ministerial officials into my enemies? I confined them to the Privy Council's duty room to save them from His Majesty's wrath. At the same time, I have pulled all of the surveillance reports from the Interior Ministry's archives and submitted them to His Majesty for him to review. The imperial agents have monitored Hai Rui's residence since his arrival in Beijing. Apart from Wang Yongji, an official at the Audit and Inspection Commission, and Chee Dazhu, an agent with the Imperial Investigative Agency, Hai Rui had no contact with any other officials. Once His Majesty has read these reports, his suspicions will inevitably dissipate. I'm certain that Grand Secretary Xu and his cabinet members will be allowed to go home and resume work tomorrow morning. Your Royal Highness, please tell me in no ambiguous terms, what else I could have done. Am I trying to sabotage and wreck our Great Ming Empire?"

The Prince of Yu lowered his head ruefully as Chen Hong prostrated himself on the floor and wept loudly.

7

Since its founding in the late fourteenth century, the Imperial Investigative Agency had evolved from a private guard military institution to a secret police organisation. It became the emperor's eyes and ears throughout the empire. The imperial secret agents were bound to the service of the emperor and took direct orders from him. Their role was simply to keep the emperor on the throne by spying on his ministers and nullifying his political opponents. The omnipresent spies monitored the daily activities of senior ministers and submitted their reports to the Interior Ministry. Occasionally, there were exceptions. Low-level officials who had been accused of conducting suspicious activities also fell into the scope of surveillance.

In the case of Hai Rui, a mere grade-six official at the Ministry of Treasury, Chen Hong placed him on the watch list following the incident at Home of Six Necessities on the day he arrived in Beijing.

In the ensuing months, the Criminal Investigative Division kept daily records of his movements. This evening, Chen Hong pulled out Hai Rui's files and spread them out on Emperor Jiajing's desk. After Chen Hong left, Emperor Jiajing held a lamp and walked over to his desk to study each page. A few entries in the surveillance report drew his attention.

Three o'clock in the afternoon on 22 December in the forty-fourth year of Emperor Jiajing's reign: Wang Yongji, an inspector at the Audit and Inspection Commission, delivered a basket of New Year groceries to Hai Rui's residence. Hai Rui declined the gifts.

Ten o'clock in the morning on 27 December: The wife of Chee Dazhu, an agent with the Imperial Investigative Agency, delivered a basket of food to Hai Rui's residence, but Hai Rui's family refused to open the door for her. At noon, Hai Rui returned home and accepted four eggs before sending Chee's wife away. At about three o'clock in the afternoon, Hai Rui left home with a bolt of cotton cloth. He entered the Prosperity Fabrics Store on Qianmenwai Avenue, and sold the cloth for fifteen strings of copper coins. With the money, he bought a chicken, a fish and seven kilograms of rice.

Emperor Jiajing worked his way through the trivial details of Hai Rui's everyday activities, which somehow triggered unexpected feelings of sadness and sympathy.

Six o'clock in the afternoon on 27 December: A messenger at the Ministry of Treasury visited Hai Rui with an urgent letter. Hai Rui left for Tongzhou to retrieve grain from a military warehouse.

Ten o'clock in the morning on 28 December: Hai Rui escorted ten grain carts and departed for Daxing County to assist with disaster-relief efforts.

New Year's Eve in the forty-fourth year of Emperor Jiajing's reign to 5 January in the forty-fifth year of Emperor Jiajing's reign: Hai Rui's residence remained closed. Neither his mother nor his wife left the house. At five o'clock in the afternoon on 5 January, Hai Rui returned home from Daxing. He suddenly fell ill. His wife sought help from a neighbour, who contacted Wang Yongji. An hour later, Wang and Li Shizhen arrived. At midnight, Wang left Hai Rui's house and went to the Audit and Inspection Commission to compose his congratulatory letter to His Majesty. Li Shizhen stayed overnight at Hai Rui's house.

On 7 February, the Grand Canal was open for navigation. Hai Rui bid farewell to his wife and mother, both of them went south on a passenger boat with Li Shizhen.

From July in the forty-fourth year of Emperor Jiajing's reign to the present: Hai Rui received three visitors – Wang Yongji, Chee Dazhu and Li Shizhen. He paid no calls to friends or colleagues.

When he reached the last page, Emperor Jiajing raised his head contemplatively and let out a soft sigh. The surveillance report was supposed to provide some clues as to who was behind Hai Rui's bold scheme. Instead, it seemed to confirm the junior official's virtue and noble intent. Rubbing his eyes, the emperor stared into the distance. Dawn light filtered through the south-facing window. He could hear roosters crowing in the distance.

A junior eunuch on duty came in to report that Zhao Zhenji and the supervisor at the Criminal Investigative Division had just concluded their preliminary interrogation of Hai Rui. "They have requested an audience with you," said the eunuch.

"That was fast," Emperor Jiajing sneered. "Bring them in."

The supervisor scurried inside. Zhao followed him. They knelt before Emperor Jiajing. The supervisor held the one-page transcript above his head.

"Throw the transcript on my desk," Emperor Jiajing said dismissively. "I'm not reading it now."

"Yes, Your Majesty," said the supervisor who rose and placed the paper on the emperor's desk. He bowed and exited the meditation room.

"Do you know if the cabinet members and ministerial officials have finished with their defence statements?" the emperor asked Zhao. "I assume they're simply going through the motions."

"Your Majesty, if you wish, I can go and collect the statements for you," Zhao replied without raising his head.

"Why don't you bring everyone here."

"I shall do it now." As Zhao kowtowed to the emperor, he looked puzzled. Was it a tacit signal that the emperor had cleared his ministers of wrongdoing? What had caused his sudden change of mind?

After Zhao left, Emperor Jiajing strolled over to his desk and picked up the sheet of interrogation transcript. His empty gaze shifted from the paper to the south window. Day had broken.

"Your humble servant Chen Hong is back from the Prince of Yu's mansion," Chen Hong's voice sounded outside.

Emperor Jiajing put the transcript down and returned to his prayer mat. "Come in," he said as he closed his eyes.

As Chen Hong trotted in, Emperor Jiajing opened his eyes. When he saw that the chief eunuch was returning empty-handed, he became suspicious. "Did you get a written response from the Prince of Yu?" he asked.

"Yes, Your Majesty, I... I did," Chen Hong replied nervously.

"Where is it?"

"Please forgive me," said Chen Hong, dropping to his knees. "The Prince of Yu wrote a letter in response to your edict, but he insisted that his correspondence be delivered by Princess Li and your grandson. The mother and son are here now. They have requested an audience with Your Majesty."

Emperor Jiajing fell silent. He knew instinctively that the letter contained subversive content. Otherwise, his son wouldn't have gone to the trouble of sending his family members to present the letter. Sadness flashed across his face. "Bring them in," he said.

"Yes, Your Majesty." Chen Hong sprang to his feet and hurried out.

As Emperor Jiajing was adjusting his robe and posture, his daughter-in-law and grandson appeared at the door.

Princess Li kowtowed to the emperor. When she was about to instruct the young prince to kowtow, Emperor Jiajing stopped her. "There's no need," he said, waving his hands. Chen Hong put an embroidered ottoman on the left side of Emperor Jiajing's prayer mat. The princess bowed before sitting nervously on the edge of it. The young prince, who stood in front of his mother, silently stared at his grandfather.

"Come here," said Emperor Jiajing, beckoning to the young boy. With hesitancy, the boy walked over. The emperor hugged his grandson, trying to lift him from the floor, but quickly realised that he no longer had the strength to do it. The sharp-eyed Chen Hong rushed over. He held the boy in his arms and placed him on the emperor's lap.

For the first time since his emotional outburst the previous night, Emperor Jiajing broke out into a broad grin. "I haven't seen my grandson for only a few months," he said. "But now, he's too heavy for me to even carry him."

Princess Li's eyes glistened with tears, but she forced a smile. Dropping on her knees, she said: "Your humble daughter-in-law has been entrusted with the Prince of Yu's letter, and I hereby present it to Your Majesty."

Emperor Jiajing shifted his gaze from Princess Li's face to the letter in her hands. He did not comment.

Chen Hong stood with his head down. He could feel his heart thumping violently.

"Chen Hong, please go out and check if those loyal courtiers of mine have arrived," Emperor Jiajing said with a hint of sarcasm in his tone.

"Yes, Your Majesty," a startled Chen Hong replied. He was not aware that the emperor had invited members of the Privy Council to the palace.

"Xu Jie and members of the Privy Council are awaiting your orders," Grand Secretary Xu's voice sounded outside the meditation room.

"Speak of the devil," Emperor Jiajing mused. "Please enter."

Having been confined to the Privy Council's duty room overnight, Grand Secretary Xu looked weary. There were dark circles around his eyes. Deputy Li Chunfang, Gao Gong and several ministerial officials walked behind Grand Secretary Xu. Their eyes had also lost their lustre. They each held what was supposed to be a defence or confession statement. Once inside, they fell to their knees.

"What do you have for me?" Emperor Jiajing asked deliberately, knowing that his ministers would have nothing to offer.

"We are here to present our defence statements," Grand Secretary Xu replied with a hint of defiance in his tone.

"Anything worth reporting?"

"Your Majesty, we held an extensive discussion. I'm pleased to report that none of us here was aware of or involved in Hai Rui's remonstration. I entreat you to read each individual statement."

Emperor Jiajing glanced at Chen Hong, signalling for him to gather the submissions.

After Chen Hong collected the statements, he knelt in front of Emperor Jiajing and presented them with both hands.

Emperor Jiajing peered at the papers in Chen Hong's hands and then at Princess Li who was holding her husband's letter above her head.

"My boy, do you know what your father and those ministers have written?" Emperor Jiajing asked the young prince who was sitting stiffly on his lap.

"Grandfather, they have written things that will make you upset," the young prince replied timidly.

Several cabinet members raised their heads slightly to get a glimpse of the boy, whose precocious remarks surprised them.

"My grandson knows me better than anyone else," Emperor Jiajing said, pinching the boy's face. "Now let me ask you another question. If Grandfather is not happy with what they have sent me, shall we read them or not?"

"Burn them," the boy blurted out and clapped his hands.

"Excellent!" Emperor Jiajing shouted. "Your wish is granted. Chen Hong, take these statements along with the Prince of Yu's letter. Burn them. I won't read a word."

"Long Live Your Majesty… a wise decision, indeed," Chen Hong said loudly as he quickly took the Prince of Yu's letter from Princess Li's hands and walked over to an incense burner. Removing its lid, Chen Hong tossed the letter and the defence statements into the fire one by one. They burst into flames.

Everyone in the room, including Princess Li, prostrated themselves before Emperor Jiajing and his grandson.

"We are deeply indebted to Your Majesty for your benevolence and heavenly wisdom," Grand Secretary Xu articulated excitedly on behalf of all the ministerial officials.

"That brute attacks me relentlessly, trying to nullify everything I have done for our nation," Emperor Jiajing fumed. "Hai Rui thinks he is the reincarnation of the mythical minister Bi Gan of the Shang dynasty. Bi Gan remonstrated with King Zhou, but King Zhou punished him by ripping his heart out. I hate to disappoint

Hai Rui, but I'm no King Zhou. Hai Rui wants to destabilise our empire so he can go down in history as a martyr like Bi Gan. Having given it some thought, I have decided not to be deceived. I will share with all of you what he has written. You read it, and I'll let you be the judge."

Chen Hong still had a stack of statements to burn when Emperor Jiajing beckoned him. "Your Majesty, what can I do for you?"

"Hand that brute's remonstrance to Grand Secretary Xu and distribute it to all ministerial officials."

The Privy Council, the Department of Justice, the Imperial Judiciary, and the Audit and Inspection Commission had decided to hold a joint inquisition. Such a manoeuvre involving a mere grade-six official was unique in the history of the Ming dynasty.

The inquisition took place in the Privy Council's duty room. The four cabinet members – Grand Secretary Xu, Deputy Li Chunfang, Gao Gong and Zhao Zhenji – sat behind a desk in the middle. Officials from the other two agencies occupied two desks on the left and right. There were ink stones and calligraphy brushes on their desks. Each official was required to take notes during the interrogation so Emperor Jiajing could compare them later.

Hai Rui arrived in a special police wagon, escorted by the supervisor at the Criminal Investigative Division and two imperial agents. When the supervisor scurried into the Privy Council's courtyard and announced Hai Rui's arrival, the room quietened down.

"Bring him in," ordered Grand Secretary Xu.

The wagon's back door flipped open. Two imperial agents reached inside and pulled Hai Rui out of the vehicle. Hai Rui steadied himself. The bright sunlight lit up his face. Breathing fresh air, he raised his head and squinted at the rising sun.

"Go inside!" an imperial agent urged him. "They're all waiting for you."

Hai Rui turned around. It was his first visit to the Privy

Council's complex. The duty room door was open and officials inside were quietly observing him. Hai Rui avoided their stares and looked up at a plaque that bore the characters 'The Cabinet' above the door. He stopped before a flight of stone stairs. Even though the stairs were neither high nor steep, the chains around his ankles made it impossible for him to climb. Since the charges against Hai Rui involved insulting the emperor, none of the imperial agents dared unlock his shackles or lend him a hand.

In the past, shackled criminals who had been summoned to face inquisition at the Privy Council lumbered up the stairs on their knees. For a proud man like Hai Rui, would he be willing to bear the humiliation of climbing the steps on his knees? The ministerial officials inside watched him anxiously.

Hai Rui sat down on a step, tried strenuously to move his legs, but failed. He stopped and closed his eyes.

"Hai Rui, please move!" Zhao shouted before banging his gavel on the desk. "You're attending trial here at the Privy Council. Stop acting like a spoilt child!"

"Excuse me, sir, may I ask a question? Am I a convicted felon?"

"We will reach a verdict after the inquisition today," Zhao replied loudly.

"Your Highness has not answered my question. Am I convicted or not?"

As Zhao was about to bang his gavel again, Gao Gong glanced at Zhao and interjected: "Hai Rui, what do you mean by that?"

"According to the *Great Ming Code*, serving officials summoned for interrogation are not supposed to wear shackles before they are convicted."

"You are right," Gao Gong confirmed as he glanced at his colleagues. "The *Great Ming Code* does contain this provision. Your shackles shall be removed."

Gao Gong's words were met with silence. He rose from his chair and ordered the supervisor: "Did you hear me? Please take off his shackles."

Before the supervisor had time to respond, Zhao intervened. "Is there a reason why Hai Rui is shackled for the hearing?" he asked the supervisor. "Have you received special instructions from above?"

"Yes, Mr Zhao. We have specifically been told not to remove Hai Rui's handcuffs and manacles."

"Who told you that?" Gao Gong enquired.

"Chen Gonggong," replied the supervisor.

"Was it Chen Gonggong's own idea or did he simply follow His Majesty's order?"

"I wouldn't dare speculate."

"If His Majesty has not issued a decree on this, we should comply with the *Great Ming Code*, which stipulates that an official shall be free of shackles during an inquisition. Please unlock Hai Rui's handcuffs and manacles immediately."

"I'm afraid I'll have to consult with Chen Gonggong first," the supervisor insisted.

"Mr Gao, Hai Rui has perpetrated a crime that is incomparable to anything we have witnessed in the history of the Ming dynasty," Zhao maintained. "Even the *Great Ming Code* contains no reference to such malfeasance. For today's trial, we should allow the Interior Ministry to decide whether Hai Rui should wear shackles or not."

The pusillanimity of Zhao's words repulsed Gao Gong. The night before, Gao Gong was deeply moved when Zhao bravely confronted Emperor Jiajing over Hai Rui's remonstrance, but now he felt that he finally understood Zhao as a person. He was nothing but a cunning opportunist, who found every opportunity to curry favour with the emperor and Grand Secretary Xu.

"Mr Zhao, you're acting like a different person today," Gao said. "His Majesty intended us to hold an inquisition and discuss the charges against Hai Rui. We haven't even started the hearing yet, but you've already reached a verdict and found him guilty. If this is the case, why did you even bother to invite us here?"

"When did I declare him to be guilty?" Zhao retorted, his face flushed with anger.

"Didn't you just say that Hai Rui has perpetrated a crime that is incomparable to anything we have witnessed in the history of the Ming dynasty?"

"Well, I... I'm not saying or implying that he's convicted."

"If he's not convicted yet, you should request that his shackles be removed," retorted Gao Gong.

Zhao was speechless.

"Since the Privy Council is presiding over the trial, we have to follow the *Great Ming Code*," Gao Gong continued, turning to the supervisor. "I urge you to unlock Hai Rui's shackles."

The supervisor turned to Grand Secretary Xu, who remained silent.

"If you don't abide by the law, we shall withdraw and ask Chen Gonggong to come and preside over the trial."

Grand Secretary Xu decided to intercede on Zhao's behalf. "We can't go wrong if we follow the provisions of the *Great Ming Code*. Let's not waste time arguing over this. Ask them to remove the shackles."

Baffled, Zhao looked into his teacher's eyes. Even though he had not figured out the true meaning of Grand Secretary Xu's concession, he resisted the temptation to disobey him in public. "Did you hear what Grand Secretary Xu said?" Zhao told the supervisor. "Remove Hai Rui's shackles. We'll explain the situation to Chen Gonggong later."

The supervisor acquiesced grudgingly. "Now that the Privy Council has requested it, let's remove the suspect's shackles."

The two imperial agents unlocked Hai Rui's handcuffs and manacles. When they threw the iron chains onto the ground, they made a loud clanking noise.

Hai Rui rubbed his wrists and massaged his ankles before standing up. Then he turned around, climbed the stairs and marched into the Privy Council's duty room.

Under normal circumstances, a junior official like Hai Rui was required to kowtow to Privy Council members and senior ministerial officials before meetings. Following court etiquette, Hai Rui dropped down to his knees and kowtowed. When Hai Rui stood up, Zhao frowned and turned to Shen Shixing, who headed the Department of Justice.

"Mr Shen, should an official under investigation kneel down or should he stand during the inquisition?"

Like a diligent student reciting his *Four Classics*, Shen chanted:

"Based on the provisions of the *Great Ming Code*, officials who hold positions above the level of grade three shall be granted a seat during his trial. Those under grade three must stand."

"All right, you can take it from here and begin the proceedings," Zhao urged Shen.

Shen rose from his chair and saluted Grand Secretary Xu. "If memory serves me correctly, His Majesty specifically designated Mr Zhao as the chief inquisitor," he said. "If His Majesty hasn't issued any new decree, I believe Mr Zhao should preside over today's hearing."

Officials sitting on the right and left nodded in agreement. Gao Gong shot a derisive glance at Zhao while Deputy Li looked to Grand Secretary Xu for advice.

"Zhenji, His Majesty appointed you as the inquisitor at Yuxi Palace last night," Grand Secretary Xu said. "Please take over and start the questioning."

"I shall accordingly," Zhao said grudgingly before turning his gaze to Hai Rui. "Hai Rui, I interrogated you yesterday evening. But it is a different session today. The Privy Council and four other Imperial Government agencies are holding a joint inquisition. Please respond to all my questions truthfully because your answers will have a direct impact on the final outcome."

"Yes, Mr Zhao."

Zhao rose from his chair. "In the guise of a congratulatory letter, you submitted a condemnatory report, in which you fiercely attacked His Majesty, like a mad dog barking viciously at the sun. With His Majesty's permission, the Prince of Yu, members of the Privy Council and all ministerial officials have reviewed your remonstrance and we are all filled with inexpressible rage. Let me ask you, did anyone instigate you to submit it, or did you act unscrupulously out of a frenzied desire for notoriety?"

"Since His Majesty has shared my humble remonstrance with everyone present, I'm happy to answer all of your questions," Hai Rui replied slowly. "At the beginning of my letter, I clearly described it as my feeble attempt to 'rectify the monarch's conduct, define the responsibilities of his courtiers, and bring peace and prosperity to the subjects of the Great Ming Empire'. Remonstrating with His Majesty is my bound duty as an imperial official. If it's the responsibility of imperial officials to speak up, why do I need anyone to coach or encourage me? Now that you have all read my remonstrance, please tell me which aspect of it is untrue or which argument I have made runs counter to the governing principles laid out in the works of the sages? Mr Zhao, all of my inquisitors here are well versed in the books of the sages and expected to assist His Majesty with wise governing ideas. How could you denounce my remonstrance and accuse me of unscrupulously seeking fame?"

Senior officials from the four Imperial Government agencies sat hunched over their notes, trying to hide their shock and admiration. The four Privy Council members looked slightly awkward and helpless as Zhao continued his questioning.

"You're a man of chicanery," Zhao responded. "You claim that nobody instigated you and that you are not seeking notoriety. But as a mere auditor at the Ministry of Treasury, do you honestly think His Majesty should entrust you with the responsibilities of governing the Great Ming Empire?"

Hai Rui shook his head. "Mr Zhao, I have problems understanding your accusation," he said.

Zhao banged his fist on the desk. "What do you mean you don't understand? In your remonstrance, you ostentatiously claim that you intend to rectify the monarch's conduct and define the responsibilities of his courtiers. What makes you think His Majesty's conduct needs to be rectified and that the responsibilities of senior officials be defined? What right do you have to criticise His Majesty and the Imperial Government? Which part of the Imperial Government do you think you can handle, the Privy Council or the six key ministries? Your remonstrance abounds with wickedness and malice. Such lunacy is unheard of in the history of the Ming dynasty."

"Mr Zhao, I now understand what you are trying to convey," Hai Rui said calmly before raising his hand and turning to Grand Secretary Xu.

"What are you trying to say?" Grand Secretary Xu asked Hai Rui.

"The *Great Ming Code* specifically stipulates that an official who handles a criminal case shall excuse himself if there is a strong possibility that his decision is biased because of past grievances. I kindly and humbly request that the Privy Council follow the law and remove Mr Zhao from this case. If he continues, I will not answer a single question from him."

Zhao was livid. "Nonsense, pure nonsense!" he shouted. "Grand Secretary Xu, this man's a boorish and unruly scoundrel. He's no different from those notorious pirates and robbers. I strongly request that we accord him the same treatment as we would to a pirate and apply torture. Otherwise, we'll never be able to reach a collective verdict and provide a satisfactory response to His Majesty."

Gao Gong, who had been observing the fiery exchange, ignored Zhao's outburst and chose to continue with the questioning: "Hai Rui, the remonstrance you submitted last night was sacrilegious and subversive. Your argument today is equally incomprehensible. Why do you ask for Mr Zhao to be recused from your case?"

"In the fortieth year of Emperor Jiajing's reign, I served as the magistrate of Chun'an County in Zhejiang Province, where Mr Zhao was the imperial inspector. In the spring of that year, a severe flood occurred and much of Chun'an lay submerged. In May, the South China Textile Bureau acted on the order of His Majesty and issued grain subsidies to flood victims. In September, Mr Zhao urged farmers in Chun'an to pay back what had been given to them as subsidies and forced them to sell raw silk at half the market price. Through these tough measures, he aimed to fulfil the year-end quotas of five hundred thousand bolts of silk for the Imperial Palace and to amplify his political accomplishments. When I resisted Mr Zhao's order in an effort to protect the livelihood of people in my county, Mr Zhao threatened to censure me, accusing me of buying popular support and seeking notoriety. As you have just heard, he is using the same rhetoric today. Mr Zhao's prejudice is apparent. This is also the reason I called on His Majesty to define the responsibilities of his ministers. Mr Zhao belongs to the group of senior imperial officials whom I censured in my remonstrance.

Therefore, I do not believe that Mr Zhao should preside over the inquisition."

Infuriated by Hai Rui's remarks, Zhao picked up his gavel and tossed it on the floor. "Send this liar to the torture chamber," he howled.

"Let him finish, please," Gao Gong said, shooting a knowing glance at Grand Secretary Xu.

Prior to the hearing, the Prince of Yu had secretly instructed Grand Secretary Xu to protect Hai Rui. Therefore, inflicting torture was not an option. As Zhao's mentor for years, Grand Secretary Xu understood his protégé's propensity to engage in calculating and conniving behaviour. At the same time, he found Hai Rui's obstinacy and defiance intolerable. Faced with a dilemma, Grand Secretary Xu decided to obey the Prince of Yu's secret command and reject Zhao's request. "Don't bother with him," he said to Zhao. "Let him finish."

Encouraged by the grand secretary's decision, Gao Gong urged Hai Rui to continue.

"Unlike everyone in this room, I hardly have any academic credentials," Hai Rui stated. "The highest degree I have is a *juren*. Therefore, I have no desire for fame or power. Since I receive a salary from the Imperial Government, I see it as my responsibility to speak out. Over the past decades, our government coffers have been empty and the government runs into deficit year after year. Despite our fiscal restraints, His Majesty spends excessively on temples and palaces. Instead of curbing His Majesty's increasing appetite for spending and his obsession with Taoist alchemy, officials at all levels of the government ingratiate themselves by satisfying His Majesty's every whim. More egregiously, officials embezzle public funds to line their own pockets. For example, inside His Majesty's Longevity Palace, the gigantic wooden pillars were transported to Beijing from the mountains in Yunnan and Guizhou Provinces. One pillar alone costs the government fifty thousand taels of silver. As many as a hundred workers died or were injured on the road. Mr Zhao, when the Ministry of Treasury pays local governments and contractors to ship a wooden pillar from Yunnan or Guizhou to the capital city, do you not know how much of that money goes into the pockets of county and prefecture officials? Have you ever considered the cost in terms of human lives? As the minister of treasury, do you not feel responsible? This is just one example. You interrogated me last night and repeated the same questions today. I understand your intention. Since I work under you at the Ministry of Treasury, you are worried that His Majesty might suspect you of masterminding the so-called abdication attempt. I want to make it clear to everyone here that Mr Zhao has nothing to do with my remonstration. In addition, none of you would have instigated me to compose the remonstrance. I decided to speak out for two reasons – to save our Great Ming Empire and to help the common people of our nation."

Zhao stood there stunned. Grand Secretary Xu and other Privy Council members looked at Hai Rui in disbelief. Officials from other government agencies stopped taking notes. They held their calligraphy brushes and stared in awe at this headstrong, low-level official.

"Mr Zhao, I hope that by clearing your name I will help you regain His Majesty's trust," Hai Rui continued before closing his eyes. "At the same time, I don't think you have the right to interrogate me. I want to repeat, if you don't recuse yourself from my trial, I will refuse to answer any questions."

Zhao always prided himself on being a strong advocate of neo-Confucianism that emphasised self-cultivation and righteousness as a path to the formation of a virtuous and harmonious society. The night before, when he valiantly strode into Yuxi Palace and confronted Emperor Jiajing, he drew wide admiration from his peers. But Hai Rui's rebuke stripped Zhao bare. From now on, nobody would connect him with Hai Rui's treacherous plot, but Zhao's reputation as an upright official was in tatters. He was struggling for words.

Gao Gong's heart leapt with joy. "Grand Secretary Xu, how shall we proceed?" he asked. "You need to make a decision for us."

"We need to consult with His Majesty," Grand Secretary Xu replied.

Since the Privy Council's duty room was close to Yuxi Palace, Grand Secretary Xu's request reached Chen Hong in no time. He presented the inquisition transcripts to Emperor Jiajing.

Having just taken an immortality pill, the emperor was sitting on his prayer mat, feeling energised. The whites of his eyes became bloodshot. He read the record without making any comments.

"Master, the Privy Council is waiting for your order," Chen Hong reminded him.

Emperor Jiajing tossed the papers onto the floor. "This devil! The Heavenly God has sent a demon to battle me and test my stamina."

"Why don't we send him back to the Imperial Prison?" Chen Hong suggested. "I can easily subdue him through torture."

"Really?" Emperor Jiajing scoffed at his chief eunuch.

Chen Hong lowered his head.

"You are not his match. Neither is Zhao Zhenji. Deliver my edict to the Privy Council. Stop the inquisition now. Ask Grand Secretary Xu to summon all those useless scholars at Hanlin Academy and the Imperial Education Commission. They can pick a date and hold another inquisition. I shall force that demon to chew those words that he used to attack me, and then shove them down his throat."

明

As the capital of six dynasties, Nanjing had been a commercial, cultural and political centre since the third century. When Emperor Hongwu founded the Ming dynasty, many of his generals who had grown up in the south were unwilling to leave their native villages. So they selected Nanjing, rebuilt the city and made it the dynastic capital in 1368. About fifty years later, having usurped the throne from his nephew, Emperor Yongle relocated the capital to Beijing. Due to various practical considerations, Emperor Yongle decided to keep Nanjing's status as the 'southern capital' and established a parallel set of Imperial Government ministries and agencies. All provinces, prefectures and counties south of the Yellow River fell within the jurisdiction of the government in Nanjing. As a result, the so-called 'central' government in Beijing only ruled half of the territories of the Great Ming Empire. Each time the central government in Beijing issued a major policy initiative, it was required to consult with its counterpart in Nanjing. In a way, this dual system provided a certain level of checks and balances. More important, the government in Nanjing was entrusted with the task of collecting taxes from the wealthy provinces in the south, and shipping the money to Beijing to support the Imperial Palace and the Imperial Government.

Thus, among the thirteen provinces and two capitals during the Ming dynasty, two were considered strategically important to the central government in Beijing. One was Zhejiang Province, where Hu Zongxian used to rule as governor and imperial inspector. The other was Jiangsu Province, which included Nanjing, where Zhao Zhenji served as the imperial inspector before his transfer. The central government relied heavily on taxes from these two rich provinces. After the fall of Yan Song, the Prince of Yu and the Privy Council had recommended Tan Lun as the imperial inspector of Jiangsu Province.

In was March, and spring was in full bloom in Nanjing. At night, a bright spring moon and the twinkling stars decorated the sky. Along the Qinghuai River, lights flickered on the water, and the sound of oars splashing mingled with the boatmen's chatter and laughter.

A tree-lined avenue stretched parallel to the river. At this moment, a police wagon escorted by a group of soldiers on horseback burst onto the scene, disrupting the charming serenity of the river. The official who was riding at the front of the entourage was Wang Yongji. He and a group of guards from the imperial inspector's yamen had just arrested two local officials on charges of corruption and were escorting them to Nanjing.

About two hundred feet away from the Imperial Inspector's yamen, Wang spotted Tan Lun waiting for him in front of the yamen entrance, which was lit up by lanterns. Wang encouraged his horse to go faster and the whole entourage hastened.

Tan Lun came up to greet Wang when the wagon pulled up in

front of the yamen. Wang bowed while the soldiers knelt one knee to salute their imperial Inspector.

"How many did you arrest?" Tan Lun asked.

"Only two," replied Wang. "We can't touch the others until we complete our investigation."

"Send them to the provincial prison first," Tan Lun instructed the guards.

"Yes sir," a captain replied loudly before his group left with the police wagon.

"Let's go and talk inside," said Tan Lun.

The two friends entered the yamen and walked towards Tan Lun's office.

"Please leave us alone and close the door," Tan Lun told his aide. "No matter what may happen, don't barge in and interrupt us."

Once his aide exited, Tan Lun offered his friend a seat by a tea table. "Tell me about your trip."

"We talked to many people on the ground," Wang reported after taking a sip of tea. "The massive revolt was a direct result of local officials' negligence, corruption, incompetence and suppression. The coal mines in Kaihua County started to leak gas back in January. Knowing that they could cause fires, many miners went on strike. The owners bribed a eunuch who manages the Mining Bureau for the Imperial Palace. This eunuch ordered the Kaihua magistrate to send troops, forcing miners to go down the mine. Workers who held lamps in their mouths descended into the mine shaft. Barely an hour later, an explosion occurred and the mine was engulfed in flames. None of the four hundred miners were able to get out. At the same time, in Dexing County, there was a copper mine that had been in operation for four years, but the owner never bothered to spend money and reinforce the mine roof with timbers and pillars. Consequently, the mine collapsed, burying three hundred miners inside. Only a dozen survived. In both of these cases, the owners refused to pay a single penny to victims' families.

"Those poor widows and orphans petitioned their country magistrates for compensation. Rather than pacifying the victims, the magistrates of Kaihua and Dexing arrested more than a hundred petitioners. When victims' families took their cases to the prefecture yamen, the government put another hundred people behind bars. As a consequence, people felt they had no choice but to revolt against the government. There have been several riots in the region. Do you know why the county and prefecture governments in Kaihua and Dexing sided with the mine owners? The reason is simple. They split the profits with them. As we speak, riots are spreading across the region and more protesters are being locked up. When the prefecture government learned about our investigation, they quickly arrested the magistrates of Kaihua and Dexing as scapegoats. I was told that the Imperial Palace has heard about the riots. The Privy Council has assigned you and me to this case. Is this correct? We should start with these two magistrates and work with the Audit and Inspection Commission in Nanjing to expand the investigation. We're going to go after these corrupt officials one by one. I have to count on you to censure those at the Imperial Mining Bureau. We need to submit a report to His Majesty."

Tan Lun simply listened quietly. Wang noticed that his friend looked distracted.

"Has anyone pressured you to stop the investigation?" Wang asked. "This is a big scandal involving the lives of nearly seven hundred people. We can't wrap it up quickly like we did with Zheng Bichang and Ho Maocai's case."

"That case is nothing compared with what we have to handle now," Tan Lun sighed and shifted his gaze outside. "You can no longer stay in Nanjing. You have to pack and go back to Beijing tomorrow."

Wang stood up. "Hundreds of people died in these two mining accidents, and the riots are spreading. Why are you in such a rush to send me back to Beijing?"

"A much bigger incident has happened in Beijing, and I'm afraid you may be implicated. Both the Privy Council and the Audit and Inspection Commission have sent me letters, urging you to return to Beijing as soon as possible."

"Is Hai Rui in trouble?" Wang blurted out.

"Yes, they arrested him. He's now detained in the Imperial Prison."

"Did he submit a remonstrance to His Majesty?"

"Yes, the Privy Council has delivered me a copy of his remonstrance via express mail. What he has written is truly shocking."

"Could you show it to me?"

"I'm under oath to keep it confidential," said Tan Lun. "It's better if you don't read it. When you return to Beijing, you should never say that you knew about his attempt to submit a remonstrance in advance."

Wang stood there in a daze. The two friends looked at each other.

"No wonder Hai Rui urged me to request a business trip to Nanjing after the New Year," Wang murmured. "I should have thought about it... Obviously, he didn't want to implicate me... What about Amu? Hai Rui's wife is pregnant. What are they going to do now?"

"Leave that to me," Tan Lun said as he strolled to the window. "You wouldn't be able to help even if you wanted to. After all, it's my fault. If I hadn't invited him out to take the Chun'an magistrate's position, he would have avoided this scourge and lived out a quiet and peaceful life in his village... Oh well, Dr Li has brought Amu and Mrs Hai to Nanjing. Regardless of what happens to Hai Rui, I will take good care of them. When you go back to Beijing, remember two things. First, try to dissociate yourself from Hai Rui. Second, do not breathe a word of the mining accidents and the pending investigation. If Chen Hong knows that we intend to investigate his allies at the Imperial Mining Bureau, he'll retaliate and deflect attention by encouraging His Majesty to execute Hai Rui."

"Could you arrange a horse for me?" asked Wang. "I'll leave right away."

The front yard was spacious. Accompanied by Dr Li Shizhen, Amu and Mrs Hai entered the courtyard, surprised at what they saw. At the same time, there was a sense of familiarity that drew them in.

Bolts of soaked cloth lay spread out on slabs of stone, each of which was about three metres long and one metre wide. On top of each stone table was a thick log. Workers were rolling the logs back and forth over the cloth.

"What are they doing?" Amu asked a foreman who greeted them at the door.

"Amu, we use logs to smooth and tighten the fabric before we dye them over there," explained the foreman, pointing to the far side of the yard. Amu saw several large marble dye tanks positioned side by side. Next to the tanks sat a row of large vats. On the left-hand side of the yard were three-metre-high wooden racks to hang sheets of dyed cloth. Amu watched some workers who were stirring the fabric in a tank filled with an indigo solution. Using long bamboo rods, the workers scooped bolts of dripping cloth from the tank and tossed them into the air. The fabric landed securely on the tall racks.

"Please, pause for a moment to let our guest walk past," the foreman shouted to the workers.

Everyone stopped what they were doing to greet the four guests by the courtyard door.

With a beaming smile, the foreman held Amu's arm. "Your room is in the backyard," he said. "Let's go."

A teenage girl with a happy and innocent face rushed over to assist Mrs Hai. The foreman introduced her as Yu Qing. She gesticulated vigorously. Mrs Hai realised she was born mute.

Yu Qing was Madame Yun's maid. After Madame Yun received Tan Lun's letter, she sent her maid to Nanjing to take care of Amu and Mrs Hai. Yu Qing would be perfect for the job. Since she could not speak, the maid wouldn't be able to reveal Amu and Mrs Hai's whereabouts to anyone. Mrs Hai's baby bump was already visible and she felt clumsy. With Yu Qing holding her left arm, she put her right hand on her hip and carefully descended the stairs.

All of a sudden, Amu stopped. "Dr Li, what is this place?" she asked with a suspicious look on her face. "Why are we staying here?"

"This is my friend's house," Dr Li replied with a smile. "He's also a friend of Hai Rui's. He and his wife are in the cotton cloth business. The front yard serves as a weaving and dye workshop. The residential quarter is at the back. That's where you and Mrs Hai will stay. We thought you might find this place interesting. During the day, if you're bored, you can come to the front yard and watch the workers weaving and dyeing fabrics. They would love it if you and Mrs Hai could show them the Hainan style of weaving. So, the arrangement will be good for everyone. I'm sure you and Mrs Hai will enjoy your time here."

A smile crept across Amu's face. She exchanged a glance with her daughter-in-law and started moving.

"Dr Li, that's very thoughtful of you," Amu said. "But we can't stay here for free. If we could do some weaving for this friend of yours, it would make me feel better. Didn't you just say that this person also knows Hai Rui. How come I've never heard of him before?"

"I'm sure you have. When Hai Rui served as the magistrate of Chun'an County, this friend was the mayor of Hangzhou."

"Oh, I remember him. Was it Mayor Gao? He was arrested and sent to Beijing for investigation."

"Yes, that was him," Dr Li confirmed.

"Hai Rui spoke very highly of him, saying that he was a Hanlin scholar and very talented. Too bad he has to run a business, rather than working for the Imperial Government."

"There's nothing shameful about operating a business," Dr Li said. "Businessmen are just as respectable as imperial officials, scholars, farmers and workers. We need businessmen like Gao Hanwen. When he worked for the Imperial Court, he was upright and honest. Now that he's running a textile mill, he's just the same. People say he's a fair and compassionate businessman. You should trust him. He'll take good care of you here."

"It's not that I don't trust him," said Amu. "I just hope we don't inconvenience him and his wife, and cause them too much trouble."

As the guests were walking through the front yard, they noticed two weaving workshops on either side of the pathway. The loud, rhythmic sound of shuttle looms came from inside the rooms. Amu was itching to go in, but the foreman stopped her. "Amu, I'll give you a tour later," he said. "Let's get you settled in your room first."

An elaborate wooden pavilion corridor connected the noisy

front yard to the quiet residential quarter at the back. At the end of the zigzag gallery, the guests found themselves inside a quiet, picturesque courtyard house with a rock garden. Amu and Mrs Hai paused again, gasping in surprise when they saw a large pond full of lotus blossoms with a winding stone bridge and an elegant pavilion. At the end of the bridge stood a grand, two-storey house with carved pillars and curved roofs. They felt like they were stepping into an ink painting.

"Is this where we are going to sleep?" Amu asked the foreman.

"Yes, you'll be staying in the downstairs room."

Amu's face fell. "This is such an extravagant place," she said, shaking her head. "There's no way we're going to live here."

"Many courtyard houses south of the Yangtze River are like this," Dr Li explained. "In comparison, this compound is bigger because Mr Gao and his wife converted their front yard into textile workshops. Each time I visit Nanjing, Mr Gao always put me up here. Amu, this is my favourite place. I'm sure you'll like it too."

"When my master and mistress heard you were coming," the foreman said with a welcoming smile, "they were so pleased that they made special arrangements for you. If you leave, I'm afraid I'll get the blame."

Amu glanced at her daughter-in-law. They both looked hesitant.

"My master and mistress are on the way back from the Songjiang region," said the foreman. "They'll probably be here tonight. If you're reluctant to stay, you can see them first and figure out what to do next. Would that work?"

Amu turned to Dr Li. "It's already the fourteenth of April," she mumbled. "Hai Rui said he'll arrive in Nanjing in early May. We have one more month. Are you going to stay with us during this time?"

"Of course! I'll leave after Hai Rui gets here," Dr Li promised

Despite her stubborn nature, Amu was open to persuasion. After all, she had a tremendous respect for Dr Li. "Now that Dr Li is staying here as well, I guess we'll have to inconvenience them for a month," she said to Mrs Hai. "We'll move out after your husband gets here."

"Whatever you say," Mrs Hai replied obediently.

The decision pleased the foreman. "That's good," he said to Amu. "Let's cross the bridge here. Give me your arm. Be careful."

Dr Li watched as the foreman and Yu Qing led Hai Rui's mother and wife across the stone bridge. With a gloomy face, he raised his head and looked at the sky to the north.

明

The fifty-year-old Hai Rui never told Amu a single lie in his life. But this time, he would not be able to fulfil the promise he had made to his mother. Amu's wait would become indefinite.

Summer arrived in the blink of an eye. On 5 May, scholars at Hanlin Academy and the Imperial Education Commission, many of whom were members of the Clear Stream faction, gathered at the main hall of the Audit and Inspection Commission building. They had been ordered to denounce Hai Rui and rebut his arguments in the remonstrance.

Prior to the hearing, officials had removed desks and chairs from the main hall and placed rows of cushions on the floor. Grand Secretary Xu and members of the Privy Council arrived first and sat on the cushions against the north wall. Soon, other officials filed in and found their seats on both sides of the hall. Li Qingyuan, who had led a protest outside the Western Compound before the New Year, sat in the front row on the left side of the hall. Wang Yongji found a cushion at the back.

Chen Hong came with a group of junior eunuchs. He did not enter the main hall. Instead, two of his junior eunuchs placed a chair near the entrance and he sat down quietly.

The public denunciation session was scheduled to start at ten o'clock in the morning. When the hour arrived, Wang gazed at the door and waited anxiously for his friend to appear. Half an hour later, there was still no sign of Hai Rui. All eyes were on the four cabinet members. Grand Secretary Xu peered at the sun outside the window before turning to Chen Hong.

"Chen Gonggong, do you know when Hai Rui will be here?" he asked. "Shall we send someone to check with the guards at the Imperial Prison?"

"There's no rush. We're waiting for His Majesty's order," said Chen Hong, sounding nonchalant.

Grand Secretary Xu had no idea that Emperor Jiajing controlled the time of Hai Rui's appearance. He exchanged frustrated glances with other cabinet members and waited impatiently.

Chen Hong raised his head and squinted at the rising sun. He appeared equally clueless.

中

The oil lamps on the walls of the long passageway cast a faint glow, shedding some light into a corner of Hai Rui's cell. He sat on a thin layer of straw, waiting for the jailer to collect him.

On the previous day, he had received a notice that he would be summoned for a hearing in the main hall of the Audit and Inspection Commission at ten o'clock in the morning. So he awoke early to get himself ready.

People who have been in the dark for a long time tend to develop light sensitivity. Even though Hai Rui sat in the cell with his eyes closed, he could feel a patch of light moving towards him. This was followed by the sound of hurried footsteps.

"Here he is," the jailer whispered to someone.

"How come there's no bed or table in his cell?" asked another in a distinct high-pitched voice. Hai Rui knew the visitor was a senior-ranking eunuch. He kept his eyes closed and did not stir.

"Bring a desk and a chair over here," the eunuch instructed the jailer. "Set up a bed for him after I leave. Unlock the door now."

The cell door clanked open. Someone pitter-pattered inside. Soon, Hai Rui could sense that the person was standing right in front of him. Two people could be heard moving a table and a chair into his cell.

"Put them here," said the eunuch. "Wait for me at the jail entrance."

"Yes, Gonggong." The two people stepped out and the sound of their footsteps disappeared into the distance.

Hai Rui opened his eyes. The glowing lantern on the desk dazzled him. As he lowered his head to allow his eyes to adjust to the light, he noticed a pair of shiny black boots and a red robe. Slowly, he lifted his eyes and saw the pale, plump face of a middle-aged eunuch.

"My last name is Shi, and I'm first deputy interior minister," said Shi. "I have a few questions for you."

Shi Gonggong used to be ranked beneath Huang Jin, but following Huang's arrest, he was promoted to his current position. "I'm here to question you on the order of His Majesty," said Shi, who sounded business-like. "You can sit there on the chair and answer my questions. If you prefer, you can stand up. Do you want me to help you stand?"

"Shi Gonggong, please take that chair. Since you are here to deliver His Majesty's decree, it's only appropriate that I sit on the floor."

Shi glanced at the round-backed armchair, but didn't sit. He stood, gazing at Hai Rui. "You're an honest and upright official," he stated.

Hai Rui could not help looking up at him.

"I'm just quoting His Majesty," explained Shi.

Since his imprisonment, Hai Rui had managed to remain as calm as still water. But Emperor Jiajing's remark caused a small ripple in his heart.

"His Majesty said you might aspire to emulate the outspoken Bi Gan, but he is not the wicked King Zhou," said Shi.

Hai Rui gave that some thought before he answered: "The Great Ming dynasty is not a replica of the Shang dynasty. Bi Gan doesn't exist here. Neither does King Zhou."

"That's an excellent answer, and I will report it back verbatim to His Majesty. I'm here to deliver two messages. The first one is from His Majesty. Listen carefully."

"Go ahead."

"You shall attend a denunciation meeting in the Audit and Inspection Commission's main hall. The participants will be scholars and officials from Hanlin Academy and the Imperial Education Commission. They have all read your remonstrance and will rebut every single one of your claims. His Majesty wants to know if you intend to respond to their rebuttals."

"I will only respond to those that deserve answers."

"Tell me, which ones deserve an answer and which ones don't?" shouted Shi, who stamped his feet on the floor furiously. Hai Rui shot him a derisive glance. As Shi paced around, huffing and puffing, he closed his eyes.

"Why are you so stubborn?" Shi continued. "If you have a death wish, please go ahead. If you like, jump into the Tonghui River or even better, hang yourself. A piece of rope only costs two copper coins. Why are you bent on stirring up trouble and creating chaos? Mr Hai, you and those idealists probably worship that proverb – a virtuous official is not afraid to die from remonstrating, and a valiant warrior does not fear death in combat. You know what I think of this saying? It's dog shit. Only well-educated idiots believe in that stuff. Do you know how many people you have implicated this time?"

Hai Rui kept his eyes closed and did not answer.

"Let me just give you a quick list of those who have been jailed because of you. I'll start with those at the Imperial Palace. Lu Gonggong, the former interior minister, retired to Nanjing last summer. Out of nowhere, he's been accused of conspiring with you against His Majesty. Someone is trying to use this incident as an excuse to imprison him. Huang Gonggong served His Majesty for years. He has the heart of a bodhisattva. After trying to defend your behaviour, he was thrown in jail. They're torturing him daily and have broken his leg. Zhu Qi, an imperial agent who is sympathetic to your case, and your friend Chee Dazhu have both been detained. Yesterday afternoon, your good friend Wang Yongji was summoned back to Beijing. If you don't admit guilt and apologise, none of the people I have mentioned will be spared. If you don't give a damn about your own family members, you should at least show some compassion for those around you. Don't you want to save these people's lives?"

"How can I save them?"

Shi's face gradually softened. He took a furtive look outside and squatted down next to Hai Rui. "That's what I'm here for – to save you from this lunacy," he said in a gentle voice. "When you arrive at the main hall of the Audit and Inspection Commission, all you need to do is issue a public apology. His Majesty will release you. Others won't suffer on your account. Do you understand what I'm saying?"

Hai Rui remained silent, but Shi detected a painful expression on his face. He stared at Hai Rui, waiting for an answer.

"I have no intention of implicating and harming others," Hai Rui finally said.

"That's good then," Shi replied, thinking that Hai Rui had changed his mind.

"Shi Gonggong, at the beginning of our conversation, you said you were here to deliver two messages. I'm eager to hear the second one."

"Well, my second message is related to the first. If you're willing to admit guilt, His Majesty has already figured out a way to give you a means of escape. He doesn't want to make it too hard for you. You can simply say that you misinterpreted the governing philosophies of Confucius and Mencius, and made some untrue and inflammatory claims. Then, you should seek His Majesty's forgiveness. Once you voluntarily seek forgiveness, His Majesty will absolve you of guilt and transfer you to the Imperial Education Commission so you can improve your learning about Confucius and Mencius. On the surface, the transfer might sound like a punishment. But in reality, it'll be a good career opportunity. Since you only have a *juren* degree, you can use your position at the Imperial Education Commission to participate in a special imperial exam. Once you have received your academic titles, you'll have a brighter future within the Imperial Government. More important, future historians will laud the relationship between you and His Majesty as legendary and unprecedented."

Hai Rui averted Shi's expectant eyes. "Shi Gonggong, I want to use the words of the sages as my response to His Majesty's generous offer," Hai Rui said. "I hope you can relay my message truthfully. Mencius teaches us that the people are to be valued the most, followed by the state and the ruler last of all. Laozi advises us that a wise ruler has no concern for himself, but makes the concerns of others his own. I sincerely hope His Majesty thinks more about our Great Ming Empire and the millions of his subjects. In comparison, my own personal life is as insignificant as a fallen leaf that will turn into soil in the coming spring."

Shi breathed a helpless sigh. As Hai Rui closed his eyes to conclude the conversation, he could hear the soft rustling sound of Shi's silk robe. After the eunuch scurried out of the cell, Hai Rui opened his eyes. The lantern sat on the desk in the middle of his cell and the door remained open. He glanced outside. Two imperial agents and two jailers were standing motionless in the passageway as if their feet had been nailed to the ground. Shi was nowhere to be seen. Soon, more footsteps sounded at the far end of the passageway. The imperial agents and jailers quickly dropped to their knees. Hai Rui assumed that a senior official had arrived to fetch him and take him to the denunciation meeting at the Audit and Inspection Commission.

He closed his eyes, waiting for the jailers to come in and escort him out. Someone paused at the door. Then, it sounded like the imperial agents and jailers hurried away. The place fell silent. The person strode into Hai Rui's cell. From the heavy thud of cotton shoes, Hai Rui knew that the person was not Shi. He cocked an eyebrow. The person sat down on the chair and sized him up.

"You'll face another trial soon," the person finally spoke. Hai Rui had never heard this deep, gloomy voice before and he could feel a power weighing down on him. Unconsciously, Hai Rui straightened his back to compose himself. Opening his eyes, he gazed at the stranger, whose eyes resembled two deep, dark holes. Even though it was May, he was wearing a blue silk gown over a thick cotton robe. Without his official uniform, Hai Rui could not tell his rank or identity.

Unbeknownst to Hai Rui, the person in front of him was the emperor whom he had fiercely attacked in his remonstrance. Emperor Jiajing had reigned over the country for forty-five years, but seldom held audiences with imperial officials in the last two decades. Thus, the majority of officials had no idea what their monarch looked like.

Glancing at Hai Rui, who was sitting fully shackled on a layer of straw on the floor, Emperor Jiajing remarked: "You'll face the country's top Confucian scholars, who will challenge and censure you.

But I doubt their condemnation will deter you and change your mind. His Majesty has sent me here to share some of their rebuttals beforehand. He is curious to find out how you will respond."

"Since this is an order from His Majesty, I will do my best to answer those rebuttals that deserve honest answers," said Hai Rui. All of a sudden, Hai Rui was hit with an indescribable premonition about the tall, lanky stranger with thick eyebrows and long beard. "Sir, may I know which yamen you work for?"

"I work for a government agency like you," Emperor Jiajing replied without taking his eyes off the rebuttals on the desk. "Just answer my questions."

"All right, please go ahead."

"Let me read a question from Li Qingyuan, an official with the Imperial Education Commission: 'Who do you consider to be a virtuous and capable monarch in recent history?'"

"The first name that comes to my mind is Emperor Wen of the Han dynasty," said Hai Rui.

"Emperor Wen was lauded by later generations as a benevolent ruler who governed the country with policies of non-interference. His reign was marked by thriftiness and relaxed laws and low tax burdens."

Hai Rui nodded.

"Li has a follow-up question. If you consider Emperor Wen a benevolent and capable monarch, why do you rebuke him for 'his retreat, inaction and supernatural fascination'? This is nothing more than a veiled attack against the current emperor, is it not?"

Hai Rui did not respond.

"Why aren't you answering me?"

"These questions are not worth refuting."

"Is it possible that you simply don't have an answer?" retorted Emperor Jiajing, whose eyes bore into Hai Rui's.

"People like Li have not fully understood my remonstrance. They will never understand it. Therefore, his questions do not deserve my answers."

"You sound so arrogant. I'm afraid you have to respond. This is an order from His Majesty."

"All right then," Hai Rui replied in a raised voice. "In his later years, Emperor Wen began to pursue Taoism, and jettisoned the teachings of Confucius and Mencius. He adopted Laozi's philosophy of governing by doing nothing that goes against nature. His retreat and his fascination with supernatural events left many important state affairs unattended. Even so, I believe that Emperor Wen was a benevolent ruler because he cared very deeply for his people. His reign was marked by compassion and thriftiness. He listened to his advisors and put the interests of his subjects above all. His benign rule enabled the country and the people to recover from war and natural disasters. Our current emperor is under the illusion that he's following the example of Emperor Wen. For more than two decades, he has ignored imperial duties in the name of 'governing by doing nothing that goes against nature'. He regards his ministers as his house servants and treats the state coffers as his personal wallet. He imposes his will upon millions of his people. His policies have profited those at the top and led to rampant corruption at all levels of government. His unrestrained spending has depleted resources and plunged ordinary people into misery. Allow me to be blunt. Even a benevolent ruler like Emperor Wen is often criticised for his neglect of state affairs. In comparison, our current emperor is far worse."

Emperor Jiajing froze. The colour drained from his face.

"Our Imperial Government employs tens of thousands of talented people, but none would dare remonstrate with His Majesty," Hai Rui continued. "I'm the only one who steps forward. If I don't speak up, future historians will. Your Highness, please pass on my question to Li and other officials who attempt to refute my writing. They're afraid to speak up and I understand that. But when I come forward, why do they engage in character assassination? Would they rather that His Majesty earn himself eternal infamy? Someone has to tell His Majesty the truth."

Emperor Jiajing stared blankly at the ceiling without speaking. After a short pause, he said with a deep roar: "Are you saying that our current emperor is a fatuous ruler and all of his courtiers are sycophants? And that you're the only loyal, virtuous and upright official in the whole Great Ming Empire?"

"I'm just an honest, straight talker."

"A straight talker without a father and without an emperor!" uttered Emperor Jiajing as he cast a murderous look at Hai Rui.

Hai Rui was stunned. It took him a while to recover. "Your Highness, when you have the chance, could you relay my words to His Majesty?" he pleaded.

"Speak."

"I lost my father at the age of four," he said, giving way to his emotions. "My... my mother, a virtuous widow, raised me on her own. Before I left to take up a position within the Imperial Government, my mother admonished me by saying that since I grew up without a father, it is His Majesty who now clothes and feeds you, he's your father. Actually, Hai Rui is not the only one who regards His Majesty as his father. Of all the people in the Great Ming Empire, who doesn't? Unfortunately, our current emperor never treats the people as his own children. For decades, he relied on members of the Yan Clan to rule the land. Eunuchs and officials at all levels of government exploited people ruthlessly and slaughtered them like meat on their chopping boards. His Majesty lives deep inside the Western Compound, spending a great deal of his time on meditation and alchemy. Is he aware of the fact that his people are suffering? Has it ever occurred to him that millions of his subjects are ruled by an emperor who doesn't protect them like a caring father? The people he has hired to run the government act like robbers. In the two capitals and thirteen provinces, mothers and babies are dying of cold and hunger. Does my emperor father know about this?"

Hai Rui's words reverberated inside the cell. Emperor Jiajing felt as if the whole prison was shaking. He gritted his teeth and grabbed the desk with both hands so he wouldn't fall from his chair. Hai Rui stared at the stranger's face, which was turning ashen. Soon, Hai Rui noticed that the stranger's nose began to bleed. A stream of blood dripped out of the corners of his mouth.

Shocked, Hai Rui shouted. "Help!"

Urgent footsteps sounded in the passageway. Shi dashed in. Several jailers and imperial agents followed him.

"Your Majesty," cried Shi as he descended on Emperor Jiajing and wiped the blood from his nostrils with a white silk handkerchief. The jailers and imperial agents knelt around, looking lost.

"Carry His Majesty to the Imperial Hospital," Shi shouted.

The jailers and imperial agents sprang to their feet and flocked around the emperor. They lifted the chair on which the emperor sat and carried it out.

Amid the chaos, Hai Rui sank to his knees and watched in horror. A feeling of panic, guilt and helplessness welled up in him. He had never felt this way before.

"Stop for a moment," Emperor Jiajing shouted to the imperial agents, who paused outside the cell.

"Hai Rui," the emperor said with his eyes closed.

"Yes, Your Majesty," Hai Rui replied and adjusted his posture so he was facing Emperor Jiajing's back. "Your humble servant is here."

"I want to gift you two sentences. You're a man without a father and without an emperor. You have abandoned your family and your country."

Hai Rui prostrated himself on the floor.

"Let's get out of here," Shi urged.

The group of jailers and imperial agents carried the emperor away swiftly.

Things quietened down. Slowly, Hai Rui raised his head and gazed at the empty passageway. His eyes glistened with tears.

8

"What's the hold-up," Chen Hong asked as Shi, the first deputy interior minister, strode into the Audit and Inspection Commission's main hall. "It's already eleven o'clock. Has His Majesty issued a new decree?"

"Yes," Shi whispered reverentially. "I need to announce it to the whole group here."

Chen Hong nodded.

"Attention, an imperial edict has arrived!" Shi proclaimed to all the participants in the main hall.

Grand Secretary Xu and his cabinet members rose from the floor. They moved their cushions to the centre of the hall and knelt down. Members of the Clear Stream faction who were sitting on the left and right side of the hall followed Grand Secretary Xu's example and sank to their knees.

Walking to the podium, Shi declared:

His Majesty has issued a verbal decree: 'Hai Rui is nothing more than a man without a father and without an emperor. He has abandoned his family and his country. He has alienated himself from the Imperial Palace and his peers. Reasoning with him has become a pointless and impossible exercise. I hereby order Grand Secretary Xu and Chen Hong to convene members of the Interior

Ministry and Privy Council as well as a hundred representatives of Hanlin Academy and the Imperial Education Commission to deliberate over his crimes without his presence.'

The participants had spent nearly a month preparing for their rebuttals, but now Emperor Jiajing declared that "reasoning with Hai Rui has become a pointless and impossible exercise". One would assume they would be disappointed and feel horribly cheated, but the stony-faced officials reacted calmly, as if they had long expected it. The order to cancel Hai Rui's appearance struck them as inevitable as a boat folding its mast before passing under a low bridge. In fact, they would have been astonished if Emperor Jiajing had gone ahead with his previous plan.

Since Chen Hong and Grand Secretary Xu were named in the verbal edict, they stepped forward to register their responses. "We'll do accordingly," the two senior officials pledged.

A group of junior eunuchs placed eight chairs in a semi-circle along the north wall. Chen Hong and three of his deputies occupied the four seats on the left, while Grand Secretary Xu and his cabinet members sat on the right.

"Please stay seated on the floor," Grand Secretary Xu told the other participants.

"What does His Majesty intend us to do?" Chen Hong asked Shi.

"Deliberate over his crimes," replied Shi.

"All right then, let's start. Grand Secretary Xu, you tell us how to proceed."

Grand Secretary Xu did not respond immediately. His gaze swept the main hall.

Both Grand Secretary Xu and Chen Hong understood the true intentions behind Emperor Jiajing's order of "deliberating over Hai Rui's crimes". If he had wanted them to convict Hai Rui, he would have requested the joint appearance of members of the Justice Department and the Imperial Judiciary. At the moment, those who were present were scholar officials from Hanlin Academy and the Imperial Education Commission. It was obvious that the emphasis was on the word "deliberation". Even though Hai Rui was absent, Emperor Jiajing insisted that his peers denounce those claims so the whole world would know that Hai Rui's views were isolated and that the entire Imperial Government found him repugnant.

"We have distributed copies of Hai Rui's remonstrance to everyone," Grand Secretary Xu finally announced. "I know that you have all prepared your rebuttals. It's time to share what you have written with everyone."

Grand Secretary Xu's words were met with silence. The main hall felt like a pool of stagnant water.

All four Privy Council members were prominent Confucian scholars and none was willing to force others to speak on such a politically sensitive occasion. If they uttered anything inappropriate in front of so many of their peers, they would be scorned and despised, and their notoriety would spread fast. Therefore, Grand Secretary Xu simply sat there, waiting patiently.

Chen Hong could no longer bear the silence. "What is your problem?" he berated the crowd. "Is this a boycott? I want you to take turns. Let's start with the first on the left."

Li Qingyuan was sitting in that position. "Chen Gonggong, we were asked earlier to each write down our rebuttals," said Li. "We have all done our work, but we also have important questions for Hai Rui. If the defendant is not here today, to whom do we direct our questions?"

"That's a very good question," Chen Hong said sarcastically. "What you are saying… I mean, what all of you are saying is that… you cannot interrogate him and debate his arguments in his absence… Well, since you have brought along your rebuttals, why don't you just share what you have written? To make it easier, I'll ask you questions. Li Qingyuan, you go first."

"Yes, Chen Gonggong."

"Do you think Hai Rui is guilty?"

"Yes, I do."

"What kind of crimes has he perpetrated?"

"He should not have criticised His Majesty with disrespectful language."

"Is that it?"

"Yes, I think I have answered your question."

"Was he justified in attacking His Majesty with crude language?"

"I just said that it is wrong to insult His Majesty."

"You're dodging my question," said Chen Hong. "I want to know if Hai Rui's accusations are true."

"At home, we never blame our parents because they're always right. The same is true with His Majesty. The crown can do no wrong."

When Chen Hong noticed that others in the main hall were nodding approvingly, he became furious. "Are you all going to give me the same answer?" he asked in a raised voice.

"Chen Gonggong, I extrapolated the first half of my answer from one of Confucius's sayings. The Prince of Yu emphasised the second part during a recent speech he gave to us. If Chen Gonggong thinks my answer is inappropriate, I can retract it."

Chen Hong was stumped. His face turned glum, and he turned to Shi and asked: "Do you have any questions for Li Qingyuan and others?"

Shi cleared his throat and announced: "Since you have all prepared written rebuttals, I'll collect them and extract important passages from each submission. Then I will compile them into one copy. The Privy Council will distribute the compilation to senior provincial officials in the form of an internal briefing. The Justice Department and the Imperial Judiciary will take into account what you have written when they deliver the verdict."

Chen Hong narrowed his eyes and squinted at his deputy, whose determined look led Chen to conclude that it was Emperor Jiajing's idea. He suppressed his displeasure.

"I second the motion," Grand Secretary Xu chimed in. "If we ask each person to read out his statement, it will take us at least three days."

"I agree," Gao Gong said. "Please drop off your written responses here."

Seeing that the officials there were merely going through the motions, Chen Hong became worried. If anything went awry, the emperor would no doubt single him out for punishment. To avoid a repeat of what had happened with the congratulatory letters, Chen Hong wanted to make sure that he had collected a report from every single person. Moreover, he needed to review them personally before submitting them to the emperor.

"Hold on," he said when catching sight of Wang Yongji, who had just returned to Beijing the day before. "Have you written your rebuttal?"

"Yes, I burned the midnight oil and finished my report this morning," Wang replied.

"I would be interested in hearing your opinions about Hai Rui's unfounded accusations against His Majesty."

Wang handed over his report. "Chen Gonggong, please pass on the report to Grand Secretary Xu after you read it. The report details my month-long investigation into the two mining accidents in Kaihua and Dexing Counties in Jiangsu Province. Local officials' corruption and their indifference to the plight of victims have led to large-scale riots in the region. I hope the Interior Ministry and the Privy Council can brief His Majesty on this."

"It's about time you laid your cards on the table," said Chen Hong, who could not hide his excitement in sniffing out a cunning prey. "On the seventeenth of February, when imperial officials in Beijing were supposed to send their congratulatory letters to His Majesty, Hai Rui took advantage of the occasion and submitted a remonstrance to attack His Majesty. When His Majesty issued a decree, urging everyone to denounce Hai Rui and refute his unfounded claims, you submit a report on some mining accidents in Jiangsu Province. So, you two appeared to have collaborated so seamlessly. Let me ask you. Did Hai Rui discuss this with you before he drafted the remonstrance?"

Grand Secretary Xu and other Privy Council members thought they had just weathered a major political storm. Seeing that Chen Hong was about to start another, they were filled with disgust but too afraid to show their feelings. All they did was stand there, silently.

For Chen Hong, he had no intention of creating more trouble, but having known Emperor Jiajing so well, he acted out of political necessity. Over the past two decades, the emperor ignored imperial duties and relied on the Yan Clan to run the country. Yan Song successfully shielded Emperor Jiajing from attack by outspoken neo-Confucian scholars. When something went wrong, the emperor conveniently made Yan Song his scapegoat. Now that Yan Song had been toppled, Emperor Jiajing had no choice but to rely on Grand Secretary Xu and Lu Fang. Much to the emperor's frustration, Grand Secretary Xu pursued appeasement rather than confrontation. His chief eunuch Lu Fang took a similarly conciliatory approach, trying to win favour from all sides. Each time a dispute occurred and the Imperial Palace was under siege by dissenting courtiers, Emperor Jiajing had to step in to battle his opponents himself. He loathed such tasks. Chen Hong understood this. On multiple occasions, Chen Hong projected himself as a strong defender of Emperor Jiajing, and intimated that he was willing to be the emperor's substitute and do his dirty work. His relentless efforts paid off. Emperor Jiajing fired Lu Fang and installed Chen Hong as his chief eunuch. In the previous winter, Chen Hong won praise from the emperor after he brutally crushed a group of protesters outside the Western Compound.

In February, when Hai Rui delivered the remonstrance, Chen Hong was startled to find out that none of the Privy Council members and ministerial officials was willing to step up and defend Emperor Jiajing. The inquisition had been delayed for months and when it finally occurred, imperial officials were reluctant to openly condemn Hai Rui. If he reported the results of today's hearing truthfully, Emperor Jiajing would no doubt fly into a rage. Grand Secretary Xu and his cabinet members might be able to get away with it because of their support from the Prince of Yu. But if he failed to act tough and hunt down a few of Hai Rui's sympathisers, he wouldn't be able to hold onto his job as interior minister.

Meanwhile, Wang remained unfazed by Chen Hong's questioning. He felt tempted to step forward and take the blame for Hai Rui by claiming it was his idea to deliver the scathing censure. But doing so would constitute deception because Hai Rui had never consulted with him. Moreover, if he confessed to being complicit in Hai Rui's plan, he would make things worse for Hai Rui. The Imperial Palace could charge Hai Rui with the more serious crime of leading a squad of insurrectionists.

"Answer me," Chen Hong demanded.

He decided to use a different approach to defend Hai Rui and let his peers and future generations know that Hai Rui risked his life to remonstrate with the emperor.

"Chen Gonggong, Hai Rui never even notified me of his remonstrance before he wrote it, let alone consulted me," Wang responded.

"You know how much I despise cowards like you," Chen Hong berated Wang. "Since Hai Rui's transfer to Beijing last July, I was told that you contacted him frequently, and during each visit, you often spent hours talking to him. A few days before Hai Rui submitted his remonstrance, you made a request to the Audit and Inspection Commission, volunteering to handle a criminal investigation in Jiangsu Province, where you stayed until after Hai Rui's arrest. What a coincidence! You intended to create an impression that you have nothing to do with Hai Rui's crime. At the same time, you lack the guts to renounce him. So you wrote up a report last night about some mining accidents in Jiangsu to distract us. Wang Yongji, I hate to say it but you're a small and petty man, a person of low character!"

Wang was by nature a warm-hearted but mild-mannered individual. Chen Hong's insult today infuriated him, prompting him to stand up, not only to defend Hai Rui's reputation, but also his own. "It really doesn't matter if you like me or despise me," Wang replied scornfully. "I serve at the pleasure of His Majesty. Besides, of all the people in the Imperial Palace, I wouldn't call Chen Gonggong a good judge of character."

Officials in the main hall, including the deputy ministers, sat up straight, trying to suppress their chuckles.

Vindictive as he was, Chen Hong was also a master of disguise. Hiding his furore and embarrassment, he tried to laugh off Wang's insult: "All right then, if you don't like me calling you a person of low character, show me some evidence to prove me wrong!"

"Hai Rui is a patriot who never allies with any political factions," said Wang. "He doesn't need a cohort. It goes against his nature to involve others in his personal endeavour. Since he and I are close friends, he strongly encouraged me to request an assignment in the south and leave Beijing before he submitted his remonstrance. I didn't understand his true intention until today. He didn't want to implicate me. For this alone, I regard him as a truly noble and virtuous man. By comparison, I'm a small person, but not in the way that you described."

"What did you just say?" Chen Hong balked in his high-pitched voice. "Did you say Hai Rui is a virtuous and noble man?"

"Hai Rui has the guts to accept the consequences of his own action without harming others. That's what Confucius defined as a virtuous and noble man."

"Have you all heard what he just said?" Chen Hong proclaimed to the crowd. While the majority of participants cast their eyes down, the four cabinet members glanced at each other, trying to figure out how to respond.

"Wang Yongji, of the five cardinal human relationships – that between the ruler and his courtier, that between parents and children, that between siblings, that between husband and wife and that between friends – it is the relationship between ruler and his courtiers that ranks first," Grand Secretary Xu said. "The focus of our meeting today is to denounce Hai Rui's writings disrespectful of His Majesty. You shouldn't digress from our main focus by talking about your friendship with Hai Rui."

During the Ming dynasty, the Imperial Government was jointly run by the Interior Ministry and the Privy Council. When trouble occurred, the Interior Ministry tended to deflect the blame onto the Privy Council. Chen Hong found it hard to do so today. Of the four cabinet members, Grand Secretary Xu and Gao Gong were teachers of the Prince of Yu. Chen Hong did not want to get on their wrong side. Meanwhile, Deputy Li was known to be a pleasant and accommodating individual, and Chen Hong needed him as an ally. So the only person that Chen Hong always picked on was Zhao Zhenji.

"Mr Zhao, while you served as the imperial inspector of Zhejiang Province, Wang Yongji was the magistrate of Jiande County. You should know him fairly well. How would you respond to his remarks?"

Zhao felt exasperated but he had no choice but to take a stance: "I agree with what Grand Secretary Xu has just said."

"What do you mean?" Chen Hong asked. "A scholar, who is employed by the Imperial Government, fed and clothed by His Majesty. Instead of feeling grateful, the person abandoned his obligations to His Majesty and placed his personal friendship above all else. You're a prominent leader of the Taizhou school of neo-Confucianism. How do you comment on Wang's remarks relating to Hai Rui's so-called Confucian virtues?"

Zhao was placed in a dilemma. "When an imperial official puts personal friendship above the interests of the monarch, he violates the law and should be treated as an accomplice."

"I'm glad that you countenance the fact that Wang Yongji should be treated as an accomplice," Chen Hong said. "I'm certain that other members of the Privy Council share Zhao's view. Put this cohort of Hai Rui's under arrest!"

Two imperial agents stormed into the main hall and swooped down on Wang. As they pulled him up from the floor, the anti-corruption report that he was holding fell to the ground. Wang steadied himself and addressed Grand Secretary Xu: "My report contains details about how several of Chen Gonggong's subordinates at the Imperial Mining Bureau took bribes from local mine owners. Please remember to present it to His Majesty."

Wang's proclamation took Chen Hong by surprise. "Take him away," he ordered furiously. Two imperial agents seized Wang and escorted him out. All eyes were on Wang's report. Grand Secretary Xu rose from his chair and walked over. He bent down and picked up the report. Then he went up to Chen Hong and handed it to him in front of the crowd. "Wang Yongji was appointed chief investigator of the mining accidents," said Grand Secretary Xu. "Would you deliver it to His Majesty after the Interior Ministry reviews it?"

Chen Hong had not seen this coming. He regarded Wang's report as a ploy to avenge Hai Rui's arrest. Now, Grand Secretary Xu was putting him on the spot. Rejecting the report would make him appear guilty. But if he accepted it, he would be under obligation to share the findings with the emperor.

As he was hesitating, the room erupted into furious whispers.

"Be quiet," he howled as he took Wang's report from Grand Secretary Xu.

The room fell silent.

"Since the Privy Council believes it is not possible to deliberate over Hai Rui's crimes in his absence, I shall adopt your recommendation," Chen Hong declared. "As Shi Gonggong has said, we'll extract passages from each rebuttal, and hand over the compilation to the Justice Department and the Imperial Judiciary. They can review the documents and convict Hai Rui. As for Wang Yongji, Huang Jin, Zhu Qi and Chee Dazhu, they shall be charged as accomplices to Hai Rui's crime!"

When Chen Hong and his deputies strode out of the main hall, Zhao stood there with a dismal look. Chen Hong had forced him to make a judgment on Wang's remarks, and Zhao was hoping that Grand Secretary Xu would defend him and offer a few words of support to the crowd. But to his disappointment, Grand Secretary Xu was too preoccupied to take note of his protégé.

"The Privy Council shall convene a joint session with the Justice Department and the Imperial Judiciary, and submit our verdicts to the Interior Ministry," said Grand Secretary Xu before leaving.

Several eunuchs and maids huddled outside Emperor Jiajing's meditation room and listened attentively to two imperial doctors who were dictating to an assistant the names of the herbs they had prescribed for Emperor Jiajing.

Chen Hong stepped into the main hall. The eunuchs and maids dropped down on their knees. When he heard the imperial doctors' voices, Chen paused and pricked up his ears.

"Korean ginseng, fifteen grams. Pilose Asiabell Root, thirty grams. Angelica Dahurica Benth, fifteen grams…" chanted an imperial doctor.

"You're simply giving me a concoction of all the herbal tonics," Emperor Jiajing interrupted the doctor. "Where is Huang Jin?"

Chen Hong lifted his robe and scurried in. He saw two imperial doctors kneeling next to the emperor's bed. They were trembling with fear.

Emperor Jiajing was lying in bed with his eyes closed. "Huang Jin," he called out again.

Chen Hong rushed over and knelt down. "Master, I'm here," he said.

"Tell these two idiots to get out of here."

Chen Hong signalled to the two imperial doctors, who rose from the floor and slunk away.

"Go and find Li Shizhen's prescription," demanded the emperor.

Chen Hong looked baffled. "Li Shizhen?" he mumbled. "Master, what prescription are you referring to?"

Emperor Jiajing opened his eyes slowly and tilted his head. When he recognised Chen Hong kneeling close to him, he uttered a soft sound of disapproval and scorn.

Chen Hong always dreaded Emperor Jiajing's look of contempt. "Your Majesty, if you're not happy with the two imperial physicians, I'll find you another one," he said in his quavering voice.

Emperor Jiajing stared at the ceiling without answering.

Chen Hong held his breath and waited nervously for further instructions.

"How was the hearing?" Emperor Jiajing asked.

"Your Majesty, we chose one hundred officials from Hanlin Academy and the Imperial Education Commission. They all submitted their written rebuttals, but no one was willing to talk. There was this impudent person named Wang Yongji. He was so bold that he didn't even bother to write a statement. Instead, he submitted a report on a corruption scandal involving the Imperial Mining Bureau. Because he openly defied Your Majesty's order, I had him arrested."

"What did Grand Secretary Xu and other members of the Privy Council say?" Emperor Jiajing asked, giving a side glance to Chen Hong.

"The Privy Council has decided to extract passages from everyone's written statements and hand them to the Justice Department and the Imperial Judiciary. They are supposed to reach a verdict tomorrow. I'm a bit concerned that those people might slap Hai Rui with some lesser or obscure charges to protect their own interests. If this happens, we are effectively giving permission to anyone who might defile Your Majesty's name. That will create a bad precedent."

Emperor Jiajing rolled his eyes. "Bring me a calligraphy brush and a piece of paper," he ordered.

"Yes, Your Majesty." Chen Hong got up and stepped over to Emperor Jiajing's desk. A few minutes later, he returned with a stationery tray and put it on a low table nearby. Then, he propped up the emperor with a pillow and held the tray for him.

Emperor Jiajing picked the calligraphy brush from the tray, thought for a few moments and wrote four large characters – 'good rain' and 'bright moon' – on two pieces of paper.

"Deliver these two pages to the Prince of Yu," instructed Emperor Jiajing. "These four characters allude to two people. Tell him to summon Grand Secretary Xu and others. They'll be able to figure out what I want."

"I'll go right away," Chen Hong said haltingly. "By the way, may I ask Your Majesty a quick question? You just said 'Grand Secretary Xu and others'. To whom are you referring?"

Emperor Jiajing ignored him. "If Lu Fang had been around, he wouldn't have asked such a stupid question," the emperor murmured as he gazed at the ceiling, as if Lu Fang was hiding on top of the roof.

Chen Hong felt as if he had been flogged with a whip. "I… I'm such an idiot… I think I understand now," he stammered.

Did Emperor Jiajing think he was being stupid or shrewd? Chen Hong had no idea. Placing the tray back on the emperor's desk, he held the two pieces of paper in his hands and left the meditation room in a trance.

明

Emperor Jiajing's decree, which came in the form of a four-character riddle, sat on the Prince of Yu's desk. Since it was a confidential meeting to discuss the emperor's decree, Chen Hong had sent away the Prince of Yu's aide and temporarily took over tending to the Prince of Yu's personal needs. First, he rinsed a towel in a washbasin, wrung it dry and handed it to the prince with both hands so he could wash his face. As the Prince of Yu sat down at his desk, pondering the meaning of Emperor Jiajing's four characters, Chen Hong stood behind him and waved a fan gently to cool him.

Back in February, the Prince of Yu lashed out at the chief eunuch when Emperor Jiajing had sent him over to seek a written response to Hai Rui's remonstrance. Chen Hong dropped down on his knees and made a tearful confession and plea, which the prince perceived to be as acts of surrender. Since then, he no longer treated Chen Hong with the same wariness and respect as before. Like a stream of water flowing down a mountain into a river, there was no going back. Chen Hong noticed the change of attitude and accepted the irreversible reality.

Grand Secretary Xu, Gao Gong and Zhang Juzheng arrived shortly afterwards. They greeted the Prince of Yu in his study.

"Please take your seats," the Prince of Yu said to his teachers as he rose from his chair.

Grand Secretary Xu did not expect that Chen Hong would be at what he had thought was a private meeting with the prince. Hiding his disgust, he gave Chen Hong a palm-over-fist salute.

"Please sit down," Chen Hong ingratiated himself. By now, he had finally figured out what Emperor Jiajing meant by "Grand Secretary Xu and others".

The three guests sat on chairs near the south window. Chen Hong stood behind the Prince of Yu and waved his fan gently.

"We have received a decree," the Prince of Yu announced.

The trio stood up and dropped to their knees.

"Please rise," Chen Hong chimed in. "His Majesty has issued a rather unconventional decree. He has written four characters and invited you and others to decipher their meaning. Please come over and take a look."

The trio noticed two pieces of paper on the Prince of Yu's desk. They walked over. Each paper had two large characters. "Good rain and bright moon," murmured Grand Secretary Xu.

Seeing the befuddled looks on his teachers' faces, the Prince of Yu quickly explained: "According to His Majesty, these four characters allude to two people."

The room fell into an awkward silence. The Prince of Yu noted that the trio were too afraid to speak their minds in Chen Hong's presence. "There's no need to worry," he reassured them. "Chen Gonggong has a difficult job. He often has to do whatever's asked of him. But while he's devoted to His Majesty, he also has my interests at heart. Treat him like one of us, and feel free to state your opinions."

The explanation took Grand Secretary Xu by surprise, but the sincerity in the prince's tone alleviated his worries. "Can I ask Chen Gonggong a few questions?" asked Grand Secretary Xu.

"Please do," replied Chen Hong.

"Did His Majesty say anything else when he wrote the four characters?"

"Two imperial doctors prescribed some herbs. His Majesty was extremely unhappy with their diagnosis and prescription. So he kicked them out. Next, he enquired about today's hearing at the Audit and Inspection Commission."

Grand Secretary Xu exchanged glances with Gao Gong and the Prince of Yu. They all turned to Zhang Juzheng, the former child prodigy. When it came to solving literary riddles, nobody was Zhang's match. Therefore, the Prince of Yu was willing to hear him out first.

"Grand Secretary Xu and Mr Gao are handling Hai Rui's case and they're probably too close to it," said the Prince of Yu. "Mr Zhang is an outsider. You can offer us an outsider's perspective. Based on your reading, to whom do you think His Majesty is alluding?"

Zhang did not speak immediately. As a gesture of modesty, he sought the permission of Grand Secretary Xu and Gao Gong with his eyes.

"As His Royal Highness has said, a spectator observes the chess game better than the players," said Gao Gong. "Please give us your insights."

Zhang examined the four characters one more time before opining: "May I venture to say that these four characters refer to Dr Li Shizhen and Hai Rui."

"Interesting," said the Prince of Yu. "On what grounds?"

"The words 'good rain' most likely come from a Tang poem:

'Good rain knows its season/ It will fall when spring comes/ By riding on wind, it sneaks in at night-time/ And nourishes all living things slowly and noiselessly.' Dr Li Shizhen's name means 'perfect timing' and he was born in the city of Qichun, which means 'fragrant herbs of spring'. That gives me the idea that the first two lines refer to Dr Li. This makes perfect sense, doesn't it? His Majesty is feeling indisposed at the moment and intends to summon Dr Li to the palace because he's not happy with the imperial physicians. But Dr Li and His Majesty had bitter disagreements in the past. His Majesty is unwilling to issue an edict and make it known to everyone that he has reconciled with Dr Li. His Majesty's intention and dilemma are implied in the last two lines. He wants Dr Li to 'sneak in' and nurture him back to health like the spring rain. In other words, His Majesty is urging His Royal Highness to bring Dr Li to Beijing immediately."

"That's about right," Chen Hong added. "Mr Zhang's interpretation reminds me of something. When I first entered the meditation room this afternoon, His Majesty did mention Dr Li's name, but I was clueless then. Now I understand. Since His Majesty intends to invite Dr Li to Beijing without letting many people know about it, I shall give this assignment to the Imperial Investigative Agency. They can send someone to track down Dr Li in no time."

"I'm afraid we have to bother Chen Gonggong with this task," the Prince of Yu said to everyone. "Mr Zhang, please continue with the second set of characters."

"The second set, 'bright moon', is most likely taken from another Tang poem, which reads: 'From out of the sea the moon appears/ From the ends of the Earth, all share this moment.' So, a bright moon over the ocean is a propitious sign. If we examine Hai Rui's name, Hai means 'sea' and Rui is auspicious. The link is pretty obvious, is it not? But there's one thing I can't figure out: why does His Majesty use 'bright moon' to describe Hai Rui?"

"It strikes me as a bit unusual that His Majesty would refer to Hai Rui as the bright moon of the Ming dynasty," Gao Gong chimed in. "It's obviously a positive allusion. Is His Majesty implying that we should cut Hai Rui some slack when determining his crime?"

The Prince of Yu's eyes sparkled. Zhang Juzheng and Chen Hong nodded in agreement, but Grand Secretary Xu dissented. "Gao Gong's interpretation makes sense," he said with a soft sigh. "However, I think we are missing the big picture. I have a slightly different interpretation. To me, the bright moon imagery contains two layers of meanings. First, His Majesty implies that we have lost sight of the sun and allow the moon to shine too brightly."

"What do you mean?" the Prince of Yu asked.

"The character for Ming [明], as in the Great Ming Empire, consists of two parts, sun [日] on the left and moon [月] on the right. Since His Majesty is often compared to the sun, he is complaining that the imperial officials have relinquished the sun and allowed the moon to get in the way of the sun's light. That was why he withdrew Hai Rui from the hearing at the Audit and Inspection Commission earlier today because he knew many Ming officials are sympathetic to Hai Rui's views."

"Your Highness, if you trust me, let me share my thoughts with you," Chen Hong volunteered.

"Chen Gonggong, feel free to jump in," the prince said. "Your input is very important to us."

"The bright moon is often associated with the lunar festival in autumn," mused Chen Hong. "Is His Majesty hinting that Hai Rui should receive the death penalty and that the execution date should be set in autumn?"

Grand Secretary Xu nodded.

"When the Privy Council, the Justice Department and the Imperial Judiciary are meeting to convict Hai Rui tomorrow, they should sentence him to death and set the execution date in the autumn," Chen Hong continued.

Nobody objected to Chen Hong's suggestion. They simply listened.

"His Majesty currently rules the Great Ming Empire. Your Royal Highness is next in line to the throne. His Majesty wants to ensure that father and son are of the same mind. I believe that His Majesty sent me over to present you this riddle to test your loyalty. Just think about it. Hai Rui desecrated His Majesty with such harsh rhetoric, but many imperial officials seemed to be prevaricating.

Wang Yongji even refused to write his rebuttal. After I reported this to His Majesty, he issued this edict, ordering you to treat Wang as Hai Rui's accomplice. If the Prince of Yu and members of the Privy Council don't stand behind His Majesty and defend him vigorously, the Great Ming Empire will lose the protection of the sun. In other words, although everyone else can oppose capital punishment for Hai Rui, Your Highness cannot. You have to proclaim your position loud and clear that Hai Rui should be hanged and that his accomplice Wang Yongji be given harsh punishment."

The Prince of Yu appeared reluctant. Gao Gong and Zhang sat there impassively.

"I agree with Chen Gonggong's assessment," Grand Secretary Xu stated. "Your Highness, let's write down what we have just discussed and ask Chen Gonggong to take our response to Yuxi Palace immediately."

The Prince of Yu remained unconvinced.

Grand Secretary Xu decided to take the matter into his own hands. "His Majesty feels indisposed and it is important that we fetch Dr Li," he said. "Chen Gonggong, please take our response and return to Yuxi Palace immediately."

Chen Hong did not move. He waited for the Prince of Yu to give the final word.

The Prince of Yu remained sitting, looking distracted. "Please go ahead and deliver my response then," he said grudgingly.

Chen Hong kowtowed to the prince and hurried out.

"It's a pity that we are not only losing Hai Rui, but also Wang Yongji," lamented the Prince of Yu.

Grand Secretary Xu exchanged knowing glances with Gao Gong and Zhang Juzheng, and he said: "Your Highness, now that Chen Gonggong is gone, Zhang Juzheng may want to share some of his private observations with you."

"I assume that all of you would agree with me on this," Zhang said. "Paradoxically, the only way we can save Hai Rui's life is to sentence him to death."

"What do you mean?" the Prince of Yu asked.

"If you examine the four characters His Majesty has written, none contains the message of killing Hai Rui. As Chen Gonggong just mentioned, His Majesty's real intent is to sound us out and test our loyalty. If Your Highness and the Privy Council beg for leniency on behalf of Hai Rui, His Majesty might suspect we are conspiring with Hai Rui against him and kill Hai Rui in retaliation. However, if we insist that Hai Rui deserves capital punishment, His Majesty might spare Hai Rui's life as a gesture of tolerance and benevolence."

"How can you be so sure?" the Prince of Yu asked anxiously.

"Your Highness, come to think about it, Hai Rui fell seriously ill after he returned from Daxing County. Dr Li cured him. Before Hai Rui submitted his remonstrance, Dr Li fled Beijing with Hai Rui's wife and mother. Under normal circumstances, His Majesty would have put Dr Li under investigation. Instead of punishing Dr Li, His Majesty is now inviting him back to the palace to treat his illness. As the saying goes, if you like someone, you accept everything about them, including their choice of friends. I think His Majesty respects Dr Li, and he has extended that respect to Hai Rui as well."

"As Grand Secretary Xu and Chen Gonggong pointed out, the character for Ming consists of two parts, the sun and the moon," said Gao Gong. "His Majesty is complaining that we are abandoning the sun in pursuit of a bright moon. He is worried that his own son and members of the Privy Council will scheme to force his abdication. If we come out and defend His Majesty, saying that Hai Rui deserves capital punishment, we would put His Majesty's mind at ease. It is like putting the sun and moon back together to form the character Ming."

"At our joint hearing tomorrow, the Privy Council, the Justice Department and the Imperial Judiciary will unanimously find Hai Rui guilty and issue the death penalty. At the same time, we will banish Wang Yongji to the northwest. After we submit our decision to His Majesty, he has to sign off on it. The chances are high that His Majesty will commute Hai Rui's death penalty. If he does, Wang's punishment could be waived as well."

The Prince of Yu uttered a soft sigh of relief. "Let's hope you're right."

"Why don't we come up with the charges right now?" Gao Gong

suggested. "We shall charge Hai Rui with treason and sentence him to death by hanging."

The Privy Council held a speedy trial with the Justice Department and the Imperial Judiciary. Upon hearing brief statements from Hai Rui and Wang Yongji, they reached their verdicts. The results were delivered to the Interior Ministry in the afternoon.

As Chen Hong entered Yuxi Palace with the verdicts in his hands, he caught sight of a plainclothes eunuch kneeling before a stove outside the meditation room. He was boiling herbs. When the eunuch saw Chen Hong coming towards him, he quickly turned his face to the wall. Chen Hong did not recognise him. After all, thousands of eunuchs worked under him, and there was no way he could remember each one.

"Whose prescription is it?" Chen Hong paused and asked. "Has His Majesty approved it?"

The eunuch did not respond. He simply removed the lid and stirred the herbs inside the pot. Initially, Chen Hong was under the impression that the person was too scared to speak to him. But then, there was something familiar about him. As he was about to move closer and find out the stranger's identity, Emperor Jiajing's voice came from inside the meditation room: "Is that you, Chen Hong? Come in."

"Yes, Your Majesty," said Chen Hong, swiftly collecting himself. Before entering, he tilted his head and took another glance at the back of the stranger.

Emperor Jiajing's complexion had improved dramatically. He had risen from his bed and was sitting on his prayer mat.

"Master, the three agencies held a joint trial. I have their verdicts with me," Chen Hong said excitedly.

"I don't want to read them. Just give me the gist," Emperor Jiajing said with his eyes closed.

Chen Hong flipped open the cover page and explained: "The charges are listed here. Hai Rui is convicted of desecrating and insulting a monarch. The Justice Department and the Imperial Judiciary have sentenced Hai Rui to death by hanging, and the execution shall take place in autumn. Wang Yongji is charged with conspiring with Hai Rui against His Majesty. In addition to receiving eighty lashes, he should be banished to a village fifteen hundred kilometres from the capital city."

"Do you think the verdicts are fair?" Emperor Jiajing asked.

"Your Majesty, if you don't like their decisions, I can send them back and ask Grand Secretary Xu and the others to reconsider."

"Shall I order the immediate execution of Hai Rui, or should I commute his death sentence?"

"Your Majesty, as the saying goes, regardless of whether it is thunder, lightning, rain or morning dew, we should be grateful because they're all heaven's gifts. We treat each one of your orders as a gift from heaven. We will follow whatever you decide."

"Oh really? Behind my back, you and others are busy making me out to be the devil and having me take all the blame."

Chen Hong fell to his knees. "Your Majesty, we... we wouldn't dare," he spluttered.

"You wouldn't? I was told you held a vigorous, high-brow discussion at the Prince of Yu's mansion yesterday! I didn't know you are so well versed in Tang poems, such as 'Good rain knows its season' or 'From out of the sea the moon appears'."

Chen Hong was shocked, frozen like an ice statue.

"Why didn't you report to me in detail your conversation yesterday with the Prince of Yu? I sent Lu Fang away. Little did I know that I have appointed someone who tries to imitate Lu Fang! I hate to disappoint you, but you are incapable of matching Lu Fang's intellect and character. Lu Fang always reported to me any dealings he had with my son, but you try to conceal them from me. You think Lu Fang was kicked out because he was too honest with me. You think it was stupid of him to tell me everything. No, he was being smart! As the saying goes, one takes small blame to escape severe punishment. Throughout his career, Lu Fang always knew in his heart that no matter how many people kowtowed to him, calling him 'Daddy' or 'Old Ancestor', he was a slave. Who do you think you are? You even have the audacity to deceive me! Let me tell you, the only person who occasionally tells a few white lies to me is Princess Li, my daughter-in-law. That's what a daughter-in-law is supposed to do, to mediate between father and son, and maintain harmony within a family. Are you trying to be my daughter-in-law as well? Why don't you look at yourself in the mirror? That face of yours is like a hard-boiled egg without the shell. You're not daughter-in-law material."

Chen Hong placed the papers on the floor and began smacking himself hard in the face.

"Stop acting," Emperor Jiajing yelled. "If you want your face slapped, go to the Imperial Investigative Agency! The agents can do a much better job of it."

Chen Hong became scared. "Master, I never intended to be deceitful," he explained. "Since you have not been feeling well, I just didn't have the heart to tell you because I don't want to make you angry…"

"Get me a red ink brush!" Emperor Jiajing interjected.

"Yes, Your Majesty." By now, Chen Hong was shaking uncontrollably. Emperor Jiajing's rebuke muddled his mind. Instead of standing up, he crawled to the emperor's desk on his knees, picked up a calligraphy brush and dipped it in a bowl of red ink.

"Show me the verdicts," Emperor Jiajing ordered after Chen Hong handed him the calligraphy brush.

Chen Hong quickly collected the papers on the floor and hoisted them above his head.

Emperor Jiajing drew a large cross on the cover page and threw the brush on the floor.

Under normal circumstances, the emperor signed off on the Justice Department's sentencing reports by simply ticking a box on the front page. A large cross indicated his intention to pardon someone or request a retrial. But such cases were so rare that Chen Hong had not encountered a single one during his tenure there.

Chen Hong could not see what the emperor was drawing, but he could sense it was not a tick. "Master, could you tell me whether you have approved the decisions or not? Your Majesty's explicit instructions would make it easier for me to convey your orders to the Privy Council and the Department of Justice."

"It seems to me that they're all first-class riddle-solvers. Keep them guessing."

"Yes, Your Majesty," Chen Hong murmured.

"I heard that you're also pretty good at solving riddles. Take a guess now. Who am I going to assign to guard Hai Rui and Wang Yongji? I hear that they share a cell together."

Chen Hong kowtowed to Emperor Jiajing. "Master, I apologise for what I said at the Prince of Yu's mansion. Your intelligence is as limitless as the sky. Your humble servant is not smart enough to solve your riddle... I beg you..."

"Just guess," Emperor Jiajing said impatiently.

Chen Hong knelt on the floor and pretended to think hard. "Your Majesty, are you planning to send me to oversee the Imperial Prison?" he asked nervously.

"Take another guess," Emperor Jiajing demanded in an icy tone.

Beads of sweat appeared on Chen Hong's forehead. He was at his wits' end. Suddenly, Emperor Jiajing's rebuke echoed in his ears: "Lu Fang knew in his heart that... he would always be a slave." Chen Hong realised that his relentless persecution of Lu Fang's former allies must have aroused Emperor Jiajing's suspicions. Gritting his teeth, Chen Hong raised his head and replied: "Your Majesty, Zhu Qi used to take charge of the underground section of the Imperial Prison. Are you saying that we should release Zhu Qi and Chee Dazhu? Zhu Qi can get his old job back, and we can put Chee Dazhu in charge of Hai Rui and Wang Yongji."

Emperor Jiajing's face softened. His voice turned gentle. "Did you not accuse Zhu Qi and Chee Dazhu of colluding with Hai Rui?" he asked Chen Hong.

"It was my fault. I was under such pressure at the time. I was so worried that people inside the Imperial Palace would conspire with the hostile forces outside to harm Your Majesty. After some thorough investigations over the past three months, I've come to the conclusion that Wang Yongji was the only person who had direct contact with Hai Rui. I have clearly misjudged people like Zhu Qi and Chee Dazhu. Huang Jin is just a stupid straight talker. He shouldn't have talked back to you the other day, but there is no evidence to show that he colluded with Hai Rui. I beseech Your

Majesty to release Huang Jin so he can continue to take care of you."

A smirk appeared on Emperor Jiajing's face. "Do you think the Son of Heaven would be easily deceived by these little tricks of yours? You take advantage of my anger with Hai Rui to persecute Lu Fang's people and replace them with yours. Let me make it clear to you. Lu Fang served me for forty years. During his tenure here, he never dared form a clique. Given that you correctly read my mind and have apologised for your misbehaviour, I'll give you another chance. Go and deliver my message."

Chen Hong was sweating profusely. He rose from the floor and hastened out.

Emperor Jiajing noticed patches of Chen Hong's sweat on the floor. He suddenly felt dizzy and realised his own forehead was cold and sweaty as well.

"Huang Jin, bring the herbs over," he shouted.

The stranger whom Chen Hong spotted before he entered was Huang Jin. Obviously, the emperor had ordered Huang's release and brought him back to Yuxi Palace without Chen Hong's knowledge.

Huang stepped in with a bowl of herbal broth. His face looked bruised and he had a limp. The glistening sweat on Emperor Jiajing's forehead alarmed him. Dispensing with his cane, he rushed over. "Master, are you all right?" he asked.

"Walk slowly," Emperor Jiajing said with a sympathetic look. "Don't fall."

※

The secret letter inviting Dr Li Shizhen back to Beijing reached Nanjing in seven days. On the day of Dr Li's departure, Amu decided to leave Gao Hanwen's mansion as well. Hai Rui had promised to meet them in Nanjing at the beginning of May, but it was now approaching the end of the month. There was not a single message from her son. Amu was an intelligent and thoughtful woman. Even though she had detected something portentous about Hai Rui's unexplained silence, she refrained from inquiring of Dr

Li about Hai Rui's circumstances. Instead, she was determined to take her daughter-in-law to her native village in Hainan. Regardless of what had happened to Hai Rui, she intended her daughter-in-law to give birth to the family's heir safely in their ancestral land.

"Amu, please stay," pleaded the foreman who knelt in front of Amu at the backyard entrance. "If you leave, I'll lose my job over this. Can't you wait for two more days? I've already sent for Mr and Mrs Gao. You should at least say goodbye to them in person before you go."

With a cotton bag slung over her left shoulder, Amu was standing next to Dr Li. She was leaning on a cane with one hand and holding an umbrella with the other. Mrs Hai's baby bump was unusually large. Yu Qing, the mute maid, held Mrs Hai by the arm and wore a bag over her left shoulder. Dr Li's aide carried two wooden boxes on a shoulder pole and waited at the back of the group.

"Were you not treated properly or was anyone rude to you?" asked the foreman, who remained kneeling. "If that's the case, please don't take the slight personally. Regardless, you can't leave like this."

"Oh it's nothing like that," Amu explained. "You and everyone else treated us with the utmost care."

The foreman was so desperate that he enlisted the help of his co-workers who were dyeing cotton cloth in the front yard: "Everyone, get on your knees. We have to keep Amu here."

"Amu, we've just started to get to know each other," a person whose face was smeared with sweat and indigo dye entreated. "We all enjoy your company. None of us here wants you to leave. If you treasure our friendship, please stay and wait for Mr Hai to come and fetch you."

Amu felt a natural attachment to these hard-working labourers. The sincerity in their faces deeply touched her. As she was struggling for words, she turned to Dr Li, who quickly cast his eyes downward.

"I appreciate your kindness," Amu finally spoke. "While you're working hard to support your family, I have to go back to my village and take care of my family too. Please rise. Dr Li, would you help me? Ask them to resume working."

"I doubt anyone can stop Amu from going," Dr Li told the foreman. "I've tried for the last two days without success. Her departure has nothing to do with you. I will write to Mr Gao and explain the situation on your behalf. Please arrange a carriage and take Amu and Mrs Hai to the pier."

"Can't you at least stay for two more days?" the foreman asked insistently.

"I have to attend to an emergency in Beijing. Amu is eager to go home and raise her grandchild. Go and prepare the carriage."

Everyone in the front yard bowed. Amu waved at them as the foreman took the bag and umbrella from her and helped her descend the steps.

A passenger boat and a large cargo ship were moored side by side at the pier. While his aide was loading two wooden boxes onto the passenger boat, Dr Li boarded the cargo vessel with Amu and Mrs Hai. The foreman followed with Amu's baggage.

The captain came out to greet them: "Mr Li, welcome! I have arranged a double cabin for Amu and Mrs Hai."

"Please take Mrs Hai to the cabin first," Dr Li told the captain. "She needs to sit down." The mute maid held Mrs Hai and they followed the captain inside.

"You may go back now," Dr Li said to the foreman. "Thank you for taking care of us during our stay at the Gao mansion."

Placing Amu's baggage on the deck, the foreman bowed deeply to Amu. "Have a safe trip," he said. "Mrs Gao has specifically sent Yu Qing to accompany you all the way to Hainan. We have prepaid the fares and the food. When you arrive in Guangzhou, the captain of this ship will help you transfer to another one for Hainan. You should be all set."

"Mr and Mrs Gao have done so much for us. How are we ever going to repay their kindness?" Amu said after a brief pause. "Dr Li, when you see Hai Rui, please let him know about this. He needs to pay back every penny that Mr and Mrs Gao have spent on us. We are so indebted to them."

As the foreman turned around and walked towards the gangway, Amu held Dr Li's hands and made an emotional request: "Dr Li, I hate to bother you, but when you arrive in Beijing, would you find out what has happened to Hai Rui? Do drop me a line and let me know."

Dr Li's face grew grave and his lips compressed. "I don't really know the situation with Brother Hai Rui," he said. "But your son is a man of character, and I doubt he's in some form of trouble. What I'm most concerned about is his wife's health. She's seven months pregnant and I'm afraid she could give birth before you reach Hainan. I've taught the mute maid a few things about how to deliver a baby. I've also prepared some medicine. But if she's in labour, we have to rely on you to take care of everything."

"The Heavenly God will watch over us. He won't take away the Hai family heir," Amu replied.

"Amu is absolutely right, but fate is often determined by our own decisions and efforts," he replied. "Take extra care. I'm afraid I have to bid you farewell now."

As Dr Li knelt down on the deck, tears welled up in Amu's eyes.

"Captain," Dr Li called out as he rose from the floor.

The captain who was watching at the cabin door rushed over. He picked up Amu's baggage from the deck.

"Please take Amu to her cabin. If anything happens to them, I'll hunt you down."

"Dr Li, you can rest assured that they will be well taken care of," the captain promised.

"Why don't you go first?" Amu suggested to Dr Li. "I'll see you off from here."

Dr Li bowed deeply to Amu and walked towards the gangway.

Hai Rui's execution date, which had been scheduled for the first day of autumn, was fast approaching.

The sycamore tree inside the Imperial Prison's compound was

planted when Emperor Yongle moved the capital to Beijing and designated the location for the Imperial Prison. Over the past two centuries, the tree had grown so thick and leafy that guards and prisoners alike regarded it as sacred.

On the first day of autumn, a gallows was set up under the sycamore tree. A thick noose was hanging on a horizontal bar and underneath the noose was placed a wooden stool.

Under the glaring autumn sun, Zhu Qi, Chee Dazhu and several executioners stood before the gallows. They all looked up at the lush foliage, some of which had begun to turn yellow.

Two imperial agents set up an altar under the tree. On the altar were a small incense burner, incense sticks, candles and stacks of joss paper.

"Master, why don't you do the honours today?" Chee Dazhu implored Zhu Qi with a sad look.

"Light the incense sticks and seek the will of heaven," Zhu Qi ordered while fixing his eyes on the top of the sycamore tree.

Two imperial agents lit the incense sticks and handed them to Zhu Qi.

Holding the incense sticks with both hands, Zhu Qi knelt in front of the altar. "May the Heavenly God bless the honest and loyal courtiers of the Great Ming Empire," he chanted. "Shall he die or not, please give us a sign!"

At the end of his chanting, Zhu Qi kowtowed three times before placing the sticks inside the incense burner. Then, he stood and picked up the stack of joss paper on the altar. "Chee Dazhu, since Hai Rui is a friend who once saved your life, why don't you pray and finish the second part of our ceremony?" said Zhu Qi as he offered the stack of joss paper to his protégé.

Chee Dazhu took the joss paper. With trembling hands, he lit the paper with a candle flame and put it on the ground to burn. Like his mentor, Chee Dazhu dropped to his knees and kowtowed three times before getting to his feet. Walking towards the sacred tree, he chanted: "May the Heavenly God protect an honest and loyal official of the Great Ming Empire."

Closing his eyes and summoning his strength, Chee Dazhu struck the gigantic tree with the palms of his hands. Countless leaves fell from the branches. Everyone lifted their heads and watched as the leaves floated in the air. Most of them settled on the platform, rather than flew through the noose. It was a propitious omen and Chee Dazhu's eyes sparkled.

However, a single stray leaf still hovered above the noose. Zhu Qi and other executioners held their breath and observed it silently. As the lone leaf floated down, away from the noose, a gust of wind came, sending the leaf swirling up in the air. When the wind was gone, the leaf dropped down through the noose. Chee Dazhu's heart sank. He closed his eyes. It was an unmistakable sign that Hai Rui's chance of a last-minute reprieve was slim. His last hope was dashed. Chee Dazhu's legs weakened. He dropped to his knees.

明

Dr Li Shizhen's medicine failed to revive Emperor Jiajing's health, which had been harmed by years of ingesting large doses of mercury in the supposed immortality pills. He could no longer sit cross-legged on his prayer mat and meditate. At this moment, he was lying in bed, leaning against the headboard. Even in the heat of summer, he was covered with a heavy quilt.

Huang Jin was standing next to Emperor Jiajing's desk. The bruises on his face and his body had healed, but the brutal beatings inflicted by Chen Hong's supporters left him permanently crippled. He was now sorting out a stack of death warrants, each of which listed the names of offenders scheduled to be executed later in the day, and preparing them for Emperor Jiajing to sign. He paused as he came across Hai Rui's name on one of the pages. A sombre look appeared on his face. He set aside the list containing Hai Rui's name, and put the rest of the warrants on a tray before hobbling over to Emperor Jiajing.

Picking up a red ink brush from a bedside table, Huang placed it in Emperor Jiajing's right hand and handed him the tray.

The emperor's bright, piercing eyes had lost their lustre, and his vision had become blurry. He squinted, trying to read each name on the list before ticking it off. When he reached the last page, Emperor Jiajing stared at Huang. "Is that it?" he asked.

"I... I think there're a few more on your desk," Huang said.

"Bring them all."

Huang gave an involuntary shudder before limping over to the desk.

Over the past four decades, two eunuchs took turns in attending to Emperor Jiajing day and night. Huang had now become the emperor's sole caretaker. Since his release, he was never reinstalled as the first deputy interior minister. His job now was to take care of the emperor twenty-four hours a day, and run all his personal errands. At night, he slept on the floor. When Chen Hong and Grand Secretary Xu requested an audience with the emperor, they had to make a written request with Huang beforehand. Without permission, Chen Hong had no access to the meditation room. Since he was overseeing the executions today, Chen Hong paced around anxiously outside Yuxi Palace, waiting for the emperor to sign off on all the warrants. With their heads down, several junior eunuchs on duty stood around nervously.

"Are we going to carry out the executions or not?" Chen Hong barked, looking up at the sun. "What time is it?"

A junior eunuch ran inside the palace to check the water clock. "It's eleven o'clock," he reported.

"Eleven?" shouted Chen Hong. With the deadline fast approaching, Chen Hong decided to break protocol, and he strutted into the palace. At the meditation room door, he could hear Huang Jin talking. Huang's voice had lost its pig-headed vigour since his release and Chen Hong couldn't make out what he was saying. Pressing his ear to the door, Chen Hong found out that Huang was reading Hai Rui's remonstrance:

> I, Hai Rui, an auditor at the Ministry of Treasury, humbly submitted his remonstrance with the intent of rectifying the monarch's conduct, defining the responsibilities of his courtiers, and bringing peace and prosperity to the subjects of the Great Ming Empire...

"Why are you reading so slowly?" Emperor Jiajing complained. "Are you stalling for time? Hand it back to me. Let me read it myself."

Why was the emperor reviewing Hai Rui's remonstrance again? Chen Hong looked perplexed.

"Give those death warrants to Chen Hong," Emperor Jiajing could be heard telling Huang Jin. "He needs to deliver them to the Privy Council immediately."

Chen Hong adjusted his robe. As he quietly pushed open the door, he saw Huang tottering towards him with a tray in his hand. The tray contained a stack of papers with Emperor Jiajing's red ticks on them. Chen Hong tilted his head to steal a peek at Emperor Jiajing. A floor lamp illuminated the emperor's face, which was half-blocked by Hai Rui's remonstrance. From the furrowed eyebrows, Chen Hong could tell that the emperor was still nursing a grudge against Hai Rui.

"Here it is," Huang urged Chen Hong. Having suffered tremendously at Chen Hong's hands, Huang had become so resentful that he was no longer on talking terms with the emperor's chief eunuch. When he noticed that Chen Hong was using him as a shield to peek inside, he put the tray down on the threshold of the meditation room door and limped away towards the altar. Feeling exposed, Chen Hong bent down and picked up the tray. As he was slinking away, he heard Emperor Jiajing calling his name.

"Yes, Your Majesty." Chen Hong turned around and dropped down on his knees.

Emperor Jiajing, who seemed to be preoccupied with Hai Rui's remonstrance, glanced at Chen Hong out of the corner of his eye. "I hear that Grand Secretary Xu is intending to discuss an important report with me. Is that true?"

"Yes, Your Majesty, he did request an audience with you."

"Then bring him over immediately."

Four members of the Privy Council – Grand Secretary Xu, Deputy Li Chunfang, Gao Gong and Zhao Zhenji – had been waiting for the signed death warrants from Yuxi Palace. When Chen Hong appeared at the door with a tray in his hands, they all rose simultaneously.

"Did His Majesty tick off Hai Rui's name?" asked Grand Secretary Xu, who had lost his usual cool demeanour.

"All the names are in here," Chen Hong replied as he put the tray on a big desk. "I haven't had the chance to review them."

"Let's check together to see if Hai Rui's name is ticked off," Gao Gong suggested. He grabbed a stack from the tray to flip through and gave another to Zhao.

Deputy Li picked up the remaining pages and handed them over to Grand Secretary Xu.

"Hai Rui's name is not in my pile," Gao Gong declared.

"I don't see his name here either," Zhao added.

All eyes were directed towards Grand Secretary Xu, who slowly put his pile back on the tray.

"Chen Gonggong, please deliver the list to the Justice Department. All public executions shall be carried out at noon."

"Do we need to deliver any warrants to the Imperial Prison?" Chen Hong asked.

"I don't think so," Grand Secretary Xu replied. "His Majesty did not check off Hai Rui's name."

There was some cautious optimism and relief in the room as an aide rushed out to deliver the approved lists to the Justice Department. Chen Hong stood there, looking distracted. The realisation that Hai Rui might be able to get away with such a bold and vicious attack against Emperor Jiajing filled him with disappointment and anger.

This is not fair to His Majesty, he told himself, and his eyes flashed with an expression indicating he hoped Hai Rui would be hanged as soon as possible. "Grand Secretary Xu, Hai Rui's life depends on the reports you are about to submit," Chen Hong said. "His Majesty is putting a temporary hold on Hai Rui's case because he's waiting to talk with you. He requests your immediate presence."

Chen Hong's words cast a pall on the group. There was something sinister about Chen Hong's tone that they found disturbing.

Grand Secretary Xu dreaded the meeting with Emperor Jiajing. There was still an hour before Hai Rui's scheduled execution, and he was worried that the emperor would change his mind and tick off Hai Rui's name at the last minute. Like Chen Hong had mentioned, the final outcome depended on how he presented his reports. Emperor Jiajing's frame of mind was crucial to his success. "How is His Majesty's health?" he asked Chen Hong.

"His health improved after he took Dr Li's medicine, but he doesn't look too good today. Before I left, he was reading Hai Rui's remonstrance again. I think he's feeling a murderous rage right now. Therefore, I would suggest you refrain from presenting anything sensitive."

"Thanks for the advice," Grand Secretary Xu replied before turning to Gao Gong and Zhao Zhenji. "Please give me the two reports that we have discussed, one from the governor of Guangdong Province relating to Hai Rui's wife, and the other from Tan Lun."

Chen Hong watched Grand Secretary Xu intently as Gao Gong and Zhao each handed Grand Secretary Xu a folder.

"Shall we go?" suggested Grand Secretary Xu. Before Chen Hong could figure out the contents of the reports, Grand Secretary Xu marched out of the Privy Council's duty room.

9

Chen Hong led Grand Secretary Xu into the meditation room. They stopped about six feet from Emperor Jiajing's bed. As Grand Secretary Xu was about to kneel down, he was intrigued to see Hai Rui's remonstrance lying scattered on the floor.

Emperor Jiajing, who was leaning against the headboard, caught Grand Secretary Xu staring at the pages near his feet. "I just read that brute's nasty letter again," he mumbled. "You should take another look yourself."

Grand Secretary Xu kowtowed to the emperor. "Your obedient minister sincerely begs for your forgiveness."

"Are you seeking forgiveness on behalf of Hai Rui?"

"No, Your Majesty. I hope you can forgive me if I decline to reread those words. I just cannot bear to do it again."

"Good answer. As the proverb goes, if this can be tolerated, what can not?"

"Your Majesty, I absolutely agree," said Grand Secretary Xu, who kowtowed again.

Emperor Jiajing noticed two reports in Grand Secretary Xu's hands. "What do you have for me today? More dismal news?"

Grand Secretary Xu raised his head. "My wise and benevolent ruler, I have received two urgent communications today, and I feel it important to present them to you."

"Do either of these reports pertain to Hai Rui?" said the emperor, who sounded lukewarm.

Knowing that any attempt to downplay or mask his gimmick would further arouse the emperor's suspicions and complicate the situation, Grand Secretary Xu decided to give a crisp and truthful answer: "The first one is related to Hai Rui and the second is not."

"On your way over here, I assume you planned to present the second report first. Am I right? Start with the one that has nothing to do with Hai Rui."

Grand Secretary Xu didn't dare argue back. He simply couldn't because the emperor was right. "Yes, Your Majesty," he said sheepishly as he opened his folder.

The emperor smirked when he saw the report from Tan Lun was lying on top. "Just give me the gist of it," he said.

"Yes, Your Majesty. This report comes from Tan Lun, the imperial inspector in Nanjing. It arrived on the seventh of July. As we reported to you earlier, the Imperial Clothing Agency and the Department of Textiles in Nanjing entered into a joint contract with a cotton cloth mill in Songjiang in January this year. The merchants and cotton farmers are true patriots. Thanks to their tireless efforts, the mill has just produced the first batch of cotton cloth. As part of the contract, the merchants will supply the palace with fifty thousand bolts of high-quality cloth and fifty thousand bolts of medium-quality cloth, all of which has been loaded onto cargo ships. The consignment should arrive in Beijing soon."

For a brief moment, a gratifying smile flitted across Emperor Jiajing's otherwise serious and pensive face. But it soon vanished. "The report was sent on the seventh of July. How did it get here so fast?" he asked. "Is it really worth sending a super express mail about some cotton cloth?"

"Your Majesty, it is an urgent matter that warrants our immediate attention. As I briefed you previously, we're about two months away from signing a truce with the Mongolian Anda tribe. As part of the treaty, we'll supply the Anda with a hundred thousand bolts of cotton cloth. In exchange, they will gift the Imperial Palace two thousand horses. Once the truce is signed, the Anda will agree to withdraw their troops from the occupied land in our north. Starting this year, we'll be able to drastically reduce our military expenditure and save about a million taels of silver a year. The Ministry of Treasury can certainly use the savings in military spending for other purposes. Therefore, Tan Lun sent the report via super express mail because he knows that the updates will alleviate your worries."

"If you truly think so, I will take your word for it. Now, tell me what the other report is about."

Grand Secretary Xu pulled out a letter from underneath his pile and opened it. "The imperial inspector of Guangdong has notified us in his letter that Hai Rui's mother and his pregnant wife arrived on the Leizhou Peninsula on the twenty-fourth of June. They were prepared to take another ship and cross the sea to their native village in Qiongshan, but Hai Rui's wife went into labour. She experienced a difficult delivery. Since Hai Rui is a convicted official, the innkeeper could not send for a doctor. She struggled for three days. In the end, neither the mother nor her baby son survived."

Emperor Jiajing kept silent. From a side glance, he saw Huang Jin lighting three incense sticks. He didn't stop him. Huang prayed and placed the sticks inside the burner.

"Why did the Imperial Inspector of Guangdong send this report to the Privy Council?"

"Hai Rui has been charged with the crime of desecrating the crown. Local officials are bound by law to report to the Justice Department any information relating to him and his family."

Emperor Jiajing did not respond. Grand Secretary Xu had presented two reports today, one announcing a piece of good news to lift his mood and the other a tragedy to arouse his sympathy for Hai Rui. It was obviously a ploy aimed at persuading him to commute Hai Rui's death sentence. The tacit and seamless collaboration between members of the Privy Council and regional officials illustrated the colossal support and sympathy for Hai Rui. His criticism of the monarch apparently resonated with the public. The thought shocked and saddened Emperor Jiajing. He had never felt so lonely and isolated. It was a harsh reality that he could not accept.

"What do you think?" Emperor Jiajing asked of Chen Hong, who had been kneeling quietly next to Grand Secretary Xu.

"Your Majesty, as far as I know, Hai Rui is the only child in the family. As he was about to get an heir at the age of fifty, his wife and the child both died. I think this is an act of divine retribution. Your Majesty was absolutely right when you called him a man without a father and a monarch, as well as a man who abandons his family and country."

"Why don't you rise and have a seat?" Emperor Jiajing told Grand Secretary Xu.

Chen Hong moved an embroidered pouf and placed it by Emperor Jiajing's bedside. Grand Secretary Xu sat down.

"Huang Jin, hand me the last death warrant," said Emperor Jiajing.

Hobbling over to the desk, Huang picked up an ink brush and put Hai Rui's death warrant on a tray.

At his bedside, Huang handed the emperor the ink brush and placed the tray on his quilt. Emperor Jiajing fixed his eyes on Hai Rui's name on the warrant and appeared hesitant.

The suspense was such that Grand Secretary Xu, Chen Hong and Huang Jin breached protocol by raising their heads and staring at the ink brush in Emperor Jiajing's unsteady hand.

"What time is it now?" Emperor Jiajing asked Chen Hong.

"Your Majesty, it is eleven o'clock," replied Chen Hong. "The execution is scheduled to take place in three quarters of an hour."

"Didn't you just say that the death of Hai Rui's wife was an act of divine retribution? If the Heavenly God has doled out his punishment, I will follow the will of heaven as well."

That being said, Emperor Jiajing waved his red ink brush and put a big tick next to Hai Rui's name. The emperor had just signed off on Hai Rui's death warrant.

While Grand Secretary Xu's face turned ashen, Chen Hong took malicious delight in Hai Rui's impending execution. Surprisingly, Huang appeared calm and remained impassive. Rising from the floor, he took the ink brush from Emperor Jiajing and grabbed the tray.

"Hand me the signed warrant," Chen Hong demanded.

"Let Huang Jin handle this," Emperor Jiajing intervened.

Chen Hong looked baffled.

"We have three quarters of an hour left," Emperor Jiajing said to Huang. "Do you think you can reach the Imperial Prison before time is up?"

"Master, didn't you just say that we should follow the will of heaven? If I reach there on time it is the will of heaven. If not, then that is also the will of heaven."

"Your Majesty, that is pure heresy…"Chen Hong said.

"Hold your tongue," Emperor Jiajing shouted at Chen Hong before turning to Huang. "All right then. You can go now. Don't take a carriage or ride a horse. Walk at your usual pace."

"Yes, Your Majesty," said Huang. Tottering over to the desk, Huang Jin put down the tray, rinsed the ink brush and inserted it in a holder. Then he picked up the death warrant and blew on the red ink. When the ink dried, he rolled the warrant into a tube, held it reverentially with both hands and limped towards the door.

By then, Grand Secretary Xu had come to realise that Emperor Jiajing had submitted himself to the collective will of his courtiers. Deeply moved, he lowered his head. His eyes moistened.

Emperor Jiajing shifted his gaze reflectively towards the open window on the south wall. If one's eyes are windows to the soul, the emperor's soul was as inaccessible as the boundless sky. Which was more unpredictable and unfathomable, the heart of the monarch or the will of heaven?

明

Be it the will of heaven or the intent of the emperor, its outcome depended on Huang Jin's crippled leg. As Huang carried Hai Rui's death warrant and staggered towards the gate of the Western Compound, eunuchs who were on duty at the palace stopped what they were doing and observed him from close and afar.

Even though Huang had left the Interior Ministry and held no official title inside the Imperial Palace, he was a widely respected figure. When he approached the gate, the guards saluted him reverentially. Four eunuchs who had been assigned to escort Huang to the Imperial Prison waited for him at the gate. As he climbed the stone steps, two of them went up and held his arms.

"I can do it myself," Huang said. "You don't need to accompany me. His Majesty has specifically requested that I deliver his decree alone."

The eunuchs stepped aside and watched as Huang limped up step after step. At the threshold of the gate, he lifted his lame leg with one hand and carefully stepped over it.

The four eunuchs followed him, even though he declined their help. They pointed to a sedan waiting outside. "His Majesty has ordered me to walk there unassisted," he told the eunuchs, having paused for a short while. "Can any of you get a horse and ride over to the Imperial Prison? Tell the agents to wait for His Majesty's decree before they carry out the execution."

Huang waited until one of the eunuchs had mounted a horse and sped away. Then he hobbled in the direction of the Imperial Prison. Silently, the guards and the eunuchs followed Huang with their eyes.

In ancient China, most autumn executions took place around noon, especially on the day of the autumn equinox. The timing was influenced by the belief that the universe was conceived as a mirror of human society. In Beijing, the September equinox officially marks the arrival of autumn, a period of change leading to the dark of winter. During the day, the sun may still be scorching, but the autumn wind, which seemingly comes out of nowhere, blows in sharp, chill gusts, sweeping up leaves. The sky turns grey and rain falls without a moment's notice. As the saying goes, if winter means death, autumn is the dying. Therefore, executing a condemned criminal corresponds with nature's deadly mood swings.

The sun is at its highest in the sky around noon, creating the shortest shadows. Superstition had it that criminals executed at this time had no chance of rebirth or turning into a vengeful ghost. Therefore, the actual execution must occur on time, neither a minute early nor a minute late. When Hai Rui served as the magistrate of Chun'an County, he saved Chee Dazhu's life by deliberately missing the execution time. Emperor Jiajing was employing a similar tactic to save face and spare Hai Rui's life.

In Beijing, the Justice Department conducted all public executions outside a decorated archway near Xisi Street. However, secret executions took place inside the Imperial Prison's compound. A sundial was set up on the brick floor. As the sun moved across the sky, from east to west, so did the shadow it cast, forming a thin rod or gnomon.

Chee Dazhu remained kneeling under the sycamore tree. Zhu Qi and several other imperial agents who had been assigned to carry out the execution were standing some distance away. They watched the sundial anxiously, still praying for a last-minute reprieve.

"It's half past eleven," whispered an agent who was standing behind Zhu Qi.

Silently, Zhu Qi shifted his gaze from the sundial to Chee Dazhu.

"It's almost time, but we still haven't seen the signed warrant," another agent complained. "Could it be possible that His Majesty has pardoned Hai Rui?"

Zhu Qi waved his large hands, signalling for the agent to hold his tongue.

Chee Dazhu slowly raised his head and turned to peek at the sundial. His eyes glimmered with hope.

Suddenly, the cicadas hidden inside the dense sycamore leaves began buzzing. Their high-pitched shriek pierced the silence in the yard. Soon after, Zhu Qi pricked up his ears. He could vaguely hear the sound of horse hooves striking the pavement. As he directed his gaze towards the gate, his face turned tense.

The clopping sounded more distinct now. The horse stopped outside the prison gate. The eunuch whom Huang Jin had sent strode in with sweat running down his face.

There was a look of despair on Chee Dazhu's face.

"I'm here to deliver an imperial decree," announced the eunuch as he paused in the middle of the yard. Each word was dragged out in dramatic fashion.

Zhu Qi knelt down on the floor. The others followed suit, waiting for the eunuch to read the decree.

The eunuch took his time. After surveying the yard, he raised his voice and announced: "His Majesty has signed off on the death warrant. The execution shall occur at noon."

The executioners knelt there motionless.

Under the sycamore tree, Chee Dazhu reached inside his robe and held the hilt of a short sword.

"I respectfully accept the imperial decree," Zhu Qi uttered with a heavy heart as he reached out both of his hands. He thought the eunuch would hand him the death warrant.

"I do not have the decree with me," the eunuch announced.

What did that mean? Zhu Qi lifted his head. The eunuch's sheepish admission bewildered everyone.

"Instead, the warrant shall be delivered to you by Huang Gonggong," the eunuch said.

Many eunuchs who had spent their whole lives inside the Imperial Palace had developed a flair for the dramatic. They tended to exaggerate or cook up stories to create sensational effects. This particular eunuch acted like he had been cast in an opera about how Emperor Jiajing spared the life of a loyal courtier. On the way to the Imperial Prison, he smacked the horse repeatedly to make it go faster and by the time he arrived, he had woven the plot of what he believed was a once-in-a-lifetime event, a cliffhanger he could brag to his peers about for the rest of his life. Therefore, he was completely in character when he made the announcement, spacing the syllables with an unbearable falsity. One minute, he proclaimed that His Majesty had ticked Hai Rui's name on the warrant, and the next he said he did not have the decree with him. His intention was to add an element of thrill to an already suspenseful event. Unfortunately, his literary device did not play well with his audience. Zhu Qi looked dumbfounded and irate. Nobody in the yard could figure it out.

Realising that his dramatic performance could backfire and offend Zhu Qi, a powerful and intimidating person within the palace, he ceased acting and explained to Zhu Qi: "Master Zhu, Huang Gonggong picked up the warrant at about eleven o'clock.

His Majesty specifically instructed him to deliver his edict on foot, without anyone's assistance. You know about Huang Gonggong's leg. I doubt he can get here anytime soon. So, please rise and wait patiently."

From the eunuch's knowing wink, Zhu Qi seemed to have understood, but he still could not believe his ears. "Are you saying that Huang Gonggong received the decree from His Majesty at eleven o'clock and he's now walking here without any assistance?"

"Yes. He's tottering over."

"Are you sure he's not coming here in a sedan?"

"Master Zhu, what's the matter with you today?" the eunuch replied with a hint of impatience. "I just said Huang Gonggong is coming here on foot. His Majesty forbade him from riding a horse or taking a sedan. Please stand up and wait in the shade. It'll be a while."

Zhu Qi peered at the sundial. It was a quarter before noon. He finally understood.

"Chee Dazhu!" he shouted.

Chee Dazhu released the handle of his sword and turned to Zhu Qi. "Yes, master."

"Time to offer thanks to the Heavenly God," said Zhu Qi calmly.

Chee Dazhu drew the short sword from inside his robe. Scratching his left middle finger with the tip of the sword, he let the blood drip onto a fallen leaf on the altar. Then he lit the leaf with a candle and threw it onto the ground.

As the blood-stained leaf was burning, Chee Dazhu and other imperial agents kowtowed to the sacred tree.

The eunuch watched in awe. The dramatic scene exhilarated him. Real-life events were sometimes stranger than fiction.

明

There were two wooden beds in the cell, separated by two chairs and a table. Hai Rui and Wang Yongji were sitting opposite each other by the table; the jailers had removed their shackles. They both stared at Hai Rui's 'last meal' on the table – a bowl of meat, a bowl of fish, a bowl of tofu and a jug of liquor. Their cups were filled with liquor but neither had touched them.

"By now, your mother and wife should have reached Guangdong Province," Wang said, raising his cup. "May they have a safe journey."

Hai Rui also raised his cup, and the men consumed their drinks in a single gulp.

"Once His Majesty issues his edict, you will be exiled to the north," Hai Rui said as he poured more liquor from the jug into Wang's cup. "I'm sorry I won't be able to see you off. If there is such a thing as life after death, my spirit will surely accompany you to your destination."

Wang fell silent and sat there in a daze. Hai Rui finished the liquor alone. As the saying goes, a man dies the way a lamp goes out. At this moment, the light inside the cell was dimming because the candle inside the lantern had burnt nearly all the way down. The despondent-looking Wang reached inside the lantern, removed the residual wax and inserted a new candle. The cell brightened again.

"If the Heavenly God hadn't given us Confucius, we would still be lingering in darkness," said Wang, who stared at the rising flame inside the lantern. "Brother Hai Rui, you expounded and advocated the sage's ideas in your remonstrance. When you lay down your life for a just cause, you will be remembered in the history books. Your death will inspire others to uphold the Confucian ideals of governance..."

"I sought to act virtuously and righteously, and remonstrated with His Majesty to rescue the Great Ming Empire, but I have accomplished none of these goals," said Hai Rui. "His Majesty believes I'm making a name for myself and tarnishing his legacy. He will not allow me to die."

"What do you mean?" Wang exclaimed in disbelief.

"Can't you see?" lamented Hai Rui, who closed his eyes. Tears streamed down his face.

"Are you saying that His Majesty has pardoned you? How do you know?"

Hai Rui wiped the tears from his face with his sleeve and opened his eyes. "It's already past noon," he said.

Wang looked at the candle and suddenly understood. A candle would normally burn for an hour. When Chee Dazhu changed the previous one, he reminded them that it was eleven o'clock. Now, that old candle had already burned out…

"It's past noon!" Wang shouted in his trembling voice. "His Majesty has pardoned you! His Majesty has pardoned you!"

While Hai Rui sat quietly, Wang began sobbing. He rose from his chair and dashed over to the cell door. Grabbing the metal bars, he shouted into the empty passageway: "Long live the emperor! Long live our wise and holy ruler!"

His voice reverberated inside the jail. Soon after, footsteps sounded at the far end of the passageway. Men with lanterns were moving slowly towards Hai Rui's cell. Huang Jin, assisted by Chee Dazhu, appeared at the door.

"Unlock the door," Zhu Qi ordered a jailer.

Holding the death warrant, Huang limped inside. "I'm here with two imperial decrees," he announced.

Hai Rui and Wang Yongji dropped down on their knees.

"I hereby approve the execution of Hai Rui, an auditor at the Ministry of Treasury, on the charge of treason. My decree shall be delivered to the Imperial Prison by Huang Jin. He shall neither take a sedan nor ride a horse. At eleven o'clock, Huang Jin shall leave Yuxi Palace on foot. If he is unable to reach the Imperial Prison by noon, I shall follow the will of heaven and annul the enclosed warrant."

Huang cleared his throat after finishing. "Hai Rui, please kowtow and offer your thanks to the will of heaven."

Hai Rui declined. "The *Great Ming Code* stipulates that defaming and insulting the monarch is a capital offence that cannot be commuted or pardoned. I'm willing to take my punishment and die to ensure the impartiality and power of the law."

"A courtier must obey his monarch absolutely, even if he orders him to die," Huang replied. "But when a monarch orders his courtier to live, he has no choice but to live. Be grateful."

Hai Rui remained unwilling, but he kowtowed to Huang in a tacit gesture of gratitude to the eunuch's sufferings on his account.

Huang did not force Hai Rui. He turned to Chee Dazhu who was standing behind him. "Burn the death warrant," he said. "His Majesty orders you to keep a close watch on Hai Rui."

As Chee Dazhu excitedly took a candle from inside a lantern, his hands were shaking. Meanwhile, Huang pulled out another decree from his breast pocket. "Wang Yongji, are you ready to receive an imperial edict?" he asked.

"Yes!" said Wang, who kowtowed. Hai Rui raised his head and listened attentively.

Huang unfolded the decree and read aloud: "I have received the corruption case submitted by Wang Yongji, an inspector at the Audit and Inspection Commission. Given the shocking nature of the scandal involving the Imperial Mining Agency and two local mining companies, I hereby reinstate Wang's position at the Audit and Inspection Commission and dispatch him to Nanjing, where he shall assist Imperial Inspector Tan Lun and conduct a thorough investigation. Those who are found guilty shall be put under immediate arrest and sent to Beijing for sentencing. The Ministry of Treasury shall confiscate their assets and provide proper compensation to victims' families."

"Long live my wise and holy ruler!" Hai Rui shouted.

明

Emperor Jiajing had sent Chen Hong on an errand, and he was alone in the meditation room with Grand Secretary Xu.

"Grand Secretary Xu," the emperor called out in a melancholy tone.

"Yes, Your Majesty," Grand Secretary Xu responded affectionately as he stood up.

The usual brutal cynicism and indifference were absent in Emperor Jiajing's eyes. Grand Secretary Xu saw a lonely man desperately searching for understanding. "If the public thinks I have made so many errors during my forty-five years on the throne, why is it that none of you have come forward to remonstrate with me?"

"Your Majesty, the crown can do no wrong," Grand Secretary Xu replied. "You have your own set of challenges. As your courtiers, we try our best to assist you and share your responsibilities. How could we shift the blame to Your Majesty?"

"With all the grievances against me, how did you manage over the years?"

Grand Secretary Xu's eyes moistened. "Everything we did was guided by two words – respect and loyalty."

"That sounds like pretentious jargon," Emperor Jiajing countered. "Drop all of that. Follow Hai Rui's example and speak truthfully. You won't be held culpable."

Grand Secretary Xu could detect the change in Emperor Jiajing's attitude. Hai Rui's harsh censure, coupled with the emperor's own mortality, had triggered his self-reflection and remorse. The thought both saddened and emboldened Grand Secretary Xu. He decided to jettison his usual fear and replied: "Now that Your Majesty has asked, let me say a few words that you probably don't want to hear."

"Go ahead."

"Our country is governed with filial piety, a central tenet of Confucianism, because our empire is like one big family. If Your Majesty is the father and the people of two capitals and thirteen provinces of the Great Ming Empire are your children, the Privy Council is rather like the daughter-in-law of the family. We at the Privy Council run the family to the best of our abilities, obeying and serving our in-laws and husband, and raising our children. When conflicts occur, we try to endure our grievances and cover up flashpoints to appease both sides so we can maintain harmony in the family. When it is impossible to attend to the needs of all sides, we always succumb to the demands of the in-laws at the cost of our children's interests. That's how we manage it. I don't think there's any better way."

Emperor Jiajing paused for a moment. "Hai Rui also stated in his remonstrance that the world is the monarch's family, and he criticised me for neglecting my duty as a parent. But I'm old and plagued with illness. Even if I recover, I don't think I can ever fulfil my parental responsibilities. Over the past few days, I've been pondering abdication and letting the Prince of Yu take over…"

"Your Majesty, I beseech you to reconsider," Grand Secretary Xu pleaded as he fell to his knees. "There are thousands of things that require your leadership. The revival of this country depends on you recovering your health. Your courtiers are in awe of your talents and strategic wisdom. If you resign abruptly, you'll no doubt jolt the world, placing the Prince of Yu in a dilemma because he is not ready for the throne. It is my sincere hope that Your Majesty regains good health and moves to your new palace where you can resume your control of state affairs. If we could redirect our resources to nation-building, eliminating corruption and regaining trust in the Imperial Government, we shall be able to rejuvenate the Great Ming Empire in no time. By taking hold of the reins once more, you will benefit our country and future generations."

Emperor Jiajing looked visibly touched. Straightening his back, he said: "Grand Secretary Xu, could you find Dr Li's herbs inside one of those cabinets? Since Huang Jin is not here, I'm afraid you must boil them for me."

"Yes, Your Majesty," replied Grand Secretary Xu. He was surprised by the renewed vigour in the emperor's voice.

※

Once the Chongyang Festival in early September was over, the leaves in the north started to turn yellow.

There were many tall trees outside the Prince of Yu's mansion. When the west wind blew, the square in front of the mansion was covered with a thick layer of fallen leaves. By the time they were swept away, a new layer began to form. Since the Prince of Yu was expecting an entourage of honoured guests, the eunuchs on duty could not use brooms for fear of stirring up the dust. Instead, the Prince of Yu's personal aide convened a large group of servants to rake or scoop up the leaves with their bare hands.

"Stop, stop," shouted the aide, rushing out. "The first uncle is arriving."

The eunuchs who were raking leaves quickly lined up on both sides of the avenue at the front of the gate.

The Prince of Yu's horse guards who had gone to the city gate to welcome the guests were now leading the way. They were followed by two carriages and a cargo cart. As they approached the Prince of Yu's mansion, the eunuchs and maids bowed collectively.

Gao Hanwen and Li Qi, Princess Li's younger brother, were sitting inside the carriages. The Imperial Palace had requested that they produce a hundred thousand bolts of cotton cloth and ship them to the northeastern border before the winter solstice, as part of the government's upcoming peace treaty with the Anda tribe. To ensure that the goods arrived first in Beijing before frost, Gao Hanwen and Li Qi personally escorted the cargo ships. They handed over the cotton cloth to officials at the Ministry of Treasury and came directly to the Prince of Yu's mansion.

The two side gates were opened. A small group of officials and eunuchs, led by Zhang Juzheng and Feng Bao, were waiting in the front yard. The young prince, who had heard about his uncle's visit, was ready to burst with excitement. He held Feng Bao's hands. In front of Zhang, who mentored both his father and him, he tried to suppress his enthusiasm. With his eyes wide open, he eagerly watched the gate. But soon, he started to fidget. Pinching Feng Bao's hands, he whispered: "I can hear clopping outside. Why aren't my uncle and his friends coming in?"

Feng Bao lifted the boy and held him in his arms. "Your Royal Highness, close your eyes and count to ten," he said. "By the time you finish, your uncle will be here."

"What if I finish counting and he's still not here?" the boy asked in a raised voice. "You'll have to bark like a dog for me, will you not?"

Zhang shot a stern glance at the young prince. "Your Highness, behave yourself," he chided, intimidating the boy into silence.

The boy's face fell and he pinched Feng Bao hard on the bottom. Feng Bao grimaced, pretending that the pinch had hurt him badly. Worrying that Zhang might see what he was doing, the young prince stopped.

"The guests have arrived," the aide announced as he appeared at the archway.

Li Qi walked in with a huge smile on his face. Gao Hanwen followed him. Despite the long trip, the two looked spirited. They bowed to Zhang.

When Feng Bao carried the young prince in his arms and stepped forward, all three bowed to the boy and greeted him: "Your Royal Highness, it is a pleasure to see you."

The boy was too impatient to observe the ritual. "Put me down," he shouted, struggling in Feng Bao's arms. The second his feet touched the ground, he ran up to Li Qi. "Uncle, did you bring me the gifts you promised in your letter?" he asked.

Li Qi was beaming with joy. Squatting down, he hugged the boy and said: "Your Royal Highness, I wouldn't dare forget. I've packed them in more than a dozen boxes. But the best gift you will receive is stored in a vat. You can't keep it to yourself, though. Within the next couple of days, you should present it to your grandfather."

"My grandfather lives inside the palace and has everything he needs," the boy argued. "Everything he has is the best. Do I really need to give him another gift? He won't like it."

"This gift that I'm giving you is very special," Li Qi whispered in the boy's ear. "I can guarantee that His Majesty will like it. In fact, he'd be elated if you present it to him."

"What is it then? I want to see it now."

"Carry the vat inside!" Li Qi shouted to his porters.

Four workers appeared at a side entrance carrying a large gilded bronze vat. As they stepped over the threshold, some water spilled out from inside the vat.

"Be careful," Li Qi shouted nervously as he directed the workers. "Easy, easy…"

The workers hauled the vat into the front yard, bowed and retreated straight away.

The young prince was now burning with curiosity. When Li Qi carried the boy over, he peeked inside and was shocked by what he saw. Inside the vat was a turtle that was nearly a metre long and half a metre wide. It seemed that the turtle's shell, which looked golden and shiny, had been polished. A few characters were discernible on its back.

"This turtle is huge!" the young prince exclaimed. "I see characters on its back, but I can only recognise a couple of them."

Gao Hanwen, who was standing nearby, laughed. "Only a learned scholar can understand the meaning of those characters," he said. "A calligrapher inscribed them on the back of the turtle many, many years ago. Ask Mr Zhang to explain them to you."

The young prince turned to Zhang, who did not act surprised at all. Tan Lun and Gao Hanwen had written to him about the turtle several days before. Exchanging a knowing glance with Gao Hanwen, Zhang stepped closer to the vat.

"Let me see," he said before pausing to read the characters. "It reads: 'The first year under the reign of Emperor Wen of the Han dynasty.'"

"How old is the turtle then?" asked the prince.

"I would say the turtle has been around for at least one thousand, seven hundred and thirty years."

"It's a miracle!" the young prince marvelled. "He's lived longer than my grandfather!"

Staring at the miracle creature, Zhang was lost in thought. He became keenly aware that a grand scheme that he and his fellow reformers had been devising for years would finally have the chance to come to fruition. Emperor Wen of the Han dynasty was a devout Taoist. He governed the country by adopting the Taoist principle of non-interference, and historians referred to him as a wise ruler who brought stability and prosperity to his empire. Emperor Jiajing, who had neglected state affairs for more than two decades, often deflected criticism by comparing himself to Emperor Wen. If Emperor Jiajing saw this ancient turtle, he would no doubt be pleased with the Prince of Yu. For a while, Zhang was worried that the emperor, whose illness had rendered him more capricious, could depose the Crown Prince. The gift would help restore the emperor's trust in his son. Once the prince ascended the throne, he and other courtiers could initiate the reforms that they had been planning for years.

"It's a rare species, a propitious talisman," Zhang said to the young prince. "This miracle turtle was released into the river during the reign of Emperor Wen of the Han dynasty. Emperor Wen was a wise and virtuous ruler. So is your grandfather. If you and your father present it to His Majesty, you will make him very happy."

"Where did you get this magic turtle?" Feng Bao asked Li Qi.

"It's truly a divine creature, and the timing of its appearance couldn't have been better. Ten days before we departed, a fisherman caught it in Lake Tai. When he saw those characters carved on the turtle's back, the fisherman knew it was a very special reptile. So he delivered it to the imperial inspector's yamen. When Mr Tan heard that we were leaving for Beijing, he told us to give the turtle to the Prince of Yu and his son so they could present it to His Majesty."

Throughout his young life, adults around him had been teaching him various ways to please his grandfather. So the young prince was more than eager to have this opportunity to put what he had learned into practice. "I want to personally take the turtle to my grandfather now!"

"We need to show it to your parents first," Zhang said before turning to Li Qi and Gao Hanwen. "The Prince of Yu is waiting for you in his study. Feng Gonggong can take Li Qi to see Princess Li."

The group began to disperse.

The four workers were called back to move the bronze vat to the backyard. Several eunuchs were unloading the cart outside the mansion. They came in carrying gift boxes of various sizes.

明

"We are greatly indebted to you for your contribution," the Prince of Yu greeted Gao Hanwen, who took a deep bow.

"Sit down and have a cup of tea," the prince continued, pointing to a chair against the south wall. "It is impressive that you were able to produce a hundred thousand bolts of cotton cloth at such short notice. If the peace talks with the Anda tribe succeed, we can save thousands of lives and significantly reduce our military spending."

"Your Highness, you are probably not aware that Gao Hanwen

and his wife have donated fifty thousand bolts of cotton cloth. That's the reason we were able to put it all together so fast. An imperial official owes his first loyalty to the monarch because he's fed and clothed by the Imperial Palace. But Mr Gao was stripped of his position at Hanlin Academy. As a commoner, he is under no obligation to do this. He's a true patriot!"

Zhang Juzheng's praise failed to excite Gao Hanwen. In fact, he looked rather forlorn. "As the proverb goes, we're cutting out a piece of our flesh to treat a boil. Even though the hundred thousand bolts of cotton cloth will enable us to prevent wars and save thousands of lives along the northern border, cotton farmers and textile workers in the south are being robbed of their livelihood."

"What do you mean by that?" asked the Prince of Yu, who appeared startled.

"Why don't you share your observations with His Highness," Zhang said to Gao.

"Your Highness, the Imperial Palace has implemented this cotton cloth production programme to encourage farmers to improve their livelihoods by growing cotton near Songjiang region," Gao stated. "But major landowners are snatching all the profits. For each bolt of cotton cloth that is woven, sixty per cent of the profits go to big landowners and textile merchants like me. Only thirty per cent is given to the Imperial Palace. Farmers and weavers get only ten per cent. It's a hopeless situation. Grand Secretary Xu's family owns a large swath of land near Songjiang and he is a key proponent of the plan. So, we're in a bind."

"When Grand Secretary Xu presented me with this plan, he vowed to keep his family out of things. He never mentioned this sixty-thirty-ten split," said the Prince of Yu, looking visibly upset. "This is no different from the previous rice-to-mulberry conversion policy under the reign of Yan Song. Farmers were encouraged to grow mulberry leaves and sell them to big silk mills. They ended up with hardly any profits. We are repeating the same mistakes. Mr Zhang, please go and summon Grand Secretary Xu."

"Your Highness, to be fair, Grand Secretary Xu has nothing to do with this situation," Gao said earnestly. "If you summon him here, the most he could do is write to his family in Songjiang and issue them a rebuke. The Xu family can very well choose to leave the business. If they do, no other landowner would dare get into textiles and enter into a contract with the Imperial Palace. Our grand plan to expand cotton farming and replenish the state coffers would come to naught."

"The key problem is that the law has given members of the imperial family and senior imperial officials tax-exempt status," Zhang interjected. "Regardless of what they grow on their land, be it rice, wheat or cotton, the Imperial Government cannot collect any taxes."

"Big landowners annexed the land of small farmers, and they don't pay any taxes on what they grow on their land," said Gao. "No matter how much cotton cloth we produce, neither the Imperial Government nor ordinary people benefit from it. Moreover, the programme has imposed a heavy burden on the farmers."

"Then what's the point of advancing the programme? Why not revoke it?"

"It's more complex than that," Zhang murmured.

"For this plan, big landowners set aside a hundred seventy-thousand acres of their land for cotton production," the Prince of Yu continued. "They've netted at least two hundred thousand bolts of cotton cloth in profits. But the Xu family and other landowners are only willing to contribute fifty thousand bolts to help with the Imperial Government's peace treaty. Where is Imperial Inspector Tan Lun? Why didn't he do something about it?"

"Tan Lun has a very difficult task," Zhang explained. "The big landowners have their own textile mills to process the cotton they harvest from their own fields. After they produce the cotton cloth, they don't sell it directly on the market. Instead, they wait for textile merchants to come and buy the products wholesale. So, the Imperial Government can only impose a ten per cent tax on the profits that merchants make after they resell the cotton cloth at retail stores. Fortunately, we have Tan Lun and Princess Li's brother there. They personally pressured big landowners to pay their share of taxes at the wholesale phase. As a result, we were able to collect fifty thousand bolts of cotton cloth for the peace treaty, and Gao Hanwen pitched in the remaining bolts. Otherwise, we could have ended up with far less. Your Highness is absolutely justified in complaining about the sixty-thirty-ten split, but you should understand Tan Lun's dilemma. He fought relentlessly and offended a large group of noblemen and families of senior imperial officials in the process. To me, the real problem lies with our tax laws."

"Our founding father made the laws. It would be political suicide to change them," sighed the Prince of Yu. "At the same time, Grand Secretary Xu controls the Privy Council, and he won't feel motivated to change the current arrangement that hurts the financial interests of his family. So there isn't much we can do about this, is there?"

"There is a way, but it cannot be done now," said Zhang.

"How?"

"Revamp the whole tax system," Zhang said in a near whisper.

"Watch what you say," warned the Prince of Yu, glancing around furtively.

"Your Highness, I understand that certain things are not meant to be said at the moment. Aristocrats and senior imperial officials own the majority of land in our country. If they don't pay taxes on their income, commoners are shouldering a disproportionate share of the tax burden. The high taxes have made it unaffordable for ordinary farmers to own their land. They are forced to sell it to the wealthy. If we allow the land annexation to continue, our state coffers will continue to remain depleted and more people will be pushed into poverty. If we don't reform the system, people will rise up and the dynasty will be lost."

"Mr Zhang, mind your tongue. It's premature to make such statements."

Zhang was persistent. "Your Highness, there are things that you should start thinking about," he said in a low voice. "Conventional wisdom has it that without a long-term strategy, a short-term plan never accomplishes anything. But sometimes, working out a short-term plan might help with a long-term strategy. Dr Li has said that His Majesty's illness is incurable and that he probably has just a few months to live. So you have to have a plan in place."

The Prince of Yu's face turned grim. "The only plan we have

now is to urge Dr Li to try everything possible to treat His Majesty and restore him to health," he said with determination. "As his filial son, I cannot covet his throne and plot to take over. Mr Zhang, I also urge you not to have any such illicit thoughts."

"Your Highness, I admire your filial piety, but we have to be practical. Otherwise, the peace and stability of the Great Ming Empire, and the livelihoods of millions of your subjects, could be at stake."

"What on earth are you trying to convey?" the Prince of Yu asked impatiently.

"Your Highness, let me give you an example. The Anda tribe lives in the Mongolian desert and their people are in dire need of our cotton cloth. As part of the peace treaty, we promise to supply them with a hundred thousand bolts of cotton cloth every year. Thanks to the generous donation by Gao Hanwen and his wife, we are able to fulfil our obligation. But what about next year and the year after? If we can't produce a hundred thousand bolts next year and renege on our promise, war would ensue. Therefore, reforming the taxation system in the south is an urgent matter. Whenever one engages in restructuring, it takes time and meticulous planning."

The Prince of Yu nodded in agreement, but still appeared hesitant. "What do you expect me to do?" he asked. "We cannot propose our ideas to His Majesty now. At the same time, it is wishful thinking to take over the throne early so we could implement these strategies."

"Your Highness, these are not my intentions," said Zhang. "I just want to remind you that you should start preparing so that, when the time comes, you'll be ready."

"How do I prepare? What kinds of things do I need to prepare?"

"There is one thing you can do right now," Zhang proposed. "You should try persuading His Majesty to save this person's life. Some day, when we decide to initiate the taxation reform, he will be there for us. He's crucial to our success."

The Prince of Yu was an intelligent person and knew exactly who Zhang had in mind. "Are you referring to Hai Rui?"

"Yes, Your Highness. In the future, if we continue to expand cotton production in the south and require big landowners to pay taxes like everyone else and force them to give back the land that they have annexed to small farmers, we will run into tremendous resistance. There is only one person who can fend off the attacks of thousands against us. That's Hai Rui."

The Prince of Yu finally understood the painstaking intention of Zhang's argument. "But His Majesty has already pardoned Hai Rui, has he not?" the Prince of Yu asked, sounding perplexed.

"Your Highness, His Majesty is plagued with illness, which is largely caused by those immortality pills he's been taking. The pills make him capricious like the summer weather. Thunder and rain can strike at any minute. Hai Rui might have been pardoned this morning, but His Majesty may decide to behead him the next day. You must let His Majesty understand that preserving Hai Rui's life is like looking after a sharp weapon to protect our Great Ming Empire."

"You mentioned Hai Rui's crucial role in our future taxation reform in the south," the Prince of Yu said pensively. "Grand Secretary Xu's family would be the first to be affected by the reform. As you know, Grand Secretary Xu has taken extraordinary risks to save Hai Rui's life. If we send Hai Rui to tackle the task, how will he face Grand Secretary Xu?"

"Your Highness, that's a very thoughtful and insightful observation. I don't dispute the fact that our programme could harm the financial interests of Grand Secretary Xu when his family may be forced to pay taxes. But reforming the taxation system is imperative, and Grand Secretary Xu understands its inevitability. He has made tremendous contributions to our country, and he's well-respected by both imperial officials and the public. Grand Secretary Xu understands that if we send someone who fails to implement the new policy, his reputation would be tarnished. At the same time, our continued financial crisis would push the Great Ming Empire to the verge of collapse. Grand Secretary Xu will agree with us that Hai Rui is a valuable asset. With his fearlessness and foolhardiness, Hai Rui would be the perfect person to carry out the reform and attend to Grand Secretary Xu's concerns. Even for the sake of Grand Secretary Xu, we have to save Hai Rui."

The Prince of Yu's face lit up. "Why don't you draw up a report on my behalf and I will submit it to His Majesty tomorrow. He can castigate me or depose me, I don't care."

Zhang Juzheng and Gao Hanwen exchanged glances. "We've made a special arrangement for your visit tomorrow," Zhang said. "I don't think His Majesty would be displeased with you. Gao Hanwen, could you show that special gift to His Highness?"

The Prince of Yu turned to Gao expectantly.

"It's truly a divine creature," said Gao. "Right before we departed, a fisherman captured a turtle. The characters inscribed on its back show that the turtle was released into the water during the Han dynasty, at the onset of Emperor Wen's reign. So we brought this magical creature all the way here. If Your Highness visits His Majesty with your son and presents it as a good luck charm, it would be easier for you to bring up Hai Rui's case."

"Do such creatures really exist?" the Prince of Yu asked. "How could it live so long? I refuse to present to His Majesty a fake relic or a so-called divine creature because it could backfire on us. We know that from experience. Remember Grand Master Zhang's blood scripture?"

"I can assure you that this one is authentic," said Gao. "The turtle was released into the water in the first year of Emperor Wen's reign. It's been around for at least one thousand, seven hundred and thirty years. We're keeping it in a special vat in the backyard. You're welcome to inspect it."

"Take me there," said the Prince of Yu, who strutted out with a sceptical look on his face.

10

THE BOWL WAS FILLED TO THE BRIM WITH HERBAL BROTH. HUANG JIN held it with both hands and cautiously limped to the emperor's bed in order to prevent the medicine from spilling. Emperor Jiajing leaned against the headboard. Huang brought the bowl up to his mouth. The emperor took a sip before reaching out his bony hands and taking the bowl. After inhaling deeply, he drank the broth in one gulp.

Huang's eyes moistened. He picked up a wet towel from the night table and gently sponged the residue off the corner of Emperor Jiajing's mouth and his overgrown beard.

"Help me up," the emperor ordered. "Wash my face and comb my hair."

"Master, you're only seeing your son and grandson. They're family. You don't need to exert yourself and get dressed up, do you? Just lie down and rest."

"They're the future monarchs of the Great Ming Empire. I need to set a good example for them. Go and find that official robe for me."

"Yes, Your Majesty, I understand." Huang choked up. Turning around, he wiped away his tears and trotted over to several wardrobe trunks along the wall. He unlocked a trunk lid. Underneath a piece of bright yellow silk brocade lay a crown and a dragon robe. Huang removed the brocade and carefully brought out the emperor's ceremonial attire.

"Take the prayer mat away. Ask them to bring the throne chair from the main hall."

明

Donning their official yellow robes, the Prince of Yu and his son were kneeling on prayer cushions outside Yuxi Palace. Chen Hong stood next to them, with his back arched. They were waiting for the emperor's summons. Behind them was the gilded bronze vat that contained the magic turtle.

Inside the meditation room, two eunuchs on duty placed the emperor's horseshoe dragon chair in the place where he used to meditate on a prayer mat. They bowed and exited.

Huang leaned forward to help Emperor Jiajing put on a pair of official boots. Wrapping his arm around Huang's neck, the emperor slowly got up from his bed and trudged towards his throne chair. Once he was seated, Huang combed his hair, created a bun on the top of his head and massaged his face with a warm towel. Dipping a different comb into a basin of warm water, Huang groomed his unruly beard.

"Get me my dragon robe," demanded the emperor.

Huang picked up the outfit from a nightstand. Since the emperor was sitting, Huang paused, trying to figure out how to do it without too much manoeuvring. But from a side glance, he saw that Emperor Jiajing had straightened his back and managed to stand up.

Spreading out the robe, Huang stood behind the emperor, who slipped his arms into the sleeves and lifted up the bulky outfit. Huang quickly moved to the front to fasten the buttons and tie the jade belt. Once the emperor sat back down on his chair, Huang placed the crown on his head and inserted a long jade hairpin through a hole on the left side of the crown. It came out through a hole on the right side.

Adjusting the shoulders of the robe, Huang stepped back to take one more look at Emperor Jiajing. Tears streamed down his cheeks.

It had been twenty years since he last saw the emperor wear his crown and dragon robe. Decked out in his majestic ceremonial attire, he looked so foreign. The experience felt surreal.

"Do I look awful?" asked the emperor.

"Your Majesty, you look heavenly!"

"Why are you crying then?"

"I'm simply overjoyed."

"Bring me the mirror."

Huang limped over to the emperor's desk and brought him a mirror. He squatted down in front of his master and held it up.

In the mirror, Emperor Jiajing saw an unfamiliar figure staring back at him – an illusory, after-life version of himself. "Every Taoist practitioner pursues the enlightened state of having three forces of vital energy condense into one's body," he murmured. "I guess it is just as elusive as riding on the wings of the wind. Oh well, time to bring in the guests."

Huang put the mirror away and stepped out of the meditation room to fetch the Prince of Yu and his son.

Soon the special guests appeared at the door. They knelt outside the threshold. "Your son, Zhu Zaiji, and your grandson, Zhu Yijun, kowtow to Your Majesty."

There was sadness in Emperor Jiajing's eyes when he heard the Prince of Yu's lacklustre voice. But the sight of his ebullient grandson lifted his mood. "Come in," said the emperor.

The Prince of Yu rose from the floor, held his son's hand and entered.

Huang placed an embroidered pouf next to Emperor Jiajing. "His Majesty has offered that seat to the Prince of Yu," he said, pointing to the pouf on the left side of the throne chair.

The Prince of Yu bowed to his father before sitting nervously on the edge of the pouf.

The young prince had always felt deeply attached to Emperor Jiajing even though everyone around him saw his grandfather as a much-feared figure. But it was a different story today. When the boy saw the emperor donning his crown and dragon robe, and sitting high up on the throne chair, he became timid and simply stood there. The emperor noticed the boy's reluctance. Managing a weak smile, he gently clapped his hands. "Zhu Yijun, come over here," he beckoned to the boy in his feeble voice.

The young prince stepped towards him. Emperor Jiajing stretched out his hands and the boy grabbed them timorously.

"In the *Book of Rites*, there is a famous line advising a monarch on who is allowed to sit on his lap. Has your teacher taught you this yet?"

"Yes, Your Majesty, my teacher has taught me about the special relationship between the grandfather and the grandson. The *Book of Rites* says that a monarch is allowed to hold his grandchild on his lap, but not his son."

Emperor Jiajing laughed. "It sounds like you have a very competent mentor," he said. "But Grandfather is too ill to hold you on my lap. I shall ask Huang Jin to get you a pouf. You can sit next to me."

Huang carried another embroidered pouf and placed it on the right side of the throne chair. As Huang was about to lift the young prince off the floor and put him on the pouf, the boy struggled free from his grip. "Hands off," he insisted. "I can manage myself."

Much to the emperor's delight, the boy jumped up to the pouf, straightened his back and sat on the edge of the seat with his legs dangling in the air.

"My grandson is just like me!" Emperor Jiajing raved. "I hear that you have brought something to show me. What is it?"

"Father," said the Prince of Yu, glancing at his son nervously, fearing that the boy might misspeak.

"I'm not asking you," Emperor Jiajing chided the Prince of Yu. "Let my boy speak."

The young prince stared at his father and became reticent.

"You can answer His Majesty's question."

"Yes, Father," the boy replied before turning to Emperor Jiajing. "Grandfather, my father and I intend to present an auspicious talisman from heaven. It's not an ordinary something."

"All right, show it to me then."

Huang rushed outside. "Bring the propitious gift inside," he ordered.

Chen Hong was supposed to oversee the Prince of Yu's gift outside the palace. Looking dispirited, he stood there sulking. His excessive purges in the aftermath of the Hai Rui incident provoked the ire of Emperor Jiajing, who had banned Chen Hong from serving him in the meditation room. On this important occasion when three generations of rulers gathered inside Yuxi Palace, he was assigned a menial task and had to wait outside with some junior eunuchs. At this moment, he was so preoccupied with these angry thoughts that he did not even hear Huang's calling.

One of the four junior eunuchs who had been designated to carry the bronze vat prodded him gently. "Chen Gonggong, His Majesty is calling us," he said. "We need to take the vat inside."

Chen Hong awoke from his reverie. "What are you waiting for?" he scolded. "Go quickly."

The four eunuchs lifted the vat off the floor and staggered into the palace. Since Emperor Jiajing was too emaciated to get up from his throne chair, the eunuchs placed the vessel on a spot about two feet away from him.

Emperor Jiajing peered at the turtle inside. His illness caused blurry and dimmed vision. He squinted hard but still couldn't read the characters on the back of the turtle. "Zhu Yijun, what do those characters say?" he asked.

The young boy saw an immediate opportunity to show off his newly acquired knowledge. "Yes, Your Majesty," he replied in a raised voice, full of confidence. "The characters on the back of the turtle read: 'The first year under the reign of Emperor Wen of the Han dynasty.' This is a propitious talisman from heaven. The magic turtle is nearly one thousand, seven hundred and thirty years old!"

"Oh I see," marvelled Emperor Jiajing whose eyes brightened.

The young prince had rehearsed his lines multiple times the previous day. Once he started bragging, he found it hard to stop and began rambling: "Grandfather, historians say Emperor Wen of the Han dynasty was a good ruler. Everyone in the country compares my grandfather to Emperor Wen. But that Hai Rui person speaks ill of both Emperor Wen and my grandfather. So the Heavenly God has sent this magic turtle into this world to inform them that what Hai Rui has said is wrong."

The Prince of Yu and Huang Jin looked towards Emperor Jiajing, waiting for the grandfather's proud smile. But all they could see was a blank, expressionless face. Of course, they could not hear Hai Rui's voice echoing in Emperor Jiajing's ears:

> Emperor Wen began to pursue Taoism in his later years and jettisoned the teachings of Confucius and Mencius. He adopted Laozi's philosophy of governing by doing nothing that goes against nature. His retreat and his fascination with supernatural events left many important state affairs neglected… In comparison, our current emperor is far worse.

The emperor's deadpan response disappointed and scared the young prince. He couldn't help blurting out in dismay: "Grandfather, did I say anything wrong?"

The boy's question jolted Emperor Jiajing. He realised that his mind had drifted off. The eagerness on the faces of his grandson and the Prince of Yu made him feel guilty. "Zhu Yijun is absolutely right," the emperor said with a forced smile. "Now that you have dedicated this rare and auspicious creature to me, how may I reward you?"

The grandfather's endearing gesture melted away the boy's fear. "Grandfather, I don't need any rewards from you," said the boy, who decided to go off script. "But if you insist, I do have a request. Could you release Hai Rui?"

There was a look of panic on the Prince of Yu's face. He had not expected his son to bring up this sensitive topic so bluntly. Emperor Jiajing would surely suspect that the Prince of Yu had orchestrated the plot. "Hold your tongue," the Prince of Yu chastised.

Huang Jin, who seldom showed any emotion following his ordeals, tensed up.

Emperor Jiajing's inscrutable countenance gave little away.

The boy felt wronged. He was under the impression that the whole idea of presenting the turtle was to persuade his grandfather to pardon Hai Rui. Now that he had said it, why did his father look upset? What did he do wrong? Scared by the tension in the air, the boy slipped down from the pouf and sank to his knees before his grandfather.

Emperor Jiajing glanced at his grandson who was kneeling at his feet and uttered a sigh. "My boy, do you know the poem, 'From out of the sea the moon appears/ From the ends of the Earth, all share this moment'? Deep down, everyone wants me to pardon Hai Rui. They all share this secret thought, but nobody dares say it. My grandson is the only person who's not afraid of speaking his mind. I like that. Zhu Yijun, please rise."

The boy raised his head and stood up grudgingly. "Grandfather!"

"Let's make a deal. If you can do this for Grandfather, I will pardon Hai Rui."

The young prince shot a furtive glance at the Prince of Yu.

"Don't look at your father. He doesn't have your guts."

The young prince shifted his gaze to Emperor Jiajing.

"I shall ask Huang Jin to carry this turtle to a lake nearby. Do you dare pick it up and set it free yourself?"

"Yes, Grandfather, of course!"

Emperor Jiajing beckoned to Huang and instructed him: "You accompany my grandson to the lake. If Zhu Yijun fulfils his pledge, you can bring Hai Rui over here."

"Yes, Your Majesty, I will do accordingly," replied Huang, who held the boy's hand and walked away.

"Wait," Emperor Jiajing called out. "Ask Chen Hong to send a message to Zhu Qi and Chee Dazhu. The two of them can escort Hai Rui here, but nobody else should know about this."

"Understood," replied Huang Jin.

After the imperial edict was issued, Chen Hong ordered eunuchs and maids to vacate the public areas inside the Western Compound. Thus, the large square outside Yuxi Palace looked deserted. When Huang returned with the young prince after they had released the turtle into the lake, there was not a single person in sight. They paused on the stone steps outside the palace main hall and surveyed the empty compound.

"They're here!" the boy shouted, pointing to the Western

Compound gate. In the distance, Huang saw Chen Hong rushing towards them. Close behind Chen Hong, two imperial agents were carrying a sealed sedan.

Knowing that Hai Rui was coming, the boy clapped his hands and called out. Huang hushed him down.

During the Ming dynasty, only a prince or a sick minister was allowed to visit the Forbidden City in a two-carrier sedan. After Emperor Jiajing moved into the Western Compound in the twenty-first year of his reign, the two-carrier-sedan rule was modified to regulate visitors at the Western Compound. As grand secretary, Yan Song was granted such a privilege after he had turned seventy, but since his downfall, the Prince of Yu was the only person who could ride a sedan inside the Western Compound. Emperor Jiajing never bestowed the privilege on Grand Secretary Xu.

Now, for the first time in history, a prisoner was allowed inside the Western Compound in a sedan – Hai Rui sat inside the tightly sealed vehicle with his limbs in shackles. The two carriers happened to be Zhu Qi and Chee Dazhu, who hurried over upon receiving Emperor Jiajing's secret decree. Transporting a tiny man like Hai Rui, the two kungfu masters hardly felt the weight on their shoulders. They walked in vigorous strides behind Chen Hong. Before long, they reached the stone steps outside Yuxi Palace. Even though Chen Hong was carrying nothing, he was out of breath. Zhu Qi and Chee Dazhu set the sedan down on the ground. When they spotted the young prince, both of them got down on one knee and saluted him, but the boy did not even bother to look at them. He fixed his gaze on the sealed sedan.

Zhu Qi lifted the sedan curtain. Reaching a hand inside, he helped Hai Rui step out. Chee Dazhu moved the sedan aside so it wouldn't block Hai Rui's path.

As Hai Rui dragged his fettered feet and lumbered towards the stone steps, the young boy who was standing at the top of the steps moved forward to size up the much-admired loyal courtier. Wearing an old linen robe, Hai Rui did not look at all like what the young prince had imagined. He did not possess the stately appearance of Grand Secretary Xu, and nor did he appear to be learned or refined like his mentor, Zhang Juzheng. Even though Hai Rui had combed his hair and cleaned his face, he struck the young prince as a pig-headed country bumpkin. A sense of disappointment washed over him.

"You are Hai Rui, are you not?"

From the apricot-coloured robe and the crown, Hai Rui knew that the boy was the young prince. Adjusting his shackles, Hai Rui bowed to the boy. "Your Royal Highness, I am Hai Rui."

"You're a bold man! How dare you insult His Majesty?"

The boy's remark amused Hai Rui. His vigour and intelligence gave Hai Rui a glimmer of hope for the future of the Great Ming Empire. "If I do it now, nobody will criticise His Majesty in the future."

Hai Rui's reply took the young prince by surprise. Looking perplexed, he tried to figure out what it meant. The sparkle in Hai Rui's eye drew him in. He could not help liking this shackled, unimpressive-looking prisoner. Descending a few steps, he approached Hai Rui and whispered: "I have pleaded with the emperor to pardon you. When you get in, behave yourself and answer His Majesty's questions tactfully."

The young prince's precocious advice warmed Hai Rui's heart. He bowed and replied in a rough yet tender voice: "Your Royal Highness, thank you. I think I know how to respond to His Majesty truthfully."

"Your Royal Highness, His Majesty and the Prince of Yu are waiting for you," Chen Hong interjected with an ingratiating smile. "Let's get going."

When Zhu Qi and Chee Dazhu attempted to unlock Hai Rui's fetters, Chen Hong stopped them. "Leave them on," he said. "Carry him up there."

Inserting their hands under Hai Rui's armpits, Zhu Qi and Chee Dazhu hoisted Hai Rui in the air and walked up the steps.

The scene seemed a little strange.

Emperor Jiajing was perched on his round-backed throne chair. The Prince of Yu sat on an embroidered pouf on the left and his son on the right, with his legs dangling. The current and future rulers of the Great Ming Empire stared down at Hai Rui. The expressions in their eyes were vastly different from each other.

Much to Huang Jin's surprise, Emperor Jiajing granted Hai Rui a prayer pillow so he could kneel on it.

Zhu Qi and Chee Dazhu had left and were waiting outside Yuxi Palace. Huang retreated to the main hall and was squatting down before a boiling medicine pot on a stove next to a window in the east wall.

Emperor Jiajing had contemplated today's royal 'trial' for quite some time. Several days ago, he secretly ordered Huang to seek out Dr Li and ask the physician to prescribe some medicine that would boost his strength and enable him to sit straight for two hours. That was his specific intent. Dr Li, who was then widely considered as the best and most knowledgeable doctor in the country, certainly knew how to concoct a few single doses to satisfy the emperor's request. Early this morning, Emperor Jiajing gulped down a large bowl of Dr Li's herbal broth, which seemed to have achieved its intended effect. Even though he had been sitting for a solid hour, he was energetic and felt he could go on for another hour without lying down.

"This person has a famous nickname," Emperor Jiajing started by addressing the Prince of Yu and his grandson. "Do you know what it is?"

Tan Lun had mentioned this to the Prince of Yu years before, but he decided to feign ignorance. "Your Majesty, I've never heard of it before," he said. "Please advise."

"People used to call him a 'calligraphy brush holder'," the emperor explained, turning to his grandson.

"Grandfather, may I ask why he is called that?"

"He used to be a teacher in Nanping County, Fujian Province. One day, the county magistrate came to visit his school. Hai Rui and two other teachers were summoned to a meeting with the magistrate. While his two colleagues who were standing on each side of him got down on their knees to greet the official, Hai Rui refused to kneel and remained standing throughout the meeting. Thus, the three of them resembled a calligraphy brush rack that is shaped like a mountain range, with the tallest peak in the middle and smaller ones on either side. Thus, locals gave him that endearing nickname. As you can see, he is a rebel by nature and challenges authority out of habit."

"Your Majesty, I don't challenge authority out of habit. If I can be a calligraphy brush holder, I would like to provide a port for your brush with which you can write a glorious chapter in the Ming history book."

"You are not my calligraphy brush holder and nor could you ever be one," Emperor Jiajing asserted in his stern voice. "Raise your head and look at the three figures in front of you. What do we resemble?"

Hai Rui slowly lifted his head and saw Emperor Jiajing sitting on his tall throne chair in the middle. The Prince of Yu and the young prince occupied two low embroidered poufs on each side of him. He quickly understood what the emperor attempted to convey: the three generations of the royal family formed a trinity and they were the true brush holders of the Ming dynasty.

Hai Rui did not respond.

"You cannot work it out can you?" the emperor said sarcastically before turning to his grandson. "Zhu Yijun, you know the answer, do you not? Tell him."

The young prince gladly obliged. "Grandfather, when the three of us, Your Majesty, my father and I sit here, we look like a calligraphy brush holder."

"Do you happen to agree with what my grandson has said?" Emperor Jiajing asked Hai Rui.

"Your Majesty, I beg to differ. What I'm seeing is not a brush holder, but the character for 'mountain' [山], the mountain of the Great Ming Empire."

The Prince of Yu was shocked that Hai Rui would have the impertinence to openly challenge the assertions made by Emperor Jiajing and his grandson. And yet, the analogy sounded quite grandiose. In fact, it was hard to refute. Worried that Hai Rui's reply could further provoke Emperor Jiajing, the Prince of Yu spoke up: "Hai Rui, how can you be so self-righteous even at this point in time? Straight talking and foolhardiness alone don't make you a wise and intelligent courtier. Traditionally, the word 'empire' consists of two characters, 'mountain' and 'river'. If you compare the unity of His Majesty, his son and his grandson to the character for 'mountain', who do you think is the river? The mountain and river cannot be separated."

Hai Rui lowered his head but remained persistent. "Your Royal Highness, I stand by what I just said. His Majesty, his son and his grandson are the mountains of the Great Ming Empire. The people and the imperial courtiers are the rivers."

One of Emperor Jiajing's favourite hobbies, in addition to his fervent pursuit of Taoism, was to play word games, and he took perverted delight in tormenting his courtiers with his endless riddles. Over the years, he kept everyone wandering inside his maze as they tried to pick up and follow the subtle clues and find their way out. He toyed with them and nobody dared to stray from the path and disobey the rules of his game. Before today's meeting, Emperor Jiajing had incorporated Hai Rui into what could probably be the last riddle of his life. As expected, Hai Rui fell right into his trap. The thought reinvigorated him. Instead of rebutting Hai Rui's claim, he tilted his head towards the Prince of Yu. "Do you think what he said is true?" he asked.

Of course, the Prince of Yu agreed, but as usual, he chose not to speak his mind in front of his father. "Father, forgive my ignorance. I want to hear your views about his claim," he mumbled.

"Zhu Yijun, what do you think? Answer me honestly."

"Grandfather, it sounds about right," replied the boy, staring at Emperor Jiajing nervously.

"Your analogy sounds noble but it's intrinsically wrong," the emperor argued forcefully, his eyes fixed on Hai Rui's. "You're all familiar with the Tang poet Liu Yuxi's famous lines: 'Red blossoms of mountain peach crowd the uplands/ The spring water of the Shu River surrounds the mountain as it flows.' You ostentatiously state that the current and future monarchs of the Great Ming Empire are mountains, and that the people and the courtiers are rivers. Let me ask you this. Rivers almost always flow away from the mountain sources. How do you explain the true relationship between the mountains and the rivers?"

Hai Rui was stumped. "Your Majesty, you are right," he admitted after a brief pause. "My analogy is truly inappropriate."

While Hai Rui's meek apology eased the Prince of Yu's worries, it excited the boy, who looked impressed by his grandfather's oratory prowess. He shot Emperor Jiajing an admiring glance.

"Great nations rise and fall," continued Emperor Jiajing. "Empires come and go, the endless Yangtze River flows inexorably. You think you can control the tide of history and save the world? Just because you have read a few books and attended some neo-Confucian lectures, it doesn't mean you are entitled to freely give your views on state affairs and make wild accusations against me and the Imperial Palace. Speaking of your inappropriate analogy, you heaped praise on the so-called virtuous monarchs, and cited Emperors Yao and Shun in Chinese mythology, Emperors Wen, Xuan and Guangwu of the Han dynasty, as well as Emperors Taizong and Xianzong of the Tang dynasty. Let me ask you again. If those virtuous monarchs and sages to whom you alluded in your article are immortal like the mountains, tell me which of the mountains still exists for them?"

"Your Majesty, there may not be any vestige of the sages' existence, but they are remembered in history books and in the hearts of the people."

The Prince of Yu and the boy held their breath and looked on nervously.

Surprisingly, Emperor Jiajing did not seem to be bothered by Hai Rui's seemingly insolent reply. "My son and grandson, remember his words," he said calmly.

"Yes, Your Majesty," the two princes replied.

By then, Emperor Jiajing could feel that his medicine-boosted energy was sapping fast. He told himself to hasten his remarks. "Even though the word 'empire', which, like my son has pointed out, consists of the two characters 'mountain' and 'river', it doesn't really mean mountains and rivers as you understand the words. I want you all to remember this. A monarch is not a mountain. His courtiers and subjects are not rivers. Since ancient times, the character 'river' that makes up the word 'empire' commonly referred to the Yangtze River in the south and the Yellow River in the north.

The Yangtze is notable for its clarity and the Yellow River has always been turbid and muddy. Both rivers have been flowing since time immemorial. There used to be a popular saying: when the Yellow River flows clear, a sage will emerge from the water. But when was the last time the Yellow River flowed clear? The water in the Yangtze irrigates the fertile land in multiple provinces. So does the Yellow River. One cannot favour the Yangtze River because of its clarity and abandon the Yellow River for its murkiness. This is a basic law of nature that Hai Rui doesn't understand. In his remonstrance, he urges me to rely on the Yangtze River and discard the Yellow River. How could it be done? On the other hand, we try to harness and control the Yellow River when it overflows its banks. That was the reason I dismissed Yan Song and executed Yan Shifan and other members of the Yan Clan. By the same token, when the Yangtze floods, I apply equally tough measures to control it as well. Now you will understand why I ordered the arrests and executions of members of the Clear Stream faction."

This plain but shocking truth not only stupefied the Prince of Yu, but also dazed Hai Rui, who widened his eyes in disbelief. Emperor Jiajing pointed at Hai Rui, who now looked defeated, and uttered the words that the Prince of Yu was dreading: "Take this Hai Rui, for example. He thinks he is a loyal defender of the Great Ming Empire, like a clear river flowing around a mountain. But when the clear water submerges the mountain peak, it's also called a flood! I know very well that he wants me to kill him. In this way, he turns himself into a martyr and makes a good name for himself in the history books and in the hearts of the people, while I would live in infamy and be forever remembered as the evil monarch who killed an upright courtier. For this reason alone, he deserves the death sentence!"

The Prince of Yu's face turned pale and the grandson appeared on the verge of tears.

"Our founding father rules the country with filial piety. Even if I don't kill you, my son will after he takes over the throne," he said to Hai Rui. "If he doesn't kill you, he would be regarded as unfilial. To make it easier for my son, I will allow you to live until the end of this year."

Hai Rui prostrated himself on the floor. "I'm willing to accept my death sentence as Your Majesty wishes," he said.

"Anybody here?" Emperor Jiajing shouted.

"Your Majesty, do you need me?" Huang Jin replied. While squatting quietly by the stove, he had overheard the soul-searching conversation inside the meditation room. By the time the emperor called him, Huang began sweating profusely and his heart was beating fast. Removing the medicine pot from the stove, he put the lid back on the stove. As he hobbled through the door, his mind was flooded with trepidation.

"Tell Zhu Qi and Chee Dazhu to escort him back to the Imperial Prison."

"Yes, Your Majesty," replied Huang with a heavy heart.

Tears were welling up in the young prince's eyes. He stared blankly at his grandfather.

"Zhu Yijun, are you mad because Grandfather has gone back on his word?" Emperor Jiajing teased the boy.

"I wouldn't dare," the boy replied as he wiped away his tears.

"It's good to know you wouldn't dare. Let me teach you something. Nothing that others have promised you counts. Only the decisions you make yourself matter. Understand?"

How could the young boy comprehend the profound meanings of these words? He felt betrayed but learned to conceal his emotions. "Grandfather, I understand," he mumbled meekly.

"Your Majesty, your humble servant Chen Hong is waiting for your orders," Chen Hong's voice sounded from outside the door.

"Escort Hai Rui back to the Imperial Prison!"

"Go in there, grab Hai Rui and bring him out," Chen Hong was heard directing Zhu Qi and Chee Dazhu, both of whom were standing next to him.

By the time Hai Rui was taken away, Emperor Jiajing felt exhausted. "Huang Jin, take my grandson to the imperial gift room," he instructed. "Reward him there with anything he likes."

The boy slid off the pouf and knelt in front of Emperor Jiajing. "Grandfather, I wouldn't want to receive any rewards from you."

"Nonsense," said the Prince of Yu. "How dare you reject His Majesty's gifts. Go there immediately."

Huang bent down and held the boy's hands. "Your Highness, the Prince of Yu is right," he said as he carried the young prince on his back. Before reaching the door, he turned around and instructed the Prince of Yu: "The herbs are cooked. I left the broth on a counter next to the stove."

"I'll take care of it," the Prince of Yu said.

As Huang tottered away, Emperor Jiajing watched the back of his grandson, eagerly waiting for the boy to turn his head and give him one last glance. But the boy never looked back. When Huang pivoted his body slightly to cross the threshold of the meditation room door, the boy deliberately shifted his gaze away towards the south window.

It was heartbreaking for Emperor Jiajing. His eyes dimmed.

"Even my grandson is turning his back on me," Emperor Jiajing murmured. There was a sombre note in his voice that was frightening. The Prince of Yu raised his head. Emperor Jiajing's face was bleak and his body suddenly went limp. Before the emperor slipped off his chair, the Prince of Yu dashed over and held his father in his arms. "Father, Father, are you all right?" he shouted.

Emperor Jiajing clung to his son tightly so he wouldn't fall to the floor. "Carry me to the bed," he mumbled. "Can you manage?"

The Prince of Yu had inherited from his mother a highly delicate constitution, but at this moment, his fear and desperation gave him a temporary boost of strength. With one hand holding his father's back, he grabbed the ailing emperor's legs and lifted him off the chair. Step by step, he plodded forward. Then, bending down slowly, he laid the emperor flat on the bed. By then, sweat and tears streamed down his face. "I shall summon Dr Li immediately," he said.

"Don't go..." commanded the emperor as he seized the Prince of Yu's sleeve.

The Prince of Yu paused. Seeing the vacant look on his father's face, he realised that he could not leave him alone on his deathbed. Pulling out his father's jade hairpin, the Prince of Yu carefully removed his crown, pulled off his boots and covered him with a blanket.

Having rested for a few moments, Emperor Jiajing gradually

regained his strength. "Get down on your knees," he ordered his son.

The Prince of Yu knelt next to a step stool in front of the bed and gazed at his father.

"They're under my pillow," said the emperor. "Take them out."

The Prince of Yu put his hand under Emperor Jiajing's pillow where he could feel a stack of papers wrapped in a piece of silk cloth. He sensed that this was the emperor's will. Slowly, he pulled the package out.

"Unwrap the silk cloth and read my first decree," said the emperor.

On the cover of the first decree, the Prince of Yu saw the following words: 'A declaration to return the Duke of Chu's land to the people.'

There was a glimmer of understanding in the Crown Prince's eyes.

"The Duke of Chu just passed away. Since he has no heir, several of his relatives who live nearby are coveting his land, which is about two hundred and forty thousand acres. Our family owes too much to the people of our country. I shall not give the land to other members of the royal family. Let's distribute it to the Duke of Chu's tenants. Assign this case to officials at the Ministry of Treasury and Ministry of Civil Affairs. Count this as my last contribution to the people of the Great Ming Empire."

"Father, thank you for this wise decision," said the Prince of Yu, who rose and kowtowed to Emperor Jiajing.

"Move on to my next decree."

The Prince of Yu rose from the floor and carefully put aside the first decree. When he saw the characters on the cover of the second edict, 'Granting a full pardon to Hai Rui, an auditor at the Ministry of Treasury', tears came rolling down.

"Zhang Juzheng once called Hai Rui 'our nation's sharp weapon'. There's nothing extraordinary about his claim. Even if Hai Rui is a magic sword of our Great Ming Empire, only the competent and the virtuous are fit to hold the sword. I'm not known for my virtues. In comparison, you're more benevolent and caring. I'll leave this sharp weapon to you to handle those corrupt officials. At the same time, if you push for your new policies, Hai Rui is the only one who can blaze a trail for you. He's certainly unstoppable."

By now, the Prince of Yu was weeping.

"Don't cry," Emperor Jiajing consoled his son. "Let me finish. The remonstrance that Hai Rui submitted is harsh, but I have read it more than a hundred times. He claims that nobody can understand what he's written. In a way, he's right. The core argument in his report is that the monarch should act benevolently by adopting people-oriented policies and sharing responsibility in government. Although an emperor holds supreme power, he seeks and listens to the advice of his cabinet before making decisions. I have been in power for forty-five years, and I always preferred autocracy. But you're not as strong-willed as I am, and you lack the talents to govern alone. Delegate your power and let the Privy Council and other senior ministers shoulder some of your responsibilities. Employ an honest and loyal person to run the cabinet."

"But Father, are you aware of any truly virtuous courtiers in the Great Ming Empire? Please advise."

"There are none. A virtuous courtier sometimes goes astray through force of circumstance. Hire them when they are virtuous, and dismiss them when they betray you. For this, I have made arrangements for you. Keep going."

The cover of the emperor's third decree baffled the Prince of Yu. The page was actually blank.

"Open it," said the emperor.

The Prince of Yu turned the cover page and inside were listed three names: Xu Jie, Gao Gong and Zhang Juzheng.

"I assigned these three people to be your teachers when you were a boy. You can use them in the order that I list their names here."

Cupping the list with both hands, the Prince of Yu choked up. "In addition to these three people, do you have anyone else to recommend to me?" he asked.

Emperor Jiajing looked lost and his eyes became hazy. He stared blankly at the canopy of his bed, as if he intended to look up at the sky. "Only the Heavenly God knows…"

The Prince of Yu rested his head and arms on the bed frame and burst out crying.

明

Despite being huddled around two large charcoal braziers, Deputy Li Chunfang, Zhao Zhenji and Zhang Juzheng still felt cold. Dressed in their official robes, they appeared tired. Since Emperor Jiajing's health had deteriorated a few days ago, they had been holding a vigil. If Dr Li's words were to be trusted, the emperor could pass away at any moment.

Feeling stifled and restless, Zhang got up from his chair and walked over to the door. When he lifted the thick cotton cloth door curtain, an icy blast of air blew snowflakes into the room. His colleagues shuddered as they stared at the grey sky and heavy snow outside.

"Grand Secretary Xu has been gone for two hours," Zhang said. "Shall we all go and wait outside Yuxi Palace?"

"He said he would summon us immediately if anything happens," Zhao advised. "We should stay put."

Zhang let go of the door curtain grudgingly and walked back to his seat near the fire. All of a sudden, his body jerked forward as if someone had pushed him. The palace chimed in the distance, and everyone in the room sprang to their feet.

"His Majesty!" Zhao cried out.

Zhang spun around and dashed out the door. The others followed and swarmed into the yard. In the howling wind, the bell sounded bleak.

明

It was past midnight and Hai Rui was still sitting by his table, reading a collection of annotated articles by neo-Confucian scholars. Since his private audience with Emperor Jiajing in October, he had stopped trimming or combing his hair and beard. In a matter of two months, his hair, tied on the top of his head with a cotton cloth strap, had reached down to his shoulders. His scraggly beard covered most of his face. Since Chee Dazhu changed his sheets and clothes regularly, and secretly took them home for his wife to wash, Hai Rui was able to maintain good hygiene and dress neatly. The floor was scrubbed clean and the cell remained spotless. Even in the winter, Hai Rui walked around in a pair of straw sandals without socks.

Urgent and heavy footsteps sounded in the passageway outside his cell.

Hai Rui put his book down and turned his gaze to the door. He sensed that something momentous was about to happen.

A jailer carrying a lantern appeared with Chee Dazhu, who was wearing a white linen mourning belt around his waist. With a large food basket in his arm, he looked grief-stricken.

Hai Rui's eyes fixed on the mourning belt, which was a clear signal that his life was coming to an end in the morning. Slowly, he rose from his chair.

The jailer unlocked the door and Chee Dazhu walked in without his usual greetings. Not looking at Hai Rui, he removed the lid on the food basket and placed a jug of liquor and several dishes on the table.

Chee Dazhu poured some liquor into Hai Rui's cup and then his own. Hai Rui raised his cup. "I want to thank you and your wife for taking care of me during the past few months," he said. "But let's drink to your wife first. Please give my best regards to her."

Chee Dazhu simply gulped down the liquor silently.

Hai Rui reciprocated by filling Chee Dazhu's cup and then his own. "Zhu Qi and your colleagues at the Imperial Investigative Agency have treated me well," said Hai Rui, emptying his cup. "Please thank them on my behalf."

"My saviour, don't just drink, take some of the meat and vegetable dishes," said Chee Dazhu as he tried to fill his cup again.

"All right then," said Hai Rui, who glanced at what he believed was his last meal. At home, he always ate rice with vegetables and meat. So he picked up a large bowl of rice that Chee Dazhu had prepared, put some vegetables and meat on top, and devoured the food in no time. Soon, the bowl and dishes were empty. He poured more liquor into Chee Dazhu's cup and said: "Dazhu, could you do me one more favour?"

"What is it, my saviour?"

"I have written a letter to Mr Wang Yongji," said Hai Rui, pulling out a thick letter from his breast pocket and handing it to Chee Dazhu. "Could you find a way to deliver this to him as soon as possible? I'm afraid I have to leave Amu, my wife and young son to his care now."

Hai Rui's request stunned Chee Dazhu, who paused for a few seconds before dropping down on his knees. He started sobbing.

Hai Rui laughed. "You're a warrior who risked your life to battle against the pirates," he said to Chee Dazhu. "I thought death no longer fazes you. Please rise. If any of your subordinates see you crying like this, they'll mock you."

"I'm sorry, I have lied to you," Chee Dazhu mumbled.

Hai Rui sensed something ominous. "Tell me now so I can die with no regrets," he demanded.

"I have hidden it from you because I was worried the news would ruin your health. I once told you that your wife had given birth to a healthy baby boy. That was not true. Your wife died in childbirth. The baby did not survive either…"

Hai Rui's mind went blank. He stood there in a trance. Tears slowly filled his eyes and rolled down his cheeks. Grabbing the liquor jug on the table, he emptied it with one gulp.

Chee Dazhu knelt on the floor, looking helpless.

"I'm not a filial son," Hai Rui murmured, wiping away his tears. "I have failed Amu and my ancestors… It is vital that you deliver the letter to Wang Yongji immediately. I'm entrusting him with my ailing mother. I hope he can take care of her until she passes away."

Chee Dazhu rose from the floor and helped Hai Rui sit on his chair. "Do you have any more liquor for me?" Hai Rui asked.

"I'm afraid not."

"Is my execution at noon? I still have several hours left. Could you get me another jug?"

It was Chee Dazhu's turn to shed tears. "My saviour, I have received an imperial edict early this evening. His Majesty has pardoned you. I'm actually here to pick you up and send you home."

Hai Rui felt like he had been struck by lightning. His eyes widened and he could not breathe. "Then, why... why are you wearing a mourning belt?" he asked.

Chee Dazhu pulled out another white linen belt and gave it to Hai Rui with both hands. "His Majesty... His Majesty just departed for heaven."

Hai Rui reeled back from the news. His face turned ashen and his body started shaking uncontrollably. Suddenly, he clutched his chest and doubled over.

"Are you all right," asked Chee Dazhu, who pounced on him, trying to stop Hai Rui from collapsing. Hai Rui pushed Chee Dazhu's hands away. All of a sudden, he let out a sorrowful wailing. As Chee Dazhu looked on in horror, Hai Rui began throwing up violently. When the vomiting stopped, he passed out and lay on the floor like a piece of dry wood.

On 14 December 1566, Emperor Jiajing passed away, having ruled the country for forty-five years. According to historians, Hai Rui vomited violently upon hearing the news of the emperor's passing and collapsed on the ground.

明

Overnight, Emperor Jiajing's obituary was distributed to all ministries and agencies in Beijing. The next morning, the winter blizzards blew fiercely. Several hundred senior officials donned mourning clothes and converged in front of the Meridian Gate, which had remained closed for twenty-four years after Emperor Jiajing moved out of the Forbidden City in the aftermath of a failed assassination plot against him. Officials knelt in the snow. Their howling reverberated in the air.

At seven o'clock, a side door on the left opened. Grand Secretary Xu and other Privy Council members filed out. Attired in their white mourning outfits, they lined up to the left of the Meridian Gate. A side door on the right opened. Chen Hong, the interior minister and his deputies walked outside, also wearing mourning clothes. They lined up on the right side of the Meridian Gate. With tears glistening in their eyes, members of the Privy Council and the

Interior Ministry waited for the central door to open. The new emperor was supposed to come out of the central archway and announce Emperor Jiajing's will.

At this moment, the snow ceased and the wind died down. All eyes were on the central archway.

Chen Hong waved his right hand. Two eunuchs strode towards the Meridian Gate, each holding a three-metre-long whip. Stopping in front of the central door, they shook their hands slightly, and the long whips lay flat on the snow-covered ground like two snakes.

Chen Hong waved his hand again. The two eunuchs raised the whips and swung them high in the air. The whips swirled in two circles and produced a loud, crisp crack.

The wailing stopped. The whips cracked a second time and then a third time.

The Meridian Gate's central door slowly creaked open.

Countless pairs of tearful eyes were directed towards the central archway, which led to the inner palaces. To their surprise, the archway looked deserted. The new monarch was nowhere to be seen. There was total silence.

Suddenly, imperial officials heard wheels rolling on the snow-covered pathway behind them. This was followed by the sound of soldiers marching in the crunchy snow. Members of the Privy Council and Interior Ministry turned around and knelt with their backs to the Meridian Gate.

"We welcome the arrival of our new emperor," Grand Secretary Xu proclaimed in a resonate voice.

Realising that their new monarch had come from the opposite direction, they quickly turned around and kowtowed to the Prince of Yu, who had just ascended the throne.

Draped in a white linen cloth, the new emperor's sedan moved slowly on the pathway under the escort of Zhu Qi, Chee Dazhu and several imperial guards. About halfway to the Meridian Gate, the sedan stopped. Zhu Qi who stood on the left and Chee Dazhu on the right opened the sedan door. The Prince of Yu, who was attired in a white mourning robe, appeared. While Zhu Qi held the new emperor by the arm, another imperial guard placed a step stool on the ground.

As the Prince of Yu disembarked, the crowd erupted in greetings: "Long live, long live, and long, long live."

The Prince of Yu waved at the imperial officials, but stood by his sedan without moving. He seemed to be waiting for someone.

Baffled, officials craned their necks to find out what the delay was about. A second person emerged from the emperor's sedan. Chee Dazhu held the person's arm as he stepped onto the stool and got off. That person was Hai Rui.

Under the shocked glare of hundreds of imperial officials, the Prince of Yu held Hai Rui's hand. They trod on the snow-covered pathway and marched towards the Meridian Gate.

On 25 December 1566, the Prince of Yu assumed the throne. His era name was 'Longqing', meaning 'grand celebration'.

Before his death, Emperor Jiajing issued a set of decrees as a gesture of repentance over his persecution of those who had remonstrated with him. "The survivors shall be summoned back, the deceased shall be posthumously honoured and their families compensated, and those who are imprisoned shall be released and reinstituted," stated one decree. Thus, the new ruler, Emperor Longqing, promoted the outspoken Hai Rui, and reinstated a group of loyal and talented officials who had been banished by his father. This moment served as the prelude to what later became known as the 'Longqing New Deal' which lasted a mere six years.

ABOUT THE AUTHOR

Liu Heping was born in Hunan Province, southern China in 1953. He spent his childhood in the theatre and went on to become an acclaimed screenwriter, novelist and historian known for his deep insights into the events of Chinese history. His pioneering historical drama about the Ming dynasty, *Da Ming Wang Chao 1566,* was first published as a novel in 2006 and sold nearly a million copies. The following year, it was broadcast as a 46-episode TV series that garnered popular and critical acclaim in China. His Chinese Civil War TV drama, *All Quiet in Peking*, gained a cumulative 400 million online views in the month following its first broadcast in October 2014. The series made waves among China's intellectual circles and was picked up for international distribution by Netflix. Liu's realist approach to the historical and contemporary transformation of China has been hugely influential and well received in the Chinese-speaking world.

ABOUT THE TRANSLATOR

Wen Huang is a Chicago-based writer and translator. His memoir about growing up in Xi'an in the 1970s, *The Little Red Guard*, was a *Washington Post* Best of 2012 pick. He started translating Chinese non-fiction works in 2005, and since then his translations have been published by Pantheon, Harper Collins and Amazon. In 2007, he was the recipient of a PEN Translation Fund Award. His writings have appeared in *The Paris Review*, *Harper's Magazine*, *The Asia Literary Review* and *Words Without Borders*.

ABOUT THE SERIES

In 2007, *Da Ming Wang Chao 1566* captivated Chinese readers and TV audiences with the true story of a humble scholar-official named Hai Rui who stood up to the rampant corruption within the court of the Jiajing Emperor.

The Emperor's Nemesis is the final entry in a series of four English-language novels that have been translated from the original Chinese. The first three volumes of the series, *The Taoist Emperor*, *The Imperial Governor* and *The Chief Eunuch* were also published by Sinoist Books.

About **Sino**ist Books

We hope you enjoyed this story of political intrigue set in China's Ming dynasty.

SINOIST BOOKS brings the best of Chinese fiction to English-speaking readers. We aim to create a greater understanding of Chinese culture and society, and provide an outlet for the ideas and creativity of the country's most talented authors.

To let us know what you thought of this book, or to learn more about the diverse range of exciting Chinese fiction in translation we publish, find us online. If you're as passionate about Chinese literature as we are, then we'd love to hear your thoughts!

sinoistbooks.com
@sinoistbooks